Appellate
Civil Practice and Procedure
Handbook

Appellate
Civil Practice and Procedure
Handbook

Neva B. Talley-Morris, Esq.
A.B., M.Ed.

Prentice-Hall, Inc.
Englewood Cliffs, N.J.

Prentice-Hall International, Inc., *London*
Prentice-Hall of Australia, Pty. Ltd., *Sydney*
Prentice-Hall of Canada, Ltd., *Toronto*
Prentice-Hall of India Private Ltd., *New Delhi*
Prentice-Hall of Japan, Inc., *Tokyo*

This publication is designed to provide accurate and authoritative information with regard to the subject matter covered. It is sold with the understanding that the publisher is not engaged in rendering legal, accounting, or other professional advice. If legal advice or other expert assistance is required, the services of a competent professional person should be sought.

> *...From a Declaration of Principles jointly adopted by
> a Committee of the American Bar Association and a
> Committee of Publishers and Associations.*

Library of Congress Cataloging in Publication Data

Talley-Morris, Neva B
    Appellate civil practice and procedure handbook.

    Includes bibliographical references.
    1. Appellate procedure—United States. I. Title.
KF9050.T34   347'.73'8   74-34596
ISBN 0-13-039065-8

Printed in the United States of America

This book is dedicated to my secretary,

Mada Teague Larmore

—a life member of the National Association of Legal Secretaries.
Her expertise as a legal assistant and her loyalty as a true friend
are among the prized assets of this author.

————————————

Also by the author:
    FAMILY LAW PRACTICE AND PROCEDURE HANDBOOK

A Word from the Author

This handbook of appellate civil practice and procedure is designed as a time alarm and a motivator for the general practitioner. It is applicable to the mature lawyer handling an occasional appeal, to the lawyer anticipating appellate work, or to the overworked busy lawyer with a big backlog of pending appellate cases. Recent trends in appellate volume and court reforms have imposed demands on the talent of private practice from the most remote areas. Broadened scope, constitutional issues, and increasing litigation of the current decade require a new look at appellate advocate's availability.

This manual is a ready reference tool. It is prepared as a guide and a stimulus toward best legal services in appellate litigation. It covers applicable procedures and effective practices. The actual technical requirements of various appellate courts are set forth. Pertinent illustrations and examples are given from the heartland sources of many smaller states.

Chapter 1 concentrates on the psychology of appellate endeavors, laying foundations, evaluating merits, and considering caseloads. The ultimate goal of winning the case on appeal must come into focus from the very first communication in attorney-client interviews. Emphasis is directed toward professional responsibility for guidance in appellate image of client, attorney, court, and legal assistants. The lawyer builds his appellate practice from client to client in communication exchange, as the banker builds his bank from customer to customer in monetary exchange.

PART I of the book is devoted to state supreme court appeals. It provides check lists, cross-references, and practical applications of procedure rules. Current appellate jurisdictions are compared. Tables of innovation trends are compiled, and sample forms are given. New systems of appellate and intermediate levels of court organization are reviewed in Chapter 2. The migrant client and branch office or factory expansions demand continuing legal education and professional alert to give best services to clients on the move. Learning how and where to process a civil appeal in a sister state today may provide the exact procedure applicable in tomorrow's appellate problem for you. This book attempts to provide the over-view which is not only basic in current appellate situations, but also preparatory for procedural awareness in forthcoming court reform and jurisdiction revisions.

Principles revealed are the most common to the 50 states, with specific concerns for the non-metropolitan centers. In Chapters 3 and 4, topics are devoted to procedure for eliminating retrial by appeal de novo, abstracting testimony, preparing the record and appendix. Illustrations of briefs in appeals by right, by writ of certiorari, mandamus, prohibition, and amicus curiae proceedings are found in Chapters 5, 6, and 7. By permission of the appellate advocates, briefs from three different states are reproduced as examples of how-to-do-it. Selections were based on substantive issues of universal interest. Annotations are made on both form and content. Chapter 8 directs attention to current limitations imposed on oral arguments. Reference tables are given to reveal time allowances from many states.

PART II of this handbook reveals some practical answers to the title question, "How to Proceed with Civil Appeals in U.S. Court Jurisdictions." New federal rules of procedure are cited from all circuits. Tables are included to convey statistics reflecting apparent urgency for appellate advocate-jurist cooperation in coping with increasing dockets. Chapter 9 is devoted to appeals as of right and the many new rules of procedure in all U.S. Circuit Courts of Appeals. Chapter 10 is devoted to new rules in bankruptcy appeals. Chapter 11 explores extended scope of certiorari proceedings which demand new methods for expediting, to avoid delayed justice. Chapters 12 and 13 give specific directives from revised rules for preparing the written record, brief, abstract, and appendix. The last chapter summarizes the critical issues pertaining to closing argument and final disposition of the case on appeal. New trends are recognized toward non-record decisions.

Many experts refer to this area of law practice as being where the real action is located and the most gratifying professional skills are developed. It is in the appellate courts that the law itself is on trial, and the skill of the legal profession is at its zenith. Some jurists have recently expressed the opinion that the Bar as a whole has been remiss in its failure to provide institutes, produce books, or promote journal articles for the continuing legal educational guidance in this so-called initial link in the legal process—the art of appellate advocacy. It is hoped that this *Appellate Civil Practice and Procedure Handbook* may, in part, meet this need.

Neva B. Talley-Morris

Table of Contents

PART TWO: APPELLATE CIVIL PRACTICE AND PROCEDURE IN FEDERAL COURT JURISDICTIONS

List of Forms and Tables

FORMS

TABLES

Appellate
Civil Practice and Procedure
Handbook

PART ONE

Appellate Civil Practice and Procedure in State Court Jurisdictions

1

How to Build a Foundation for Civil Appeal Procedures

Firm foundations for appellate advocacy may rest on research and knowledgeable understanding of legal patterns from past and present. Successful practice in upper level is frequently developed by the lawyer's willingness to blend experiences from past legal endeavors with energetic acceptance of today's broader challenges. Historical over-views provide stimulating injections of zeal and motivating impulses for effort toward higher ground of client representation. Lower level jurisdictions did meet the need of pioneers in processing courtroom traffic to finality. Early judicial history of the United States reveals slow development for the remedy of appeal to a review court.[1] From our heritage not only among litigants but also among thousands of members in the legal profession, there lingered a reluctance to proceed beyond the familiar realm of trials in courts of original jurisdiction.

A. ACCEPT NEW TRENDS IN APPELLATE HISTORY.

Decisions of the nineteenth century recognized appeal as a writ of right at common law under certain circumstances. The following examples are typical of early common law rulings in the State of Illinois where the court said:

---

[1] Irwin S. Rhodes, "Legal Records as a Source of History," *American Bar Association Journal,* Vol. 59, 1155 E. 60th Street, Chicago, Ill. (June 1973), p. 635.

(1832) "At common law, the only mode of removing a cause from an inferior court of record to a superior court for reversal, was by a writ of right, which could not be denied except in capital cases."–*Bowers v. Green*, 1 Ill. 42.

(1860) "A writ of error is a writ of right by the common law and lies in all cases, civil and criminal, except capital cases, but can of course be regulated by statute." *Unknown Heirs of Longworth v. Baker*, 23 Ill. 484.

Increasing concerns in the twentieth century developed a realization of growing need for availability of appellate review from all final judgments. The last state in USA to remain without *statutory* provision for appeal as a matter of right is Virginia, which continues the pattern of England. It provides only for appeals discretionary with the court. (Va. Code §8.462.)

By 1970, several states had specifically provided for appeal as a *Constitutional* right, to wit:

ILLINOIS: Const. Art. VI §5 and 7;
FLORIDA: Const. Art. V: §4 and 5;
LOUISIANA: Const. Art. VII: §10 and 29;
DELAWARE: Const. Art. IV. § 11.
NEW JERSEY: Const. Art. VI §6.

Once a state establishes avenues of appellate review, Supreme Court decisions have recently held that the equal protection clause of the U.S. Federal Constitution requires that: "The avenues must be kept free of unreasoned distinctions that can only impede open and equal access to the courts." See:

Rinaldi v. Yeager, 384 U.S. 305 (1966);
Williams v. Oklahoma City, 395 U.S. 458 (1969);
North Carolina v. Pearce, 395 U.S. 711 (1969).

1. Recognize Today's Demands for Appellate Advocacy.

The demands for equal access to the machinery of justice and to professional legal counseling, have increased the caseload throughout all appellate levels. Clamors are loud for more available appellate services to the poor, to the minority groups, and to the middle income American families. Today's greater utilization of the appeals as vehicles for social and political changes is paramount everywhere. The pressure is mounting for the legal profession to promote and to protect equality, due process, and the *public interest.* Specifically, the average citizen has become more involved in court processes from original jurisdictions to the highest appellate forum.

Statistics reveal that the courts in the United States produced approximately 50,000 reported decisions in the first half of the nineteenth century. The next fifty years produced 450,000; and the reported cases of the twentieth century are now estimated at more than two million published decisions.[2] In 1817, only 42 cases were filed with the U.S. Supreme Court, but in 1970, over 4,000 were filed.[3]

The past decade has brought a deluge of appellate practice to the unsuspecting and frequently unprepared general practitioner. Demands are increasing for skilled attention to the challenges of appellate legal endeavor. The lawyer reaches for tools and gears his speed, in an effort to meet the demands and to serve the appellate court litigant in whatever applicable court review he may be competent or with due diligence may become competent. If the outreach is too far distant to be practical, then he must be in touch with referral to serve his client with greater skill and expediency. Unfortunately, some of the present log jam in the crowded appellate courts may be caused by the busy lawyers who are unaware of changing rules, or procedural aspects currently involved in designation of the record, abstracting, brief writing, and recent case decisions in point.

2. View Potentialities and Possibilities of Appeal from the Outset.

The new professional outlook perceives potentialities of every case in the light of possible review by a superior court. Trends toward permanent court records and uniform procedures are rapidly permeating every level of the client's cause of action. Alert leadership will be forthcoming in phases where the law itself will be on trial. Take a good hard look at each case merit, the human aspect, time factor, cost element and tomorrow's potentiality before another forum. Best effort is a priority at the scene of original court jurisdiction. Appellate successes are built on the firm foundation of basics at the lower level. A brief look backward can promote daylight saving time on tommorrow's sprint forward to win appellate goals.

B. APPRAISE CASE MERIT AND TIME FACTORS.

In preparation for appeal, the law searching can be by computer,[4] if

---

2 Bert H. Early, "National Institute of Justice—A Proposal," *West Virginia Law Review,* Morgantown, W. Va., Vol. 74, No. 3, Reprint, April 1972, p. 241.

3 Clifford P. Kirsch, "A History of Court Administration—The American Experience," *Judicature,* Journal of American Judicature Society, 1155 East 60th Street, Chicago, Ill. (April 1972), p. 329.

4 David T. Link, "Law Searching by Computer," *Legal Economics News,* Standing Committee on Economics, American Bar Association, 1155 East 60th Street, Chicago, Ill. 60637, Vol. 38 (Nov. 1972), p. 1.

you have a technical question of law to be decided. It is conceded that the attorney's time should be centered on legal analysis. Yet there are clerical and research activities which must precede analytical talents. The appellate advocate has the opportunity of know-how through the advance projects and research activities of the American Bar Association. He may now upgrade his continuing legal education through membership in the newest Section of Law, Science and Technology. Rapid changes in science and technology affect people's rights and require legal accommodation.[5]

1. Use Automated Research Aids for Appellate Resources.

Professional automated research aids are available to the sole practitioner in remote areas as well as to the large firms in metropolitan centers. Justice on review is frequently based upon advocate's finding the right case. Better legal searching is therefore a commendable part of continuing education to promote modern appellate advocacy. Organized bar activities provide many new and modern tools for updating skills for the lawyer who handles an occasional appeal in connection with a vast caseload of general trial practice. The First National Conference on Automated Law Research was held in March, 1972, sponsored by the American Bar Association Standing Committee on Law and Technology. This committee also publishes the new quarterly, *Jurimetrics Journal* which deals with the newest developments in science, technology and the law.

2. Rely on Office Teamwork for Control of Appeals Timing.

Today's appellate advocate will need a trained staff of alert assistants. Experienced secretaries can be appeal timekeepers for the work load and guideline progress. They will put the legal records into their right perspective to reach best progress of each specific case. The secretary and other legal assistants are to be assigned supportive tasks pertinent to their respective skills for appeal processing. In appellate realm of law practice, the legal secretary should be your expert on rules of limitations. Move the case forward on well-defined schedule within time limits. Each co-worker wants a productive part in the blueprint you have analyzed and established as the priority appellate. Goals are set. and time notes are posted for completion of each phase. Office staff is made an integral moving part of your team as the project unfolds within the designated limitations, and justice is achieved for the client in appellate court!

---

5 See *American Bar News,* Vol. 19, No. 5 (June 1974), p. 4.

C. RELIEVE CROWDED COURT DOCKETS BY CAREFUL CASE AND CLIENT SCREENING.

Your client's cause may be one which should not enter appellate levels. If the issues for review are very, very weak, you will advise the client of the potential "lost cause" and the traumatic concerns in further processing. Some clients may exhibit personal temper tantrums and sheer vengeance motivation. Losses incurred by the client who urges a fight to "the highest court in the land" may outweigh anticipated satisfaction of getting to that forum. In final disposition, the attorney will have a client who shouts, "Why didn't you tell me?" Better to give him a release at the time of first outburst when he declares, "If you won't take the appeal case for me, I'll find another attorney who will!" The screening of case acceptance and the screening of clients are both important to the successes of upper level practice. This applies to acceptance at the lower level, or at any of the appellate levels. Groundwork screening may have been overlooked prior to processing the case in court of original jurisdiction, or circumstances may have changed to the extent that a reevaluation is imperative at each instant of employment consideration in taking the cause to higher court.

The cautious advocate will consider all merits and circumstances at each level. He will quote fee and accept employment for each forum.

1. Negotiate Compromises for Client Best Interest Prior to Appeal.

If your client is open to compromise and recognizes the wisdom of your counsel, appeal may be avoided with mutual satisfaction. Compromise negotiations are often the wiser course on both sides. The adversary may be just as reluctant to proceed into potential overcrowded appellate dockets. The winner of a trivial case could be the economic loser who gains no stripes on his status merit badge.

Authorities propose many solutions toward easing the crowded dockets at the State Supreme Court level. Screening can be done by the addition of intermediate appellate courts, by the use of masters, magistrates, referees, mini-courts, administrative judges, and various pre-litigation conferences between lawyers and appeal clients.

2. Use Pre-Appeal Conferences as a Parallel to Pre-trial Solutions.

In today's world of crowded appellate jurisdictions, the pre-appeal settlements have a parallel thrust to that of the pre-trial conference at the lower level. This legal tool was implemented to relieve crowded dockets. It flowered into wide usage during the depression period of the 1930's.[6] This was a time when court dockets became overcrowded on civil debt collections arising out of the economic collapse of 1929. Presiding Judges, practicing attorneys, and litigants have found great satisfaction in the continued growth and expansion of the use of pre-trial as a screening device. This procedure lays a good foundation for pre-appeal review on screening the more vital issues.

Pre-appeal conferences frequently open doors for compromise negotiations and final settlement. Adversary litigants, attorneys, and the Court all gain relief as time savers and psychological winners. Potential frustrations from over-delayed final hearings are avoided. Tensions are relaxed and each litigant becomes a more useful member in community activities and economic endeavors. Each can declare himself the silent winner!

D. NOTE NON-EMPLOYEE LIAISON ELEMENT IN APPEAL PROCESSING.

Attorneys who handle appeals from the locations of American heartland and hinterlands will thrive on cooperative endeavors, not only within the small office staff but also from court personnel, county law librarians, brief printers and bondsmen. These are people he sees every day in the normal leadership activities in small communities, and he knows each by his first name. For best image, the attorney considers this human element by timely delivery of his material and prompt payment of all costs. There lies good will in the cohesive potential of many hands through which appellate records must be processed.

1. Maintain Open Communication Channel with All Court Staff.

Professional courtesy should be extended in recognition of human alertness of court reporters, record clerks, and transcribers. This may provide untapped resources of error detection, information, assistance, and guidance which a reserved "stuffed shirt" fails to recognize. Cultivate respect with all personnel and treat each as a co-worker in the appellate processing. Minute technicalities and small details can be easily overlooked by the attorney or the busy Judge who signs the court orders with a mere scanning glance.

In the event attention is not readily called to correction of said errors, unnecessary delays may ensue. Statute of limitations may run, and appellate's cause could be lost.

---

6 "Editorial," *Judicature,* Journal of American Judicature Society, 1155 E. 60th Street, Chicago, Ill. 60637, Vol. 55 (May 1972), p. 356.

2. Seek Advice When Time Is Short.

It would appear that the human element in a word of caution on statute of limitations, might frequently be available from a court clerk, reporter, or transcriber of record. They work daily with designation of record and may acquire great awareness and knowledge of rules on appeal limitations. The busy lawyer and the Judge with a heavy backlog might save themselves time and embarrassment by merely recognizing "our Girl Friday" as this human storehouse of on-the-spot knowledge. Try a compliment for teamwork with a question: "Miss Friday, how about our timing on this proposed appeal?" Her answer might reflect just the caution that you need: "Mr. Jones, I think this appeal must be filed prior to_____,but perhaps your law clerk could check it out to be certain." She lets you know she is just a court assistant, but she is honored by your request for her advice, and she will respond by showing greater interest in minute details at her fingertips where the important paper work is being compiled for your case.

3. Apply Illustrated Case to Local Setting.

To illustrate a situation where a word to the wise might have been heeded, we cite the case of *C. K. Hester and Rose Keefer, Appellants v. Tom Keefer, Administrator of the Estate of Caroline Casey, Appellee* [497 S.W. 2d 642]. The Opinion as handed down by Justice James of the Court of Civil Appeals, Waco, Texas, on July 16, 1973, with Rehearing Denied on August 9, 1973, states, in part, as follows:

OPINION–JAMES, JUSTICE

This is a case wherein Appellee Tom Keefer, Administrator of the Estate of Caroline Casey, deceased, brought suit against Appellants G. K. Hester and Rose Keefer for cancellation of certain instruments executed by deceased, and for the recovery of certain funds alleged to belong to the deceased's estate. Based upon a jury verdict favorable to Appellee Administrator, the trial court entered its judgment in favor of Appellee, from which Appellants prosecute this appeal. We have determined that this court lacks jurisdiction for the reason that the appeal bond was not timely filed, and hence dismissed the appeal.

All pertinent dates concerning the appellate steps herein referred to occurred during the year 1973. The following is a resume of the sequence of events considered by us in our determination of the question of jurisdiction:

Date of entry of Judgment; February 2.
Motion for New Trial filed: February 9.

Order overruling Motion for new trial entered: April 6.
Appeal Bond filed: April 30.

[1] The Motion for New Trial was overruled by operation of law forty-five days after February 9, the date of its filing. The forty-fifth day was Monday, March 26. (Rule 329b. Texas Rules of Civil Procedure.) Therefore, since the motion for new trial had been overruled by operation of law after March 26, the trial court's order of April 6 overruling said motion was a nullity.

[2] The Appellants had thirty days from Monday, March 26, in which to file their appeal bond, the thirtieth day being Wednesday, April 25. Since the appeal bond was filed April 30, it was five days late. (Rule 356, Texas Rules of Civil Procedure.) The thirty-day period of time in which the appeal bond must be filed, which commences with the date of the overruling of the motion for new trial. is mandatory and jurisdictional.

In the case at bar, the trial court on February 13 entered an order setting a hearing on the Motion for New Trial for one o'clock p.m., March 2; however, the record reflects that no action was taken on the Motion until April 6, when the order was entered overruling the motion for new trial. In the light of the foregoing, this court is without jurisdiction, and the appeal is accordingly dismissed. Appeal dismissed.

OPINION ON APPELLANTS' MOTION FOR REHEARING

On July 31, 1973, after the entry of our original opinion, Appellants caused a Supplemental Transcript to be filed containing an order of the trial court signed by the trial court on July 27, 1973, shown to be filed with the District Clerk on July 31, 1973, which reads as follows:

"Order Re-Setting Hearing

"Be it remembered on this the 26th day of February, 1973, the Court on its own motion, determined that Defendants' Motion for New Trial heretofore filed on the 9th day of February, 1973, and set for hearing by this Court for 1:00 o'clock p.m. on March 2, 1973, should be re-set and hearing should be had before this Court on Defendants, Motion for New Trial on April 6, 1973, and counsel for Plaintiff and counsel for Defendants having agreed to said re-setting of the hearing on Defendants' Motion for New Trial:

"IT IS THEREFORE ORDERED that said Motion be set for hearing before the Judge of this Court, sitting in the regular Courtroom in the Courthouse at Madisonville, Madison County, Texas, on the 6th day of April, A. D. 1973, at 1:00 o'clock p.m.

SIGNED this 27th day of July 1973

James F. Warren
JAMES F. WARREN, JUDGE

> 12th Judicial District Court
> Madison County, Texas."

[3] Appellants contend that since the order shows on its face that the trial court on its own motion determined that the hearing on Motion for New Trial should be re-set from March 2, 1973, to April 6, 1973, and the order further recites that counsel for both sides agreed to such re-setting of the hearing, that this was a compliance with Rule 329b, Texas Rules of Civil Procedure, and that the effective date of the order overruling the motion for new trial was extended to April 6, 1973. If this contention were correct, then Appellants' appeal bond (filed on April 30, 1973) would have been timely filed.

We overrule this contention.

[4] As stated in our original opinion, the forty-fifth day from the date the Motion for New Trial was filed was Monday, March 26, 1973. Since the trial court had not determined or disposed of this Motion for New Trial on or before Monday, March 26, 1973, this means that as of Tuesday, March 27, 1973, the Motion for New Trial was overruled by operation of law. Therefore, the trial court's order signed July 27, 1973, filed with the District Clerk on July 31, 1973, and shown in the Supplemental Transcript was late and is a nullity. Moreover, the recitation in the order that counsel for both sides agreed to the re-setting of the hearing fails to meet the requirements of Section 3 of Rule 329b, which required "one or more successive written agreements of the parties in the case filed with the clerk of the court, postponing a decision on the Motion to a day certain specifically set out in any such agreement." See Texas and New Orleans Railroad Co. v. Arnold (Tex. Sup. Cr. 1965). [388 S.W. 2d 181.]

Appellants' Motion for Rehearing is accordingly overruled.

Truly the human touch will alert appellate advocate and the cooperating staff toward greater attention in the direction of various statutes of limitations. It is important to have communication between the lawyer's office and court assistants who may be processing appellate papers. A small error, if timely corrected, could parallel the old cavalry story of the nail that lost the battle: For the need of a nail, the shoe was lost; for the need of a shoe, the horse was lost; for the need of a horse, the rider was lost; and for the need of a rider, the battle was lost!

That short delay, that off-the-record agreement to postpone hearing, that unauthorized waiver, that belated filing of omitted ORDER, or that omission of some other vital precaution prior to the designation of the record, could lose the appeal. With increasing complexities of modern life, our judicial system is serving crowded urban areas. It must face greater administrative pressures. Lawyers can relieve some of these burdens by being more alert on rules and limitations.

E. CHECK ALL COURT COSTS AND FEE POTENTIAL.

Priority is established for ample time to be given in first interview with client considering appellate processing. Mutual trust, respect, confidence, and sincerity are basic elements in considering attorney-client teamwork in appeal cases. The breakdown in communications will ferment client hostility into a spewing pot of suspicion over money matters. The items of immediate retainer, early advances applicable to court costs and research fees, advocate fees, and method of final payment, should be thoroughly explored and accepted by the client.

1. Get Estimates on Court Costs.

The lawyer will supply estimates on court costs and case facts requiring additional fee expenditures. Litigants are rarely aware of clerk's filing fees, court reporter's fees, transcript costs, designation of record, off-set or printer's costs for abstract of testimony, brief costs for legal research and format preparation, final printing or duplicating and binding the pamphlet paperback in the required number of copies for court use. The terms may be strange to the litigant as he looks at the cost estimate sheet. Show him samples of each item so that he will know what is meant by "Record to Be Lodged," "Abstract of Testimony," and "Written Brief." These will be available in the lawyer's office from prior appeal work. Samples might be available from the Office of the Supreme Court Clerk who may have disposal stacks of old copies ready for the shredding machines. This may seem very elementary to NYC lawyers, but it will be time well spent in the orientation period with the potential appellate client. You will not be teaching him a law course on how-to-do-it, but you will be acquainting him as to his financial expenditures for these services.

2. Discuss Overall Financial Matters with Client.

Gains to be anticipated in the specific case at hand may be minimized in comparison to the client's hardship in financing an appeal. Lower level jurisdiction costs may have depleted the client's moneys to the extent that appeal processing is not a sound economic venture when considered in the light of other pressing obligations to be met. He may have a sick wife and helpless child whose hospital care and medical expenses are more important at this time of his life span than further litigation involvements. On the other hand, the appeal client may be the impoverished wife defending her rights in a divorce action, and the husband-appellee may be liable for her appellate costs for filing fees, transcripts, and legal fees, all of which can be requested in proper Motion procedures. Or the client with a meritorious appeal case but no finances, may be eligible for assistance through Legal Aid.

F. REVIEW ETHICAL CONSIDERATIONS MOST PERTINENT IN APPEAL CASES.

The new *Code of Professional Responsibility* should be brought into focus at all stages of appellate processing. Certainly there is no greater foundation stone to be considered in this area of limelight than strict adherence to this code and these rules. As adopted by the American Bar Association House of Delegates in 1969 with amendments effective March 1, 1974, these Canons, Ethical Considerations, and Disciplinary Rules do define the type of ethical conduct that the public has a right to expect, not only of lawyers but also of their non-professional employees and associates in matters pertaining to appellate practice. Copies are available through American Bar Association, Chicago, Ill. 60637.

The basic directive of Canon 2 states that "A lawyer should assist the legal profession in fulfilling its duty to make legal counsel available." In addition to "Disciplinary Rules" (DR) supporting this Canon, there are many "Ethical Considerations" (EC) which we consider of particular significance in appellate practice.

1. Appellate Counsel Employment and Fee Considerations.

Financial misunderstandings on lawyer fees too frequently send the client running to the Grievance Committees. Cases with intense emotional involvements usually give appellate advocate the most trouble. The client from Wall Street who jumps from the window of a metropolitan high rise building when stock market crashes, is of great concern to the New York lawyer who has been handling his "commercial actions." But one with this kind of emotional crisis rarely takes the hands of his children and his wife and pulls them with him in his desperate plunge. On the other hand, the client who is involved with family law problems could be the one who turns with gun in hand and takes the lives of all members of his family, in-laws, and spouse's lawyer. Because of increasing concerns of the legal profession for this area of law practice, this author has made use of appellate illustrations and examples to focus attentions on the family and its legal problems in the wide-open spaces of America as well as in the urban communities. No longer can we say "who cares" about the laws and court systems across state lines where the deranged parent may have taken the children of our appellate litigant! What other area of. dedicated practice could be more concerned with appellate procedures and with the daily application of "Ethical Considerations"!

2. Prepare Written Memorandum or Signed Contract on Fee Agreement.

Examples of application of EC 2-19 and EC 2-20 are included on the following pages to illustrate forms used to reduce to writing the employment of counsel who may become appellate advocate.

a. *Example 1* illustrates the point that potential appeal should come into focus at the initial outset of what appears to be a very simple case. Your client is able to pay for representation in defense on a divorce action, but prefers to make installment payments on the entire contracted fee. Oral agreement between lawyer and client is ratified by the simple use of a confirmation letter (Form No. 1). Note that the letter provides space for client signature on returnable copy to indicate approval of this fee arrangement; and that it stipulates total fee must be paid prior to final date of case closing. It also puts the client on notice that a further contract must be negotiated, should this case evolve into later appellate procedures.

EC 2-19. As soon as feasible after a lawyer has been employed, it is desirable that he reach a clear agreement with his client as to the basis of the fee charges to be made. Such a course will not only prevent later misunderstanding but will also work for good relations between the lawyer and the client. It is usually beneficial to reduce to writing the understanding of the parties regarding the fee, particularly when it is contingent. A lawyer should be mindful that many persons who desire to employ him may have had little or no experience with fee charges of lawyers, and for this reason he should explain fully to such persons the reasons for the particular fee arrangement he proposes.

FORM #1

Dear Client:

Re: Case #_____
Court of Original Jurisdiction

Your letter of April 21 has reached my office together with the enclosed check in the amount of $_____ paid as temporary retainer toward my legal fees, as agreed for representing you in your defense on the above action.

This reply is written to acknowledge receipt of this payment and to re-affirm our agreement as to legal fees which we discussed upon your telephone call to my office last week, to wit:

1. You pay as temporary retainer fee the sum of $_____ to apply on legal fee as quoted for my services in your defense in the above action;
2. You pay the balance of $_____, to make the total fee of $_____ on or before final disposition of the above case from the court of original jurisdiction.
3. The above said balance will be reduced by any payment made by you prior to said final date of case closing; and
4. The above said balance will likewise be reduced by any payment made by your husband to apply on legal fees due my office, which we shall urge the Court to order.
5. Should you have paid the entire $_____, then his payment amount will be reimbursed to you.
6. Should you instruct me to appeal final order of this Court to State Supreme Court, that employment will involve a different fee, depending upon time and costs incurred.

A copy of this letter is being included with the original. Please sign below to indicate approval.

Yours very truly,

_____
ATTORNEY AT LAW

APPROVED: _____
                              Client

DATE: _____

b. *Example 2* pertains to application of EC 2-20 where the contingent fee arrangement was necessary because the client had no moneys available with which to process her claim to Supreme Court for her requested review of lower court's denial of said claim. It pertains to disputed property interest in a home and rural acreage which a man and wife had acquired by their joint efforts during their marriage and prior to their divorce. At the prior date of divorce decree, the litigants had elected to keep the property, and the title had been continued for many years as an estate by the entirety under the orginal conveyance. Each litigant had intermittently lived on the premises during the interim, with the man and his second wife being in alleged possession. (See Form No. 2.)

EC-2-20. Contingent fee arrangements in civil cases have long been commonly accepted in the United States in proceedings to enforce claims. The historical bases of their acceptance are that (1) they often, and in a variety of circumstances, provide the only practical means by which one having a claim against another can economically afford, finance, and obtain the services of a competent lawyer to prosecute his claim, and (2) a successful prosecution of the claim produces a *res* out of which the fee can be paid. Although a lawyer generally should decline to accept employment on a contingent fee basis by one who is able to pay a reasonable fixed fee, it is not necessarily improper for a lawyer, where justified by the particular circumstances of a case, to enter into a contingent fee contract in a civil case with any client who, after being fully informed of all relevant factors, desires that arrangement.

FORM #2

CONTINGENT CONTRACT AND AGREEMENT
[Re: Appellate Attorney Fees]

THIS CONTRACT AND AGREEMENT made and entered into on this____day of____, by and between Appellant Mrs. TWO CLIENT, as Party of the First Part, and_____, Attorney, as Party of the Second Part, WITNESSETH:

In consideration of the mutual advantages derived and to be derived hereunder, the parties to this instrument agree and bind themselves, their heirs, executors, administrators and assigns, as follows:

Party of the First Part hereby retains Party of the Second Part and any other attorney she may associate with her in this cause of action, as her exclusive attorney to represent her in the matter of the claim said Party of the First Part has alleged against EX-HUSBAND, or any other person, firm, or corporation liable for property interest and possession of real estate located in Pulaski County, Arkansas, and described as the "NORTHEAST QUARTER NORTHWEST QUARTER (NE NW), Section X, Township 3 North, Range Y West, Pulaski County," which First Party owns as an estate by the entirety with the said EX-HUSBAND litigant, and to which property the Pulaski Chancery Court has made a ruling against her interest therein as of March____, 19____, and against said ruling appeal is now sought before the Supreme Court of Arkansas.

Party of the First Part agrees to pay, and Party of the Second Part agrees to receive as contingent fee, Forty percent (40%) of any and all sums recoverd from First Party's alleged interest in said property, or against her established interest as alleged in monthly rental income from said property until same can be sold and rights therein liquidated as to proportionate sums in partition and division, said contingent fee to be paid after the deduction of all court costs pertaining thereto, including appeal costs, transcript costs, printing and brief binding of pamphlets, or other incidentals in connection with final processing of Appeal for review of Arkansas Supreme Court; and that neither of the parties hereto shall enter into final settlement nor sign any release, transfer, or compromise settlement papers without the full consent in writing by the other party.

Party of the Second Part hereby acknowledges said employment and agrees to the terms thereof, agrees to represent Party of the First Part to the best of her ability, giving to such action as may be instituted, such time, attention, diligence, and care as shall be necessary to fully protect the rights of First Party in and to the real estate herein concerned.

In Witness Whereof, we have hereunto set our hands on this____day of April, 19____.

(Signed) _____

MRS. TWO CLIENT
PARTY OF FIRST PART

(Signed) _____

ATTORNEY AT LAW, PARTY OF SECOND PART

3. Other Ethical Considerations for Appellate Foundation Guidelines.

The following questions are propounded to evoke answers for appellate advocate who takes his basic guidelines from further "Ethical Considerations" of the new Code of Professional Responsibility:

(1) What are some circumstances under which lawyers should decline the proposed appeal case?

ANSWER: EC-2-30. Employment should not be accepted by a lawyer when he is unable to render competent service or when he knows or it is obvious that the person seeking to employ him desires to institute or maintain an action merely for the purpose of harassing or maliciously injuring another. Likewise, a lawyer should decline employment if the intensity of his personal feeling, as distinguished from a community attitude, may impair his effective representation of a proposed client. If a lawyer knows a client has previously obtained counsel, he should not accept employment in the matter unless the other counsel approves or withdraws, or the client terminates the prior employment.

(2) After losing case in court of original jurisdiction, what should appellate advocate do about prosecuting appeal as continuing counsel?

ANSWER: EC-2-31. Fully availability of legal counsel requires both that persons be able to obtain counsel and that lawyers who undertake representation complete work involved. Trial counsel ... should continue to represent his client by advising whether to take an appeal and, if the appeal is prosecuted, by representing him through the appeal unless new counsel is substituted or withdrawal is permitted by the appropriate court.

(3) Should appellate advocate make monetary advances to his client?

ANSWER: EC-5-8. Although this assistance generally is not encouraged, there are instances when it is not improper to make loans to a client. For example, the advancing or guaranteeing of payment of the costs and expenses of litigation by a lawyer may be the only way a client can enforce his cause of action, but the ultimate liability for such costs and expenses must be that of the client.

(4) Does the appellate advocate have professional obligation to assist in improving the appellate processes?

ANSWER: EC-6-2. He has the additional ethical obligation to assist in improving the legal profession, and he may do so by participating in bar activities intended to advance the quality and standards of members of the profession. ... A lawyer should strive at all levels to aid the legal profession in advancing the highest possible standards of integrity and competence.

(5) What must appellate advocate do if he finds he has accepted employment in an appeal matter beyond his competence?

ANSWER: EC-6-4. Having undertaken representation, a lawyer should use proper care to safeguard the interests of his client. If a lawyer has accepted employment in a matter beyond his competence but in which he expected to become competent, he should diligently undertake the work and study necessary to qualify himself.

(6) May the appellate advocate serve client as advocate and adviser?

ANSWER: EC-7-3. A lawyer may serve simultaneously as both advocate and adviser, but the two roles are essentially different. In asserting a position on behalf of his client, an advocate for the most part deals with past conduct and must take the facts as he finds them. By contrast, a lawyer serving as adviser primarily assists his client in determining the course of future conduct and relationship.

(7) Is the lawyer justified on appeal in asserting a frivolous position?

ANSWER: EC-7-4. The advocate may urge any permissible construction of the law favorable to his client, without regard to his professional opinion as to the likelihood that the construction will ultimately prevail. ... However, a lawyer is not justified in asserting a position in litigation that is frivolous.

(8) May the appellate advocate seek client's permission to forego an appeal when the action in best interest of his client seems to be unjust?

ANSWER: EC-7-9. In the exercise of his professional judgment on those decisions which are for his determination in the handling of a legal matter, a lawyer should always act in a manner consistent with best interest of his client. However, when an action in the best interest of his client seems to him to be unjust, he may ask his client for permission to forego such action.

(9) Is good faith an essential element in initiating an appeal?

ANSWER: EC-7-22. Respect for judicial rulings is essential to proper administration of justice; however, a litigant or his lawyer may, in good faith and within the framework of the law, take steps to test the correctness of a ruling of a tribunal.

(10) What is appellate advocate's obligation toward court system reform?

ANSWER: EC-8-9. The advancement of our legal system is of vital importance . . . therefore lawyers should . . . aid in making needed changes.

2

How to Prepare for Appeal to State Supreme Court
(Know Your Courts)

The first step in preparation for appellate procedure is knowledge of court locations and guidelines. What's standard in one state may be quite inadequate in another state.

A. ACCEPT EXPANDING GEOGRAPHIC SCOPE OF APPELLATE CHALLENGES.

Our court patterns grew from the bottom up. Quantity of caseload demands horizontal and vertical expansions to establish appellate systems. Each state falls into a different pattern as the population explosion increases litigation. Spreading miles of this vast country produced pioneer communication gaps which discouraged needed interchange of ideas and timely solutions to problems of court expansion for appellate services. In later years, pride has motivated preferences for existing local plans.

1. Know Your Courts and State Court Appellate Systems.

Reform movements do eliminate many so-called "lower courts" of non-record jurisdictions. Better justice and wiser economy demand a unified court system where all are courts of record with the same high quality of justice. Some of the smaller states with less entrenched habit patterns and more open-minded attitudes are leading the way in implementation of unified court systems. Appellate advocates can ill afford to say "who cares" about court reforms and good examples in other state systems. Lawyers practicing in all of the non-metropolitan states will care about reforms in adjoining states and in states of similar size and like problems of appellate court backlogs. Our new states of Alaska and Hawaii have much to offer in exemplary implementation of court systems to service today's problems. They have no obsolete habit patterns to untangle.

Thousands of appellate advocates reside and have offices located in county seats of borderlines within three or more other states. Cattle ranch appellate clients may reside in Texarkana with land appeal problems processing to State Supreme Courts of Texas, Oklahoma, Arkansas, and Louisiana. If their appeal litigation goes into Federal Courts, it could process into United States Circuit Courts of Appeals in Eleventh Circuit (Texas and Louisiana), Eighth Circuit (Arkansas), or Tenth Circuit (Oklahoma).

There are many similar examples. Certainly the appellate residing in Sundance, Wyoming, might have clients from nearby borderline areas of Montana and South Dakota with appeal litigation processing in three state supreme courts. Clients from this three-state corner could conceivably litigate in three different United States Circuits for Federal Courts of Appeals, each with its own local rules, to wit: Tenth U.S. Circuit (Wyoming), Ninth U.S. Circuit (Montana), and Eighth Circuit (South Dakota). Likewise, advocates with offices in Chattanooga, Tennessee, will care about appellate court systems and rules from that four-corner contact of Alabama, Georgia, North Carolina, and Tennessee. For Federal appellate purposes this clientele encompasses the Fourth, Fifth, and Sixth Circuits as reflected in Appendix charts. The following table reveals motivating information from all state court systems as compiled by Council of State Governments[1] and revised in April 1974:

TABLE #1

a. TABLE OF APPELLATE COURTS AND COURTS OF GENERAL JURISDICTION IN THE 50 U.S.A. STATES AND PUERTO RICO

STATE	*Appellate Courts*	*Judges*	*Trial Courts of Gen. Jurisdiction*	*Judges*
Alabama	Supreme Court	9	Circuit Courts	98
	Civil Appeals Ct.	3		
	Criminal Appeals Ct.	5		
Alaska	Supreme Court	5	Superior Courts	16

[1] See "State Court Systems (Revised 1974)," *A Statistical Summary Prepared for the Conference of Chief Justices,* RM-527, The Council of State Governments, Lexington, Ky. 40511 (April 1974).

TABLE #1 (*continued*)

APPELLATE COURTS AND COURTS OF GENERAL JURISDICTION IN ALL USA STATES

STATE	Appellate Courts	Judges	Trial Courts of Gen. Jurisdiction	Judges
Arizona	Supreme Court	5	Superior Courts	51
	Court of Appeals	12		
Arkansas	Supreme Court	7	Chancery & Probate Courts	25
			Circuit Courts	28
California	Supreme Court	7	Superior Courts	477
	Court of Appeals	48		
Colorado	Supreme Court	7	District Courts	81
	Courts of Appeals	6		
Connecticut	Supreme Court	6	Superior Courts	40
Delaware	Supreme Court	3	Court of Chancery	3
			Superior Court	11
Florida	Supreme Court	7	Circuit Courts	263
	District Appeals	20		
Georgia	Supreme Court	7	Superior Courts	52
	Court of Appeals	9		
Hawaii	Supreme Court	5	Circuit Courts	13
Idaho	Supreme Court	5	District Courts	24
Illinois	Supreme Court	7	Circuit Court (approx.) and 250 Associate Judges	360
	Appellate Courts	34		
Indiana	Supreme Court	5	Circuit Courts	87
	Court of Appeals	9	Superior Courts	63
			Criminal Courts	4
Iowa	Supreme Court	9	District Courts	83
Kansas	Supreme Court	7	District Courts	63
Kentucky	Court of Appeals	7	Circuit Courts	83
Louisiana	Supreme Court	7	District Courts	118
	Courts of Appeal	26		
Maine	Supreme Judicial Court	6	Superior Court	14
Maryland	Court of Appeals	7	Circuit Courts	57
	Court of Special Appeals	10	Courts of Baltimore City	21

TABLE #1 *(continued)*

STATE	*Appellate Courts*	*Judges*	*Trial Courts of Gen. Jurisdiction*	*Judges*
Mass.	Supreme Judicial Court	7		
	Appeals Court	6	Superior Courts	46
Michigan	Supreme Court	7	Circuit Courts	126
	Court of Appeals	12	Recorder's Court (Detroit)	20
Minnesota	Supreme Court	9	District Courts	72
Mississippi	Supreme Court	9	Chancery Courts	25
			Circuit Courts	24
Missouri	Supreme Court	7	Circuit Courts	107
	Courts of Appeal	18		
Montana	Supreme Court	5	District Courts	28
Nebraska	Supreme Court	7	District Courts	45
Nevada	Supreme Court	5	District Courts	23
New Hampshire	Supreme Court	5	Superior Court	12
New Jersey	Supreme Court	7	Superior Court	120
	Appellate Division of Superior Court	18	County Courts	103
New Mexico	Supreme Court	5	District Courts	29
	Court of Appeals	5		
New York	Court of Appeals	7	Supreme Court	257
	Appellate Divisions of Supreme Court	31		
North Carolina	Supreme Court	7	Superior Court	49
	Court of Appeals	9		
North Dakota	Supreme Court	5	District Courts	19
Ohio	Supreme Court	7	Courts of Common Pleas	291
	Court of Appeals	38		
Oklahoma	Supreme Court	9	District Courts	138
	Court of Crim. Appeals	3		
	Court of Appeals	6		
Oregon	Supreme Court	7	Circuit Courts	66
	Court of Appeals	6		
Pennsylvania	Supreme Court	7	Court of Common Pleas	285
	Superior Court	7		
	Commonwealth Court	7		
Puerto Rico	Supreme Court	9	Superior Courts	89
Rhode Island	Supreme Court	5	Superior Courts	13

TABLE #1 (*continued*)

STATE	*Appellate Courts*	*Judges*	*Trial Courts of Gen. Jurisdiction*	*Judges*
South Carolina	Supreme Court	5	Circuit Courts	16
South Dakota	Supreme Court	5	Circuit Courts	37
Tennessee	Supreme Court	5	Chancery Courts	23
	Court of Appeals	9	Circuit Courts	50
	Court of Crim. Appeals	7	Law-Equity Courts	6
Texas	Supreme Courts	9	District Courts	220
	Court of Crim. Appeals	5		
	Court of Civil Appeals	42		
Utah	Supreme Court	5	District Courts	22
Vermont	Supreme Court	5	County Courts	6
Virginia	Supreme Court	7	Circuit Courts	99
Washington	Supreme Court	9	Superior Courts	98
	Court of Appeals	12		
West Virginia	Supreme Court of Appeals	5	Circuit Courts	32
Wisconsin	Supreme Court	7	Circuit Courts	52
			County Courts	126
Wyoming	Supreme Court	5	District Courts	13
District of Columbia	Court of Appeals	9	Superior Court	44

b. Court of Last Resort and Appellate Channels Thereto.

The preceding table is designed as a ready reference for all appellate lawyers in considering litigation involvement in another state. A client from these outlying states may bring causes of concern to local counsel who is retained to inquire into potential appeal from decisions in "Supreme Court" of New York where their married son resides and requests parental financing for appeals litigation.

One trend of the mid-seventies is the gradual adoption of uniform nomenclature for signifying courts of last resort and trial courts of general jurisdiction. A total of 48 states now use the term "Supreme Court" as applicable to last resort. It will be noted that New York is the only State which applies the term "supreme" court to trial courts of general juris-diction. Because many law professors, authors, and private practitioners are acclimated to the New York area, their use of this term frequently comes through on a different communication wavelength to colleagues and litigants in the rest of the states. There is also confusion in the use of the term "District or Circuit Court" which is a court of general jurisdiction in 33 of the states, but of limited jurisdiction in New York State.

c. De Novo Appellate Practice.

Reforms are under way in most states for uniform court systems and stronger courts at the limited jurisdiction first level. Great progress has been made in the mid-seventies to establish a stronger court for all litigants in their first brush with the law. This trend of promoting a record court at all levels does give appellate advocate new zeal toward acceptance of appeal cases. It was generally conceded that these courts of limited jurisdiction provide a large portion of trouble centers and crowded dockets in upper levels. Some of the judges spent only a part of their time with their judicial duties. Their salaries were low, and the rest of their time was spent in occupations to earn a living. In effort to compensate for lack of judicial training, provision was made for the aggrieved party to appeal to a higher court where the entire case was tried *de novo* before a jurist with legal training. The court to which the appeal was taken is one of general jurisdiction already overcrowded with original trials.

The right of appeal de novo allows a defendant to avoid a sentence or stall its imposition. The defendant has an implied veto over the sentence rendered by a lower court judge. This gives the person charged with a misdemeanor, or involved in a minor civil matter, the right to have his case heard twice. The person facing a more serious crime or civil matter involving large sums of money has the right to only one trial. Therefore, it appeared to be a waste of time and money to allow two trials for the so-called minor troubles.

2. Appellate Guidance Available Through National Center.

Appellate guidance and research can be expected to emanate from the National Center for State Courts. When the National Conference on the Judiciary convened at Williamsburg, Virginia, no other item on its agenda ranked higher than the creation of a national center to stimulate and guide the reform movement for the improvement of state courts. Chief Justice Burger of the U.S. Supreme Court admonished this assembly that the time had come to make the initial decision to promote the establishment of a national center to serve all states and to cooperate with all agencies seeking to improve justice at every level. Appellate advocates from all states were represented.

a. Goals of the Center.

At the time of its incorporation, the Center adopted five major goals:

(1) To help state courts set and observe satisfactory standards of judicial administration.

(2) To support and to coordinate, but not supplant, the efforts of all organizations active in the field of court improvement.

(3) To act as a clearinghouse for information concerning state courts.

(4) To initiate and support research into problems of courts and to help states consider and implement recommended solutions.

(5) To work with the Federal Judicial Center to coordinate research into problems common to both Federal and State courts.

b. Regional Offices.

Offices have been located for accessibility to all states. Readers of the publications are urged to make known to the State Court Center their observations and criticisms.

c. State Courts Work-in-Progress Series.[2]

Among the research projects first undertaken by this new organization was the "Administration of Court Reporting in the State Courts." Not only does this project seek more efficient administration of court reporting systems already in operation, but also the study of greater potentialities of technological innovations, to wit: tape recording systems, computer-aided transcription of stenotype notes, voice writing with audio recording backups, and video-audio coverage.

All of these new concepts are of major concern to the lawyer entering appellate practice. The matters of accurate and expedient transcripts of court records are vital to improved justice and release of log jams in delayed case decisions.

3. Standards Relating to Court Organization.

Tentative draft of "Standards Relating to Court Organization" was released by the American Bar Association in 1973. Readers were urged to offer criticisms and suggestions for revision of these standards prior to final

---

2 See "Administration of Court Reporting in State Courts," *State Courts Work-in-Progress Series,* Publication No. NCSC W0001, National Center for State Courts, 725 Madison PL, N.W., Washington, D.C. (Feb. 1973).

release. Appellate lawyers, judges, court administrators, legal scholars, and agencies provided advice for consideration of the commission. Admitted problems concerned the fact that metropolitan areas faced quite different problems than those in less populated rural areas. Unfortunately New York ranks 51st in percentage of its lawyers who are members of the American Bar Association. Nevertheless, the "Standards" were approved in 1974 with finalizing the draft. These standards were developed with a view to their adoption by all state court systems.

The former *Section* of Judicial Administration has more recently become the Judicial Administration *Division* of the American Bar Association. Through its recommendation the proposed "Standards on Court Organization" were processed for approval by the Board of Governors and House of Delegates of the American Bar Association. Hopefully, appellate procedures may become more uniform, and practices may become more efficient in bringing about a higher quality of justice via these innovations. Appeal practitioners must lead the way!

B. OBSERVE RECENT TRENDS TOWARD COURT REFORMS TO UPGRADE APPEAL PLANS.

Concentrated effort by many organizations did alert the American public to the flagrant need of court reforms in all state systems. The American Bar Association, the Institute of Judicial Administration, and the American Judicature Society organized a special institute for training expert court executives. In addition, the National College of State Trial Judges organized a continuing training course for employees of administrative offices. This training in court management is specialized. It has been elevated to professional rank.

Increasing complexity of American urban life creates an administrative burden which cannot be handled by judges and routine court staff alone.[3] A professional court executive is needed to implement reforms, to organize and to administer non-adjudicative work in the courts. It is appellate advocate's duty to promote this concept and encourage progress of the new Conference of State Court Administrators. Its 1974 Convention theme was "Planning for Change: The Courts and Society."[4]

The administrative arm remains under general guidance of judges. Other aspects of more complex living have long recognized the need of an

---

[3] See "Trends in the Role of Court Executives," *Modern Court Management, U.S. Department of Justice,* L.E.A.A. ICR-70-3, U.S. Printing Office, Washington, D.C. 20402. (July 1970).

[4] *American Bar News,* Vol. 19, No. 5, Chicago, 60637 (June 1974), p. 24.

executive to organize and administer in teamwork with the specific professional endeavors, to wit: school superintendents, hospital administrators, and city managers. Effective court executives will manage courts efficiently and economically, thereby relieving judges from duties which prevent them from fully performing their adjudicative roles.

1. Selected Data on Statutory Provisions for Court Administrators—Apellate Advocate's New Friend at Court: Table No. 2.

The following table reveals data from most of the states having implemented the office of Supreme Court Administrator by 1975. Modern reform in court structure was made by constitutional revision and statutory change. Thirty-five state court executives were created within the past two decades. It is interesting to note that 46 local court executives were also employed at levels of general jurisdiction. Most of these innovations required some community group action to build up pressure for legislative enactment. The data reflects a broad and growing community sentiment at local and state levels for better court management in support of appellate procedures and court concern. The new institute for Court Management provides a source of executives formally trained in fundamentals of court administration. It has been wisely pointed out appellate lawyer has a profound obligation to see to it that all courts are properly staffed and properly performing.[5] In appeal practice, the lawyer sees the court system as a whole, and knows the deficiencies at one level which may impede justice in final outcome.

TABLE #2

SUPREME COURT ADMINISTRATORS

STATE	Title	Appointed By	Citation	Date Eff.
ALABAMA	Court Admr.	CJ	Act 1503 of 1971	1972
ALASKA	Adm. Director	SC	Alas. Const., Art. IV, §16	1959
ARIZONA	Adm. Director	CJ	Ariz. Const., Art. VI, §7	1961
ARKANSAS	Exec. Sec'y	CJ	Leg. Act 496	1965
CALIF.	Adm. Director	JC	Calif. Const. Art. 6, §6	1960
COLORADO	State Court Admr.	SC	Colo. Const., Art. VI, §5(3) C.R.S. §37-10-1	1959

---

5   Warren E. Burger, Chief Justice U.S. Supreme Court, "Remarks," Conference on National Institute of Justice, Dec. 6, 1972, Washington D.C. (Reprint). *Quest For Justice,* American Bar Association (1973), p. 13.

STATE	Title	Appointed By	Citation	Date Eff.
CONN.	Court Admr.	CJ	Conn. Rev. Stat. §51-2	1965
DELAWARE	Dir. Adm. Office		58 Del. Laws, Ch. 70	1971
FLORIDA	Court Adm.	SC	Supreme Court Rules	1972
HAWAII	Adm. Director	CJ	Act, 259, Session Laws	1959
IDAHO	Adm. Assistant	SC	Session Laws, Ch. 39, p. 61	1967
ILLINOIS	Adm. Director	SC	Ill. Const. Art. VI, §16	1970
INDIANA	Adm.-Commissioner	SC	Supreme Court, Rule 12	1968
IOWA	Court Adm.	SC	Iowa Code, §685	1973
KANSAS	Jud. Administr.	SC	K.S.A. Supp. §20-138	1965
KENTUCKY	Adm. Director	SC	Ky. Rev. Stats. 22.110-120	1960
LOUISIANA	Jud. Administr.	JC	La. Const. Rev. Art. VII §12	1954
MAINE	Adm. Asst. to CJ	CJ	Me. Stats. Chapter 467	1970
MARYLAND	Dir., Adm. Office	CJ	Md. Code, Sec. 13-101	1955
MASS.	Exec. Sec'y		Gen. Laws, Chap. 211 §3-A-3F	
	Supreme Jud. Court	SC	inserted by Acts 707	1956
			amended by Acts, Ch. 424	1963
			Ch. 755 Rev. by Ch. 650	1967
MICHIGAN	Court Admr.	SC	Const. Rev. Art. VI, §3	1963
MINNE-SOTA	Adm. Assistant	SC	Minn. Stats. Ch. 758	1963
MISSOURI	State Court Adm.	SC	R.S. Mo., §476 (320-390)	1970
			Mo. Const., Art. V, §4 - 2	
NEBRASKA	State Court Adm.	SC	Nebr. Const. Art. V, §1	1972
NEW JERSEY	Adm. Director	CJ	Art. VI, §7, Par. 1, Const.	
			N.J. Stats. 2A, §12-1	1948
NEVADA	Court Adm.	CJ	Nev. Rev. Stat. 1-320-370	1971
NEW MEXICO	Dir., Adm. Offices	SC	N.M. Stats. §16-6-1	1959
NEW YORK	State Adm. Jud. C.	Adm. Bd.	Laws of 1962, Ch. 684	1962
N. CARO-LINA	Adm. Director	CJ	Sessions Laws Ch. 310	1965
N. DAKOTA	State Court Admr.	SC	§27-02-05. 1, N.D. Code	1971
			Session Laws Ch. 124	1927
OHIO	Adm. Director	SC	Rev. Cd. §2503.05,281,282	
			Art. IV §5, Ohio Const.	1955
OKLAHOMA	Adm. Director	SC	Art. VII, §6, Okla. Const.	1968
OREGON	State Court Adm.	CJ	Ore. Laws, Ch. 193, §1-4	1971
PENN.	St. Ct. Admr.	SC	Pa. Const. Art. V, §10(b)	1968
PUERTO RICO	Adm. Director	CJ	PR Ann. Tit. 4, §331-34	1954

STATE	Title	Appointed By	Citation	Date Eff.
R.I.	Ct. Admr.	CJ	RI Pub. L., C. 3030, Ch. 239	1969
S. CAROLINA	Ct. Adm.	CJ	S.C. Const., Art. V	1973
S.DAKOTA	Ct. Adm.	CJ	Ch. 239	1974
TENN.	Exec. Sec'y	SC	Pub. Acts Ch. 86, §16-325	1964
UTAH	State Ct. Adm.	SC	UCA 78-3-18 et seq.	1973
VERMONT	Court Admr.	SC	Stats. 174, §2	1967
VIRGINIA	Exec. Sec'y SCA	SC	Va. Code An. §17-111 (1-2)	1952
WASHING-TON	Courts Admr.	SC	Wash. Cd. Rev. §2.56.010	1957
WEST VA.	Dir, Adm. Office	SC	W. Va. Code 51-1-15	1945
WISCONSIN	Admr. of Courts	SC	Wis. Stats. §257.19	1963
U.S. Courts	Dir. Adm. Office	SC	28 U.S.C. 601-10	1939

Abbr.: Cj-Chief Justice; SC-Supreme Court; JC-Judicial Council

2. Obtain Information from Appellate Court Administrator.

The appellate lawyer will find a delightful source of orientation, local information, and rules dissemination through services of Court Administrator—a friend at court. Goals established by his office may be found in check lists promoting the following:

(1) Systematic study of theory motivating more education;
(2) Specialized expertise and diplomacy;
(3) Standards of behavior and performance;
(4) Foundation for professional association;
(5) Development of a Code of Ethics for Court Administrators.

Providing information for appellate practitioner is one of the outstanding duties assumed by court executive directors. Advocates faced with congested court dockets and heavy caseloads are entitled to know procedure, policies, updated organization, and the implemented reforms as reflected in the next table.

3. Reform Trends in Appellate Guidance: Table No. 3.

The following table gives information on reform trends of the current decade when implementation has been launched in widespread areas toward more uniformity in legal practice and procedure. The following categories are presented for overview, state by state:

a. Unified Court
b. Unified Bar
c. Court Administrator Office
d. Judicial Selection by Merit System
e. Use of Judicial Qualifications Commissions
f. Adoption of American Bar Association Code of Judicial Conduct
g. Recent Revision and Application of New Court Rules

Innovations heretofore adopted[6] are indicated by the plus (+) mark on the table. Those having voluntary provisions for adoption are noted by "V"; and those not yet enacted are indicated by the minus (-) mark.

These reforms and innovations are made possible by community action under strong leadership of judges and lawyers. Appellate advocates have the most vital concerns throughout all levels of court systems. This area of responsibility rests strongly on the competent and knowledgeable leaders in every state. By cross-section study, dedicated ethical awareness, and promotion of national institutes, they may establish trends toward greater uniformity in all state court appellate procedures. Know your courts, **and** promote these standards toward greater professional efficiency in **all appellate** advocacy!

TABLE #3

TABLE 3: REFORM TRENDS IN STATE COURT SYSTEMS

STATE	*UNIFIED COURT*	*UNIFIED BAR*	*COURT ADMR.*	*MERIT SELEC.*	*JUD. QF. COMM.*	*ABA CD. CONDUCT*	*NEW RULES*
ALA.	-	+	+	+	+	+	+
ALSKA.	+	+	+	+	+	+	+
ARIZ.	+	+	+	-	+	-	+
ARK.	-	-	+	-	-	+	+
CALIF.	-	+	+	+	+	-	+
COLO.	+	-	+	+	+	+	+
CONN.	+	-	+	-	-	-	+
DEL.	+	+	+	-	-	-	+

6 See "State Court Progress at a Glance—A Special Society Report," *Judicature*, Vol. 56, No. 10, American Judicature Society, 1155 E. 60th Street, Chicago, Ill. (May 1973), pp. 427-429.

TABLE 3: REFORM TRENDS IN STATE COURT SYSTEMS (*continued*)

STATE	UNIFIED COURT	UNIFIED BAR	COURT ADMR.	MERIT SELEC.	JUD. QF. COMM.	ABA CD. CONDUCT	NEW RULES
FLA.	+	+	+	+	+	-	+
GA.	-	+	-	+	+	-	+
HAWAII	+	-	+	-	+	-	+
IDAHO	+	+	+	+	+	-	+
ILL.	+	-	+	+	+	-	+
IND.	-	-	+	+	-	-	+
IOWA	+	-	+	+	+	-	+
KAN.	+	-	+	+	-	-	+
KY.	-	+	+	-	-	-	+
LA.	-	+	+	+	+	-	+
MAINE	+	-	+	-	-	-	+
MD.	+	-	+	V	+	-	+
MASS.	-	-	+	+	-	+	+
MICH.	+	+	+	-	-	+	+
MINN.	-	-	+	-	+	+	+
MISS.	-	+	-	-	-	-	-
MO.	+	+	+	+	+	-	+
MONT.	-	-	-	+	-	-	+
NEBR.	-	+	+	+	+	+	+
NEVADA	-	+	+	-	-	-	+
N.H.	+	+	-	V	-	+	+
N.J.	+	-	+	V	-	-	+
N.M.	-	+	+	+	+	-	+
N.Y.	-	-	+	V	-	+	+
N.C.	+	+	+	-	+	-	+
N.D.	-	+	+	-	-	-	+

TABLE 3: REFORM TRENDS IN STATE COURT SYSTEMS (*continued*)

STATE	*UNIFIED COURT*	*UNIFIED BAR*	*COURT ADMR.*	*MERIT SELEC.*	*JUD'QF. COMM.*	*ABA CD. CONDUCT*	*NEW RULES*
OHIO	-	-	+	V	+	+	+
OKLA.	+	+	+	+	+	-	+
OREGON	-	+	+	-	-	-	-
PENN.	+	-	+	+	+	-	+
R.I.	+	-	+	-	-	-	+
S.C.	+	-	-	-	-	+	+
S.D.	-	+	-	-	-	-	+
TENN.	-	-	+	+	-	-	+
TEXAS	-	+	-	-	+	-	+
UTAH	-	+	+	+	+	-	+
VERMONT	-	-	+	+	-	-	+
VA.	+	+	+	-	+	+	+
WASH.	-	+	+	-	+	-	+
W. VA.	-	+	-	-	-	+	+
WISC.	-	+	+	-	+	-	-
WYO.	+	+	-	V	-	-	+

C. SUMMARY OF CHALLENGES FOR APPELLATE ADVOCATE AS COURT REFORM LEADER.

The preceding tables, charts, and discussions on current trends in court reforms are included in this handbook as motivating challenges for priority action in an area of concern where the leaders in appellate advocacy are most qualified. Who is in better position to see the needs for uniformity and unified court systems than the expert professionals handling appeals? They see the cross-section of deficiency from the action angle of the movant through all channels of court services on behalf of the litigant. They are the community leaders of whom counsel is sought by civic and other professional organizations whose group actions become involved in projects centered on updating legal services toward better justice in the courts. They are in position to attend seminars, institutes, and local committee studies of the grass-roots needs for reform. A goal can be promoted "to make judges aware of the opportunities they have to influence the way people feel and think about our judicial system."[7]

The cries of the appellate litigants for service and justice from the wildernesses of our more remote areas ring loud and clear from a thinly populated four-state corner area where the nearest appellate advocate office must service his clientele because there is no one else available. He sees the need for uniformity because he must care about processing in many states. He works actively in the American Bar Association to gain professional strength and know-how. He knows that this House of Delegates approved new standards relating to court organization in February 1974, and that it continues the work of its "Commission on Standards of Judicial Administration" from which he can obtain guidance.[8]

---

[7] See *Courts and the Community,* National College of the State Judiciary, Reno, Nev., American Bar Association publication, Chicago, Ill. (1973) p. iii.
[8] See Geoffrey C. Hazard, Jr., "A Constitution for Courts—The Standards in Summary," *Judicature,* Vol. 58, No. 1, American Judicature Society (June 1974), pp. 34-38.

3

How to Get Your Case into Appellate Court
(Know Your Rules)

The appeal case must have top priority on time and attention during these important weeks of getting your client's case properly lodged for review by the appellate court. The rules are specific, and today's Supreme Courts demand strict compliance in order that crowded dockets may ease.

A. KNOW YOUR COURT RULES.

The human error in failure to comply with appellate court rules carries a large percentage of dismissals in Supreme Courts. In an earlier day waivers could be granted; and extension of appeal time was a matter of routine expectation. In recent years the increased case load makes it imperative that rules be specific, and that motions for time extensions rarely be granted. The trend, as reflected in Table 3 of Chapter 2 herein, does portray that the majority of the fifty U.S.A. states did adopt new court rules during the mid-seventies. Many states have not provided special vehicles for distribution of these new rules. The lawyer's professional responsibility demands an alert attention to the rules as the beginning step of getting the client's case into appellate court.

1. Refresh Memory from Ready Reference Deskbook.
The lawyer's best reference for refreshing memory on appellate rules is

naturally the annotated statutes of the applicable state jurisdiction for the specific case. To supplement this office library source, some of the states do publish a paperback pamphlet on current rules in civil appellate procedure. These are distributed through the respective State Supreme Court Clerk, the Supreme Court Librarian, or the Judicial Administrator. Some state bar associations sponsor this project for members who may obtain a loose-leaf binder with annual supplements for new rules or amendments.

The pamphlets can be otained at nominal cost from whatever areas might concern each appeal. Some advocates will have dire need for current rule books from more than one state, as predicted in the following examples:

(1) Lawyers with migrant clients;
(2) Lawyers representing companies with personnel assigned to branch offices in several states;
(3) Lawyers handling probate cases involving ancillary administration in other states;
(4) Lawyers with practice located in tri-state geographic corners with limited referral potentialities;
(5) Lawyers in solo practice or small law firms with limited law library facilities and with office locations remote from any complete research library, such as Supreme Court Library, Law School Library, or Metropolitan bar association library;
(6) Lawyers who are general counsel for interstate transportation companies whose employes reside in various states;
(7) Lawyers representing personnel in outlying locations of labor union assignments:
(8) Lawyers representing traveling salesmen, field auditors, or manufacturers' representatives.

TABLE #4

a.   **SELECTED BIBLIOGRAPHY: PUBLISHER'S STATE
COURT PAMPHLETS**
(Titles Abbreviated)

ALABAMA, Rules of Court, as Amended, all courts. (1973) 380 pp.
CALIFORNIA, (West's), Rules with Amndts, all courts. (1973) 821 pp.
FLORIDA, Rules of Court, with Amndts, all courts. (1973) 281 pp.
ILLINOIS, Practice Act & Rules, Supreme & App. Courts (1973) 584 pp.
INDIANA, Rules of Court, with Amndts, all courts. (1972) 591 pp.
LOUISIANA, (West's), Statutes Ann. Rules, all courts. (1973) 573 pp.
MAINE, Rules of Court, with Amndts, all courts. (1972) 640 pp.

MASSACHUSETTS, Rules, all courts with Amndts. (1973) 573 pp.

MICHIGAN, Rules, all courts, with Amndts. (1973) 944 pp.

MINNESOTA, Rules, all courts, with Amndts. (1973) 1007 pp.

MISSOURI, Rules, all courts, with Amndts. (1973) 1145 pp.

NEW JERSEY, 1972 Rules, all courts, with Amndts. 872 pp.

NEW YORK, McKinney's Civ. Practice Law and Rules. CPLR (1972) 644 pp.

OHIO, (West's), Rules of Court, as Amended, all courts. (1972) 592 pp.

PENNSYLVANIA, Rules, all courts, with Amndts. (1973) 940 pp.

TENNESSEE, Rules, all courts, with Amndts. (1970) 289 pp.

TEXAS, Rules of Court, with Amndts. all courts. (1972) 372 pp.

WASHINGTON, 1972 Rules, with Amndts, all courts. (1972) 642 pp.

The above information highlights Court trends of the seventies on adopting new rules for many USA states as reflected in advertising flyers circulated under heading "State Court Rules," West Publishing Company, 50 Kellogg Bldg., St. Paul, Minnesota, Form 9142 (June, 1973).

TABLE #5

**b.   SELECTED BIBLIOGRAPHY: LOCAL SUPREME
COURT PAMPHLETS**
(Desk Books Paperbacks and Supplements)

ARKANSAS: "Rules of Supreme Court," *Arkansas Statutes Annotated,* Vol. 3A [1969 with Pocket Supplement 1973], 21 pp. The Bobb-Merrill Co., Inc., Indianapolis, Ind.

CALIFORNIA: "Rules of Court" [with 1973 Supplement in Loose-Leaf Binder]. Judicial Council—Supreme Court #0040-1020, 1036, Documents and Publications, P.O. Box 20191, Sacramento, Calif. 95820.

CONNECTICUT: "Practice Book—Supreme Court Rules" [1963, with Amendments 1973], 18 pp. Commission on Official Legal Publications, Office of Production and Distribution, 78 Meadow Street, East Hartford, Conn. 06108.

COLORADO: "Appellate Rules," *Colorado Revised Statutes* [Chapter 28, with 1973 Supplement], 42 pp. Supreme Court Library, Denver, Col.

DELAWARE: "Rules of Supreme Court" [1952 as amended 1970], 98 pp. Office of Supreme Court Clerk, Dover, Delaware.

FLORIDA: "Appellate Rules and *Rules of Civil Procedure"* [effective January 1, 1973], 52 pp. The Florida Bar Association, Tallahassee, Florida 32304.

GEORGIA: "Rules of Supreme Court" [1971, with Amendments to Sept. 25, 1972], 22 pp. Office of Supreme Court Clerk, Atlanta, Georgia.

HAWAII: "Rules of Supreme Court" [1968 with amendments effective January 1, 1972], 87 pp. Office of Administrative Director, The Judiciary P. O. Box 2560, Honolulu, Hawaii.

IDAHO: "Civil Appellate Rules" (1973), 15 pp. Office of Supreme Court Clerk, 451 W. State Street, Boise, Idaho 83709.

ILLINOIS: "Civil Practice Act and Rules of Supreme Court" (1971), 172 pp. Printed by Authority of State of Illinois, J-Pub. 22.2. Supreme Court Clerk, Springfield, Illinois.

IOWA: "Supreme Court Rules" [1972 with amendments effective January 1, 1973], 19 pp. Supreme Court Clerk, Des Moines, Iowa.

KANSAS: "Rules of Supreme Court" [1971, with amendments to July 1, 1973], 78 pp. Office of Supreme Court Clerk, Topeka, Kansas 66612.

KENTUCKY: "Rules of Court of Appeals" [with amendments effective January 8, 1973]. Supreme Court Clerk, Frankfort, Kentucky.

LOUISIANA: "Rules of Supreme Court" [1962 with amendments effective February 1, 1972], 48 pp. Office of Supreme Court Clerk, New Orleans, Louisiana 70112.

MISSISSIPPI: "Rules of Supreme Court" [1967, with amendments to October 2, 1972], 21 pp. Office of Supreme Court Clerk, Jackson, Miss.

NEBRASKA: "Supreme Court Rules" [Revised 1971]. Office of Supreme Court Clerk, 2413 State House, Lincoln, Nebraska 68509.

NEVADA: "Rules of Appellate Procedure" [Effective July 1, 1973], 70 pp. Handbook Issue, *Interalia, Journal of Nevada State Bar* [April 1973]. Vol. 38 No. 2, Nevada State Bar Journal, 10 State Street, Reno, Nevada 89505.

NEW HAMPSHIRE: "Rules of Supreme Court" [effective March 1, 1972], 9 pp. Supreme Court Clerk, Concord, New Hampshire.

NEW MEXICO: "Supreme Court Rules" [1970, with amendments effective March 3, 1972], 95 pp. Supreme Court Clerk, Santa Fe, New Mexico.

NEW YORK: Supreme Court "Special Aids to Practice—Method of Appeal" [1967], 10 pp. Appellate Division Third Department, Office of Clerk, Albany, N.Y.

OHIO: "Rules of Appellate Procedure" [with amendments effective July 1, 1971], 22 pp. Reprint, Ohio Bar Association, 33 West 11th Ave., Columbus, Ohio 43201.

OKLAHOMA: "Supreme Court Rules: Civil Appellate Procedure." Rules on Perfecting Appeals [1970], 24 pp. Director, Administrative Office of the Judiciary, Oklahoma City, Oklahoma 73105.

PENNSYLVANIA: "Rules of Supreme Court" [Effective 1972], 60 pp. *Pennsylvania Bulletin,* Bureau of Publication, Vol. 2, No. 29 & No. 53. P. O. Box 1365, Harrisburg, Pennsylvania 17125.

RHODE ISLAND: "Supreme Court Rules" [effective June 4, 1972], 74 pp. Supreme Court Clerk, Providence, Rhode Island.

SOUTH CAROLINA: "Supreme Court Rules" [1962, with amendments effective March 1973], 72 pp. Supreme Court Clerk, Columbus, S.C.

TENNESSEE: "Official Rules of Supreme Court" [1967], 48 pp. Clerk of Supreme Court, Nashville, Tennessee.

VIRGINIA: "Ready Reference to Rules of Court and Certain Code Sections in Appellate Procedure" [1972], 18 pp.

WISCONSIN: "Rules of Appellate Practice and Procedure" [revised to Jan. 1, 1969], 23 pp. Supplement to *Wisconsin Bar Bulletin,* Dec. 1968, State Bar of Wisconsin, Madison, Wisconsin.

WYOMING: "Rules of Civil Appeals" [amended 1973], 16 pp. Supreme Court Clerk, Casper, Wyoming.

2. Help in Updating and Distributing Local Appellate Rule Booklets for Better Justice to Litigants.

An experienced appellate advocate can render a most gratifying service in helping others to acquire ready reference bibliography and local rule booklets whether he is located in a metropolitan large law firm or in remote areas of small firms. He is recognized as a professional leader to whom others turn for guidance.

A personal copy of updated applicable court rules is needed on the desk of every appellate advocate during the entire time of appeal procedures. As one of the leading appellate lawyers in your state, it is your responsibility to promote this desk-book service as a project of your local bar association. It should be a condensed practical pamphlet which lists basic regulations in well-organized form for quick scanning. Whether you author the book or work with a committee of your colleagues, this local bar association project will provide the source and urge the availability of rule booklets. All advocates should be eager for more strict compliance with appellate rules. Good practices on the part of your adversaries and your colleagues will provide a stimulus toward your self-improvement and revived awareness of new ethical procedures in the appellate realm.

a. Examples: Format and Scope.

For your guidance in acquisition or compilation of your own desk book, and in promoting an appellate rules desk book for distribution to members of your local bar association, the following observations and examples are cited:

(1) Some of the states using paperback desk copies of appellate rules are: Idaho, Louisiana, Tennessee, Kentucky, Nebraska, Georgia, and Florida.

(2) Other states have adopted a loose-leaf form of desk pamphlet. *Hawaii* uses a loose-leaf paperback designed so that further amendments to the rules may be inserted by page in the main context, as contrasted to the former style of pocket supplement. The *State of Utah* through its Supreme Court did issue on January 1, 1973, a publication of the Utah Bar in loose-leaf binder including a complete updating of all "Utah Rules of Civil Procedure." The first page reveals that the scope of rules shall govern the procedure in Supreme Court, district courts, city courts, and justice courts of the State of Utah. The desk book issued by *Rhode Island* Supreme Court effective September 1, 1972, opens with Rule 1 on scope of rules to govern

procedure in appeals to the Supreme Court from the Superior Court, the Family Court, and the Workmen's Compensation Commission. Notes are added throughout this handbook which point out similarity to Rules of the Federal Rules of Appellate Procedure. *Nevada* uses one special issue of its *State Bar Journal* as a desk book from which a timetable is illustrated in the April issue, 1973. As a handy tool and pattern for fingertip reference we have selected this exemplary format as a "How-to-Do-It" illustration for leaders in non-metropolitan areas. Nevada is one of the smaller states, along with Hawaii and Delaware, which pull the highest ranks in percentage of its lawyers with over 70% being members of American Bar Association. We have quoted the following pages as illustrative of good directives for guidance in the many other states of comparable size and problems. Note on the following pages that their rules are now cited as NRAP in following pattern of citation FRAP from the federal appeals form.

TABLE #6

b. ILLUSTRATION: TIMETABLE FOR PROCEEDINGS BEFORE SUPREME COURT OF NEVADA RE: APPEALS

Notice of appeals
Within 30 days of service of written notice of entry of judgment or order appealed from. [NRAP 4(a)]
Time for taking appeal may be enlarged by timely motion for:
(1) judgment under NRCP 50(b)
(2) additional or amended findings of fact under NRCP 52(b)
(3) altering or amending judgment under NRCP 59(e)
(4) new trial under NRCP 59(a). [NRAP 4(a)]

Cross-appeal
Within 14 days of service of first notice of appeal, or within time otherwise prescribed by rule, whichever is longer. [NRAP 4(a)]

Fees
Payable when first documents filed in Supreme Court by appellant; additional fee payable by cross-appellant. [NRAP 12(a); 45(f)]

Bond for costs
Should be filed with notice of appeal. [NRAP 7]

Bond, supersedeas
At or after time of filing notice of appeal. Stay is effective when bond filed. [NRCP 62(d)]

Transcript of proceedings
Appellant must order within 10 days of filing notice of appeal. [NRAP 10(b)]

Transmission and docketing of record on appeal

Within 40 days from filing notice of appeal. [NRAP 11(a), 12(a)]

Where multiple appeals are taken, within time prescribed by court but not less than 40 days from filing final notice of appeal. [NRAP 11(a)]

District court may extend time not more than 90 days from filing first notice of appeal. [NRAP 11(d)]

Supreme Court may extend time beyond limit imposed on district court [NRAP 11(d)]

Enlargement of time for appeals

Time for appeal commences anew upon entry of order:

(1) denying timely notice for new trial under NRCP 59,

(2) granting or denying motion for judgment under NRCP 50(b),

(3) granting or denying motion for additional or amended findings of fact under NRAP 52(b),

(4) granting or denying motion to amend or alter judgment under NRAP 59. [NRAP 4(a)]

Enlargement of time for transmission and docketing record on appeal

Time may be extended by district court not more than 90 days, or by Supreme Court for additional time, provided orders of extension are made before expiration of last previous time period. [NRAP 11(d)]

Record for preliminary motion

On any of the following motions, a party may docket in the Supreme Court such parts of the original record as he requests, prior to docketing of complete record on appeal:

(1) motion to dismiss appeal,

(2) motion for stay pending appeal,

(3) motion for additional security for bond on appeal or supersedeas bond,

(4) motion for any intermediate order. [NRAP 11(g)]

Briefs

Appellant's opening brief; within 40 days after record is filed.

Respondent's answering brief; within 30 days after service of opening brief.

Appellant's reply brief; after service of answering brief, except for good cause shown, not later than 30 days before argument. [NRAP 31(a)]

Supplemental authorities: not later than 15 days before argument; response not later than 10 days before argument.

Amicus Curiae brief: within time allowed party whose position amicus brief supports, unless otherwise specified by court. [NRAP 29]

Time for filing briefs may be shortened or extended by Supreme Court by order for specific cases. [NRAP 31(a)]

Bill for costs

Within 14 days after entry of judgment in Supreme Court. [NRAP 39(c)]

Rehearings

Petition: must be filed within 15 days after service of written notice of entry of judgment unless time shortened or enlarged by court.

Answer: within 10 days after service of petition.

B. FILE ALL PLEADINGS PRIOR TO EXPIRATION DATE.

The prudent appellate advocate is cognizant of potential disasters, accidents, illnesses, and other unforeseen events which may delay his intended activities in perfecting an appeal. Therefore he dares not wait until near expiration date before punching his legal time clock at the designated clerk's office. His papers are stamped several days in advance of "last day" and he has ample time for serving notice of said filing on all proper parties.

1. Filing Notice of Appeal [See Form No. 3).

An appeal permitted by law from a trial court to state Supreme Court shall be taken by filing a notice of appeal with the clerk of the original court within the time allowed by the applicable state rule. Failure of an appellant to file timely notice is ground for such action as the Supreme Court deems appropriate, which may include dismissal of the appeal. In some states, dismissal is statutory with no waiver allowance. In other states, the Supreme Court rule is strictly enforced, making late filing fatal to the cause, and the appeal will be dismissed. We continue with Nevada rules and Examples:

> a. *Service of Notice.* The appellant shall file and serve notice of the filing of appeal by mailing a copy to counsel of record for each party. If a party is not represented by counsel, then a copy shall be mailed to his last known address. There shall be noted on each copy the date on which notice of appeal was filed.
>
> b. *Contents of Notice of Appeal.* The following form is suggested for a Notice of Appeal:

FORM #3

NOTICE OF APPEAL TO THE SUPREME COURT
FROM A JUDGMENT OR ORDER
OF A DISTRICT COURT

No_____   Dept. No._____

IN THE_____JUDICIAL DISTRICT COURT OF THE
STATE OF NEVADA IN AND FOR THE COUNTY OF
_____

A. B., Plaintiff   )
)
)
    v.   )
)
C.D., Defendant   )

NOTICE OF APPEAL

Notice is hereby given that C. D., defendant above named, hereby appeals to the Supreme Court of Nevada (from the final judgment) from the order (describing it)

_____

_____

_____

_____

_____

ENTERED IN THIS ACTION ON THE _____ day of _____, 19_____.

       (S)_____
          Attorney for C.D.

        _____
          (Address)

FORM #4

CIVIL APPEAL BOND
(TITLE OF COURT)

A. B. PLAINTIFF,)
Vs.   ) NO.
C. D. DEFENDANT)

CIVIL APPEAL BOND

KNOW ALL MEN BY THESE PRESENTS: That we, _____, as Principal, and _____, as Surety, are held and firmly bound unto _____, in the principal sum of _____ Dollars ($) lawful money of the United States of America, for the payment whereof, well and truly to be made, we bind ourselves, our heirs, executors, administrators, successors and assigns, jointly and severally, firmly by these presents.

  The condition of this obligation is such that whereas the above named _____, Principal herein, has entered its appeal to the Supreme Court of _____(or the District Court of Appeal) to review the judgment (decree or order) entered in this cause under date of the ____ day of ____, A. D., 19__, and filed in the records of the said Court in ____ Book ____ at page____.

NOW THEREFORE, if said_____, Principal herein, shall satisfy any money judgment contained and set forth in said judgment, in full, including costs, interest, and damages for delay, in event said appeal is dismissed or said judgment is affirmed, then this obligation shall be null and void; otherwise to remain in full force and effect.

SIGNED AND SEALED this____day of ____, A. D., 19__.

_____Principal
_____ (Surety)
_____ (Surety)

2. File Bond for Costs [See Form No. 4].

Unless an appellant is exempted by law, or has filed a supersedeas bond or other undertaking which includes security for the payment of costs on appeal, a bond for costs on appeal or equivalent security shall be filed by the appellant in the district court. It must be filed within statutory time limits and, preferably, with the notice of appeal. The bond or equivalent security shall be in the sum of [$250] unless a different amount is fixed by the district court. The bond for costs on appeal shall have sufficient surety, and it shall be conditioned to secure the payment if cost of the appeal is finally dismissed, or the judgment affirmed, or of such costs as the Supreme Court may direct if the judgment is modified. After a bond for costs on appeal is filed, the appellee may raise objections to the form of the bond, to the sufficiency of the surety, or to any alleged untimely filing.

Appeal cases are frequently lost in the State of Texas for failure to file within time limits of Texas Rule of Civil Procedure #356, to wit [example]:

Time for Filing Cost Bond or Making Deposit

(a) Whenever a bond for costs on appeal is required, the bond shall be filed with the clerk within thirty days of the rendition of judgment or order overruling motion for new trial. If a deposit of cash is made in lieu of bond the same shall be made within the same period.

(b) The affidavit in lieu of bond shall be filed not more than twenty days after the date of rendition of such judgment or order.

Source: Arts. 2253, 2258
Change: The time for filing cost bond on appeal is made uniform in all cases and in all courts.

. . .

Appeal Perfected: Rule 362 [Texas]

> The appeal is perfected when the notice of appeal is given and the bond or affidavit in lieu thereof has been filed, or if affidavit is contested, when contest is overruled. . . .

The fatal error of failure to file appeal bond .within time limit resulted in the dismissal of a typical case by the Supreme Court of Texas on January 17, 1973, No. B–3648, *W.J. Anderson et al., Petitioners, v. A.R. Casebolt, Respondent,* 493 S.W. 2d 509 in PER CURIAM, wherein the Court stated:

> Anderson and another sued Casebolt to recover either the contract price or the fair market value of a houseboat built by Anderson upon the property of Casebolt. The trial court rendered judgment for defendant Casebolt and the Court of Civil Appeals affirmed. 484 S.W. 2d 462. We conclude that the court of civil appeals was without jurisdiction to entertain the appeal because the cash deposit in lieu of a cost bond was not made within the thirty-day period required by Rule 356 [Texas Rules of Civil Procedure].

We further cite recent decisions from Missouri Court of Appeals which point out appellant's errors in time compliance, resulting in dismissal of appeals, to wit:

(1) Failure to File Notice of Appeal. On February 13, 1974, No. 35046, *Lindell L. Marler et al., Plaintiffs-Respondents, v. William H. Hart et al., Defenders-Appellants,* 506 S.W. 2d. 97, Judge Weier presiding, the Court said [in part]:

> This appeal must be dismissed because the notice of appeal was not timely filed . . . the jurisdiction of an appellate court depends upon strict compliance with the statutory procedural steps required to perfect an appeal.

(2) Failure to file transcript within statutory time limitations. On March 28, 1974, No. 9566, *First Community State Bank et al., Plaintiffs-Respondents, v. Chester D. Newhart, Defendant-Appellant,* 507 S.W. 2d 958, Judge Titus presiding, the court said [in part]:

> Notice of appeal was filed June 14, 1973, and under Rule 81.18 V.A.M.R., the transcript on appeal was due for filing here within 90 days thereafter. However, on the last mentioned date . . . the trial court extended the time an additional 90 days . . . . A transcript was received by the clerk of this court on February 22, or 73 days late . . . . Motion to extend time to file appellant's brief is overruled and the appeal is dismissed.

We propose one further time-keeper as a dismissal preventative in the time card shown in the illustration for appeal advocate's wallet.

C. TIME CARD FOR APPELLATE WALLET

The 4 x 6 inch "Time Card" is proposed for a "card-carrying" appellate advocate to use as a reminder reference to calendar priority on each case accepted for appeal to State Supreme Court.

FORM #5

TIME CARD FOR APPELLATE WALLET

1. STARTING DATE: _____   JONES VS. SMITH APPEAL SCHEDULE
   (Issue Date of Final Order)   Court of Original Jurisdiction
2. EXPIRATION DATES: GOALS MET:
   a. ____ Appeal Notice   Compliance Date: _____
   b. ____ Appeal Bond   "   "   _____
   c. ____ Designate Record   "   "   _____
   d. ____ Complete Transcript   "   "   _____
   e. ____ Lodge Record   "   "   _____
   f. ____ Appellant Brief   "   "   _____
   g. ____ Appellee Brief   "   "   _____
   h. ____ Reply Brief   "   "   _____
   i. ____ Oral Argument Notice   "   "   _____

(center fold)

TIME CARD

INSTRUCTIONS: Fill in calendar dates for specific case on left side as soon as computable upon entry of final order in court of original jurisdiction. Subsequent thereto, keep a daily watch upon each stage of timing and post successive compliance dates on right side.

D. SUMMARY OF APPELLATE ADVOCATE CHALLENGES TO "KNOW YOUR RULES."

In summary, we point out that the appellate advocate is normally considered the leader in his profession, the one whose activities, appellate practices and procedures must be exemplary to his peers and to neophytes.

He must adhere more closely not only to rules of each court, but also to the new Code of Professional Responsibility, its disciplinary rules and ethical considerations.

It is indeed an unfortunate happenstance if appellate advocate, law professor, or writer of legal articles, should by action, example or written word, transmit an attitude of "who cares" about court reforms, new rules or dispensing justice in a sister state merely because he is self-sufficient with his services and legal opportunities in one state. The over-view is available through the President of the American Bar Association who is quoted as telling the Association of American Law Schools in a recent address before Western Regional Conference in Portland, Oregon, that Law Schools must abandon their "casual attitude" toward the teaching of legal ethics. He pointed out that the legal profession should not take a defensive posture relative to some recent "outrageous activities" of a few. He urged that we use "outrageous activities" and the involvement as a clarion call to "professional re-examination." He recommended that we make it impossible for anyone to become a member of the bar without having done some rigorous thinking about ethical problems . . . . What must be abandoned is this casual attitude, this unimportant mention, this once-over-lightly consideration of ethical issues . . . . He said, "I don't believe I am wrong in saying that it is the very rare classroom teacher who regularly and thoroughly examines ethical problems directly connected with the subject matter under consideration." Rather than restrict the teaching of ethics to a single course, the ABA President said he prefers a "broad brush" approach in the teaching of ethics, supported by clinical programs and backed up by a tough three-to-six-hour essay question in the final exams.[1]

---

[1] See *American Bar News*, Vol. 19, No. 5, American Bar Association, 1155 East 60th Street, Chicago, Ill. (June 1974), p. 2.

4

How to Prepare the Record
on Appeal

Original papers and exhibits filed in trial court, the transcript of proceedings, or electronic sound recordings, if any, and a copy of the docket entries, prepared or certified by the clerk of trial court, will constitute the record on appeal in most jurisdictions.

A. DESIGNATION OF CONTENTS OF RECORD.

Local state rules are becoming more uniform in their directives for required appellate procedure. Typical guidelines are found in Rule #75 of the Supreme Court of Wyoming, and Rule #75 of the Supreme Court of Hawaii, effective January 1, 1972. These are similar to Rule #75 of Utah, which we use as example.

1. State Supreme Court Rule on Record Contents.

Within 10 days after filing of Notice of Appeal, the appellant shall serve upon the respondent [appellee] and file with the district court a designation of the portions of the record, proceedings, and evidences to be contained in the record on appeal, unless the respondent has already served and filed a designation. Within 10 days after the service and filing of such a designation, any other party to the appeal may serve and file a designation of additional portions of the record, proceedings, and evidence to be included . . . . Within fifteen days after filing Notice of Appeal, appellant shall file with the clerk of district court his certificate stating that (a) a transcript of evidence has been ordered from the court reporter, or (b) he does not intend to rely on said transcript. For failure to file such a certificate the appeal may be dismissed.

2. Proposed Form for Designation of Record.

FORM #6

IN THE DISTRICT OF_____ COUNTY

A.B., PLAINTIFF AND APPELLANT   )

) VS NO_____

C.D., DEFENDANT AND APPELLEE   )

DESIGNATION OF RECORD ON APPEAL

TO THE CLERK OF DISTRICT COURT OF_____COUNTY:

You are hereby requested to prepare, certify, and transmit to the Supreme Court of the State of Utah, with reference to notice of appeal heretofore filed by the plaintiff in the above cause, a transcript of the record in above cause, prepared and transmitted as required by law and the rules of said court, and to include in said transcript of record, the following documents*(or true copies thereof):

    1. Complaint.

    2. Answer.

    3. Order on Pre-Trial [or other temporary orders].

    4. Verdict of the Jury [if any].

    5. Judgment on Verdict [or Final Court Order].

    6. Transcript of (such parts of evidence and exhibits, as desired).

    7. Motion for new trial, with date of filing.

    8. Order denying motion for new trial.

    9. Notice of Appeal, with date of filing.

   10. Statement of points relied on.

   11. Designation of the Record on Appeal.

Attorney:_____

For Plaintiff and Appellant

_____

*(No statement of points necessary where entire record is designated.)

3. Fatality of Inadequate Record Designation.

Most jurisdictions provide that parties may agree, by written stipulation filed with trial court, that specific parts of the record need not be transmitted to State Supreme Court. Appellant may elect to designate only part of the record, and specifically request those parts as set forth in preceding suggested form. This is to be served upon appellee who may thereafter request certain other parts of evidence, exhibits, or motions over-ruled with his exceptions saved. Either party may file a short statement with the clerk to designate the entire contents of the record, including transcript of all evidence and exhibits. However, if the entire contents of the record is intended, one must beware of following that general directive by superfluous verbiage with the added phrase "relating to and pertaining to_____." These words have been ruled as words of limitation, and found to be fatal to the appeal where the rule requires that limited designations be accompanied by concise statement of points on which appellant intends to rely.

To emphasize the importance of strict compliance with the rule on designation, we refer to a Kentucky case relating to the tragic death in automobile accident of Chief Justice Montgomery and his wife, as decided by Court of Appeals of Kentucky on May 4, 1973, with rehearing denied on June 29, 1973. Under an agreed order, this case was considered and decided by a special panel consisting of circuit judges, all of whom concurred in the opinion as written by Judge Thomas A. Ballantine, Special Commissioner.

4. Motion Sustained for Appeal Dismissal: Kentucky Example.

The opinion to which we referred in preceding paragraph did reflect convincing proof of non-prejudice. Because this well-written opinion should alert every appellate advocate to the importance of rule compliance, we quote findings of this court as an example. The case is cited as *T.I.M.E.— D.C., INC., A Corporation, Appellant, v. Lydia M. Bond, Administratrix of the Estate of Phoebe Frances W. Montgomery, Deceased, Appellee*, 495 S.W. 2d 500, (1973), Special Commissioner Thomas A. Ballantine presiding, wherein the Court said:

> This appeal stems from the tragic accident which took the lives of Chief Justice and Mrs. Morris Montgomery. Judge Montgomery was driving the car in which Mrs. Montgomery was a passenger when it was struck by a truck owned by appellant, T.I.M.E.–D.C., Inc. Lydia Bond qualified as administratrix of the estate of Frances Montgomery and William Bond qualified as administrator with will annexed of the estate of Morris Montgomery. In an obvious effort to avoid diversity and removal to Federal Court, an action was filed in the Anderson Circuit Court by Lydia Bond against William Bond and TIME–DC.
>
> William Bond answered and after controverting the allegations of Lydia Bond, asserted a cross claim against TIME–DC seeking damages for the death

of Judge Bond. A jury returned a verdict for Lydia Bond on her claim against TIME–DC and for William Bond on his cross claim against TIME–DC. No appeal was taken from the judgment entered on the verdict for William Bond. A notice of appeal from the judgment in favor of Lydia Bond was filed timely and the following designation of record for appeal was filed:

> "You are hereby directed to copy and file and make a part of the record *the entire contents of the record of the above* styled case in your office, *relating to and pertaining to the* case of the plaintiff, Lydia M. Bond, Administratrix. . . including all pleadings, depositions, and a transcript of the *testimony given by all witnesses who testified for and on behalf of the plaintiff,* Lydia M. Bond. . .; all Judgments and orders entered by the Court together with Instructions of the court to the jury and those offered and refused by the defendant-appellant T.I.M.E.–D.C., Inc., a corporation."

[1] Thereafter, appellee filed a motion to dismiss the appeal for the reason that appellant failed to accompany its designation with "a concise statement of the points upon which he intends to rely on the appeal," CR 75-04. Appellant countered this motion by asserting that its designation was of the entire record. Thus we are confronted with the question of interpretation of the language of the designation. ...The designation is patently one of a part of the record. . . . The emphasized portions of the designation *supra,* cannot be understood any way except that this is a partial designation and squarely within the mandate of CR 75. . . . We adhere to the precedents long established...the Court has adopted the *policy of strict compliance.* The motion of appellee to dismiss the appeal for failure to comply with CR 75.04 is hereby sustained, and the appeal is dismissed.

Other State Supreme Court rulings reflect similar conclusions in recent decisions on proper preparation of the record on appeal and timely filing thereof:

(1) February 14, 1974, the Court of Civil Appeals of Texas (Waco) Case No. 5317, *Melvin R. Hassell and Ted Sherer, Jr., Appellants v. New England Mutual Life Insurance Company et al, Appellees,* 506 S.W. 2d 727, Chief Justice McDonald presiding, stated [in part] :

> This is an appeal by plaintiffs from summary judgment in suit for damages against defendant for alleged interference with the business relationship between plaintiffs and a client . . . .
> We cannot decide from the incomplete record before us that the judgment is erroneous. It is presumed that the omitted depositions establish the correctness of the judgment. No depositions have been brought forward as a part of the record on appeal, which is appellant's burden . . . . Affirmed.

(2) April 25, 1974 the Court of Civil Appeal of Texas (Corpus Christi) Case No. 843, *Commercial Standard Insurance Co. Appellant v. Southern Farm Bureau Casualty Insurance Co., Appellee,* 509 S.W. 2d, 387, Justice Bissett presiding, stated [in part]:

> ... Commercial Standard's brief contains 80 points of error. Most of them cannot be considered since the asserted errors were not preserved for appellate review. ... Therefore the error, if any, in allowing such questions, has been waived. ...
>
> The judgment of the trial court is affirmed.

B. ORDER TRANSCRIPT PREPARATION.

Designation for inclusion of any evidence or proceeding requires that said notice be followed by the order for preparation of the transcript. Said order and arrangement for the costs are usually the sole responsibility of appellant. New rules being implemented in practically all of the 50 states during the seventies are more specific in directives for responsibility in financial costs. Rule 10 of the Rhode Island Supreme Court sets forth procedure for ordering the transcript to be prepared by the court reporter, and specifically states that the ordering and payment of the copies of the transcript shall be in accordance with the rules of the trial court. If the appellee needs a transcript of other parts of the proceeding than those ordered by appellant, the appellee shall immediately order same.

1. New Rules Implementation: Nevada Example NRAP #10.

Nevada new rules likewise deal with the matter of ordering the transcript; said rule #10 effective July 1, 1973, states in part:

> If there be designated for inclusion any evidence or proceeding at a trial or hearing which was stenographically reported, the appellant shall order from the reporter a transcript of such parts of the proceedings not already on file as he deems necessary for inclusion in the record. Upon notice of appeal and request for record on appeal being filed with the clerk of the district court, he shall immediately mail to the reporter or reporters who reported the case a form letter including the following matters:
>
> (1) Caption of the case,
> (2) Date or dates of trial,
> (3) Portions of transcript requested,
> (4) Number of copies required, and
> (5) Either an estimate of the cost of the transcript or a form of waiver of deposit of money.

Not later than three days after mailing of the form letter, the reporter (or reporters) shall file with the clerk of the district court the estimate or waiver. Upon receipt of the estimate or waiver, the clerk shall notify counsel of record for all parties. When the money, as specified in the reporter's estimate, is deposited with the clerk of the district court, the clerk shall immediately notify the reporter. From the date of deposit of money (or waiver, as the case may be) the reporter shall have thirty (30) days for preparation and filing of transcript in a civil case. The district court, in its discretion and for good cause shown, may extend the time for preparation of transcript for an additional thirty (30) days . . . .Where the reporter waives deposit of funds, the time for preparation of transcript commences three days after the clerk of the district court has mailed form letter to the reporter. . . .

Except as otherwise required, all matters not essential to the decision of the issues presented by the appeal shall be omitted. Brevity of the record is encouraged; and the court may impose costs upon parties or attorneys who unnecessarily enlarge the record on appeal.

2. How Transcript Costs Are Provided for the Impoverished.

Realizing that most court reporters are only employed on a part-time salary, we must extend cooperative effort to see that their transcript moneys are made available when order is made. Even though the lawyer may waive his fee, he must assume responsibility to see that the reporter fees are paid for preparation of the record.

a. Appeal in Forma Pauperis.

If the case is determined by appellate advocate to have merit on behalf of his impoverished client, he may file for permission to proceed on appeal in *forma pauperis.* A party to an action desiring to proceed in this manner shall file in the district court a motion for leave so to proceed, together with affidavit showing the following facts: his inability to pay fees and costs or to give security therefor, his belief that he is entitled to redress, and a statement of the issues which he intends to present on appeal. If motion is granted, the party may proceed without further application to Supreme Court and without prepayment of fees or costs in either court, as set forth in Nevada rules. If motion is denied, district court shall state in writing the reasons for denial.

If motion is denied by district court, or if the said court shall certify that appeal is not taken in good faith, or party is otherwise not entitled to proceed in *forma pauperis,* the clerk shall serve notice of such action. A motion for leave to proceed may then be filed with Supreme Court, said motion accompanied by a copy of the affidavit filed in district court, and by a copy of statement of reasons given by district court for its action.

b.   AFFIDAVIT AND ORDER TO ACCOMPANY MOTION FOR LEAVE TO APPEAL IN FORMA PAUPERIS*

IN THE_____ JUDICIAL DISTRICT COURT OF THE STATE OF NEVADA

A.B.   )
V.   )
C.D.   )

AFFIDAVIT IN SUPPORT OF MOTION TO PROCEED ON APPEAL IN FORMA PAUPERIS

STATE OF NEVADA   )
)   SS
COUNTY OF_____)

I,_____being first duly sworn, depose and say that I am the _____in the above entitled case; that in support of my motion to proceed on appeal without being required to prepay fees, cost or give security therefor, I state that because of my poverty I am unable to pay the costs of said proceeding or to give security therefor; that I believe I am entitled to redress; and that the issues which I desire to present on appeal are the following:_____

_____

I further swear that the responses which I have made to the questions and instructions below relating to my ability to pay the cost of prosecuting the appeal are true.

1. Are you presently employed?_____

   a. If answer is yes, state amount of monthly salary or wages and give name and address of employer._____

   b. If answer is no, state last employment date and salary or wages._____

2. Have you received within the past twelve months any income from a business, profession or other form of self-employment, or in the form of rent payments, interest, dividends, or other sources?_____

   a. If the answer is yes, describe each source, and state amount received during past twelve months._____

3. Do you own any cash or checking or savings account?_____

_____
*[Author's Note: Most appellate advocates will recognize this form as identical with Form #4, "Federal Rules of Appellate Procedure—with Forms"; and the State of Nevada is to be commended for its leadership in adopting state rules and forms as NRAP, which are identical to FRAP.]

    a. If answer is yes, state the total value of items owned._____

4. Do you own any real estate, stocks, bonds, notes, automobiles, or other valuable property (excluding household furnishings and clothing)?_____

    a. If answer is yes, describe property and state approximate value._____

_____

5. List persons who are dependent upon you for support and state relationship._____

I understand that a false statement or answer to any questions in this affidavit will subject me to penalties for perjury.

_____

Subscribed and Sworn to before me this___day of____,19__.

                           _____

                                    Notary Public

ORDER

Let the applicant proceed without prepayment of costs or fees or the necessity of giving security therefor.
    DATED this___day of____19____

                   Signed_____District Judge

C. PROVIDE TRANSCRIPT AND APPEAL COSTS FOR INTRA-FAMILY INDIGENTS.

Interest is escalating in the financial predicament of indigent members of the family on appeal procedures. There are rights to be considered for the minor child who has no money, for the dependent wife who appeals her husband's divorce decree, for the indigent father who appeals his child custody rights, and for the parents in poverty who have had their parental rights terminated because of neglected and delinquent children. Appellate advocates recognize the legal profession as a service wherein family law problems are of *major interest* and *justice more crucial* than commercial actions or injunction suits with mercenary litigants.

1. Counsel Appointed for Indigent Father: California Example.

A report [1] is submitted concerning a California appeal case entitled *"In*

_____

[1] *Family Law Newsletter,* Vol. 13. No. 4, American Bar Association, 1155 E. 60th Street, Chicago, Ill. (March 1973) pp. 3-4.

Re David Scott Kitzmiller" wherein the Court of Appeals, State of California, First Appellate District, ordered that counsel be appointed for an indigent father. He petitioned the Court of Appeals to appoint counsel for him, at public expense, because he was an indigent. The Appellate tribunal granted the petition. The Court cited the Supreme Court case of *Bodie v. Connecticut*, 401 U.S. 371, which held that indigents seeking a divorce were entitled to waiver of court fees and costs, because of the importance to society of the marriage relationship or its dissolution. We agree with the conclusions of the court: "Surely the defendant of the parent-child relationship, including the process of appeal, is of equal importance."

2. Parents of Delinquent and Neglected Child: Colorado Example.

The Colorado Court of Appeals, Division II, has recently ruled that in termination of parental rights proceeding, the parents are not entitled to a free transcript where the child was found to be delinquent and neglected and no change in circumstances had occurred since first hearing. When the child failed to adapt to her new home or to a foster home, the child welfare department sought termination which the court granted. The parents appealed, raising several contentions, including that the trial court erred in refusing them a free transcript to aid in preparation of a motion for a new trial.

In Re People in Interest of A.R.S., 502 P. 2d 92 (1972), the Court said: "In the absence of a statute authorizing the furnishing of such a transcript, we hold that counsel is not entitled to a copy for preparation of a motion for new trial. ...." The Appellate Court further pointed out that under the children's Code, it was the court's duty "to consider above all else, the welfare of the child," and that where there was competent and substantial evidence supporting the trial court's determination that it was in the best interest of the child to terminate parental rights, the Appellate Court would not interfere.

3. Impoverished Wife in Divorce Appeal: Arkansas Example.

Another family law predicament of the impoverished pertains to the dependent wife who has rights for appellate court's review of divorce decree granted to her husband, but she has no separate moneys or properties of her own to use for transcript and appeal costs. Her remedy in the trial court was exhausted when her motion for appeal costs was denied. She then filed Intermediate Relief Motion in Supreme Court.

FORM #8

MOTION FOR INTERMEDIATE RELIEF

IN THE ARKANSAS SUPREME COURT

(SERVED)

A.B. APPELLANT	)	
V	)	NO. 73-3, Filed Jan. 4, 1973
C.B. APPELLEE	)	

JIMMY H. HAWKINS, Clerk

MOTION

Comes A.B., Appellant, and for her Motion States:

1) A decree for divorce was rendered by Chancery Court of Pulaski County, Arkansas, on October 10, 1972; said decree appears of record in partial transcript herein filed at T26-T29, inclusive.

2) Cost of the complete transcript and brief printing will be $1,000.

3) Appellant is without funds to pay cost of transcript and briefs.

4) Appellee is gainfully employed with annual gross earnings of approximately $40,000, and he is financially able to pay for cost of transcript and cost of the printing of briefs.

5) The parties own as an estate by the entirety real property worth approximately $40,000; the Trial Court did not dissolve the estate by the entirety and the Appellant is unable to obtain funds using the property as security in that the Appellee has refused to join with her in the obtaining of funds or in the execution of property mortgage.

6) The Trial Court denied a similar Motion, T34-T35, T37.

WHEREFORE, Appellant prays that the Appellee be required to pay the costs for the preparation of the transcript and the Abstract, and that he be required to pay the costs of preparing and printing of the Brief, and for all proper relief.

(Signed)   OSBORNE W. GARVIN, Attorney for Appellant

Fausett Plaza Bldg., Little Rock, Arkansas

4. Partial Transcript Accepted on Intermediate Relief Motion.

To the foregoing Motion, appellant attached the routine affidavit and "Citation in Support of Motion," to wit: "As incident to its appellate jurisdiction, the Supreme Court has power pending an appeal in a divorce suit to make an order allowing a wife costs and suit money." [*In re Smith,* 183 Ark 1025, 39 S.W. 2d 703.]

Said reference to a decision of June 15, 1931, was found pertinent to this 1973 case, there having been no intervening decisions in point to the contrary. In the 1973 case, careful steps were taken to see that the appellate court had jurisdiction to order intermediate relief for provision of appellant's cost money for abstract and brief. The following precautionary steps were taken to assure jurisdiction:

a. Remedy exhausted by prior motion denied in trial court
b. Notice of appeal, and designation of record timely filed
c. Certified copy of partial transcript timely filed with Clerk
d. Filing fee of $20.00 was paid to Supreme Court Clerk
e. Case accepted by Clerk, docketed, and assigned File #73-3
f. Partial transcript lodged in Supreme Court including the pre-requisite essentials of certified copy of decree and pleadings on file in trial court, including cost denial.

This intermediate procedure did result in Arkansas Supreme Court entering a preliminary order on January 2, 1973, which was also repeated in the final opinion on November 5, 1973, granting divorced wife judgment against appellee for entire cost of appellant's transcript, abstract, brief and argument. [*Reagan v Reagan*, 255 Ark 458, 500 S.W. 2d 754.]

5. Fatality of Appeal Upon Non-Compliance with Transcript Rule.

Although Supreme Courts may be liberal in accepting late appeals in criminal cases, most jurisdictions have refused to exercise their inherent powers in accepting late appeals in civil cases "except in a most extraordinary situation." With reference to the late filing of the transcript on *July 2, 1973*, the Supreme Court of Arkansas held that where transcript was obtained by petitioner 41 days before it was tendered, no unavoidable casualty was shown, and no timely request for extension of time for filing transcript was made, therefore Supreme Court would not direct clerk to accept transcript which was tendered on 91st day after filing of notice of appeal rather than 90th day as required, in *Per Curiam Order Case No. 73-136, Charles T. Bernard, Individually, and as Chairman of the Arkansas Republican Party, Appellant, v. Max Howell et al., Appellees,* 496 S.W. 2d 362 (1973). In further emphasis the Court quoted from an earlier case which had set a precedent for a long line of consistent rulings, because the Court had stated in *West v. Smith* 278 S.W. 2d 126 (1955): "*We are delivering this opinion as a precedent for future cases.*" Then as a precedent for future cases, in *SMITH*, we said: "It is not to be doubted that under our inherent constitutional power, this Court could, in a most exceptional case, allow a record to be filed after the time fixed. However, the fact that we have the power does not mean that it should be exercised except in a most extraordinary case. Here there is no such: the parties let time expire for filing the record and also let time expire in which to ask the Trial Court to grant an extension . . . . In a long line of cases we have refused . . . to allow an appellant to present evidence when it was filed too late."

April 11, 1974, Civil Appeals Court of Waco, Texas, Case No. 5327, *International Security Life Insurance Co., Appellant v. R.H. Draper, Appellee,* 507 S.W. 2d 655, Justice Hall presiding, the court found [in part], as follows:

> This is a suit on a major medical and hospital insurance policy. Trial court on October 15, 1973, ruled in favor of plaintiff and defendant filed Notice of Appeal on November 30, 1973. Judgment was formally signed and entered on December 13, 1973; Appellant caused transcript to be filed on February 6, 1974. A statement of facts was not filed . . . . Rule 386, Vernons Ann. Rules of Civil Procedure . . . required appellant to file statement of facts with this court not later than February 11, 1974, absent an extension of time for doing so. On February 19th appellant filed motion for the extension. The motion is contested by appellee . . . . The requisite deposit was not made with the reporter until February 8, 1974. This was too late for her to furnish the statement of facts for timely filing. . . .

The record failed to show why appellant waited 57 days after judgment and 32 days after its appeal was perfected to employ the court reporter for preparation of the statement of facts.

Under the circumstances, the delay was unreasonable, and the Court overruled appellant's motion for extension of time for filing a statement of facts. The case was dismissed and appellant's cause lost for failure to comply with rules of court.

D. PROVIDE RECORD WHERE NO REPORT MADE:
WYOMING ILLUSTRATION #75(c).

> If no report or recording of evidence or proceedings at a hearing of trial was made, or if a transcript is unavailable, the appellant may prepare a statement of the evidence or proceeding from the best available means, including his recollection. The statement shall be served on the appellee, who may serve objections or propose amendments thereto within ten days after service. Thereupon, the statement and any objection or proposed amendment shall be submitted to the trial court for settlement and approval; and as settled or approved shall be included by the Clerk on appeal.

E. FILE AGREED STATEMENT AS RECORD:
RHODE ISLAND ILLUSTRATION #10(d).

In lieu of the record on appeal as defined heretofore, the parties may prepare and sign a statement of the case showing how the issues presented by the appeal arose and were decided in the trial court, and setting forth only so many of the facts averred and proved or sought to be proved as are essential to a decision of the issues presented. If the statement conforms to the truth, it, with such additions as the trial court may consider necessary fully to present the issues raised by the appeal, shall be approved by the trial court and shall then be certified to the Supreme Court as the record on appeal, and transmitted thereto by the Clerk of the trial court within time provided by the rule.

F. SUMMARIZE TAPES IF ELECTRONIC DEVICES ARE USED:
ALASKA ILLUSTRATION.

Since 1960 when Alaska court system became operative upon present procedure, it has relied almost exclusively on electronic sound reporting for its trial proceedings. Their reports reflect that electronic sound reporting does not waste time and money in making transcripts which are not appealed, and the delay in preparation and filing of transcripts for appeal is greatly reduced. They also conclude that electronic sound recordings are generally less costly than other methods. Since the Alaska experience, other jurisdictions have explored the uses of sound recordings instead of the shorthand, or stenotype court reporter devices to preserve the record of evidence. Not trusting the equipment completely, some reporters prefer to supplement their tape recordings with their own shorthand or stenotype recordings.

G. ABSTRACT OR ABRIDGE RECORDS, IF REQUIRED.

All matter not essential to the decision of the questions presented by the appeal should be omitted. Documents may be abridged by omitting all irrelevant and formal portions thereof. The Utah rules provide that upon any infraction of the rule on "Record to be Abbreviated," the appellant court may withhold or impose costs as the circumstances of the case and discouragement of like conduct in the future may require; and the costs may be imposed upon offending attorneys or parties. Utah Rule #75(e).

1. Requirement in Limited Situations: Utah Rule #75(e).

"Where it appears to the Supreme Court that the transcript of evidence furnished, or to be furnished, under this rule is so extensive or voluminous that it appears necessary and desirable to do so, the court, upon its own motion, or upon application of either party, may order that such transcript of evidence be abstracted." Only so much of the record is abstracted as to give clear understanding of the question or questions presented.

2. Requirements in All Cases: Arkansas Illustration, Rule #9, 10.

Several states require that the record and testimony be abstracted and filed in printed form as part of the brief and argument pamphlet. Chancery cases are tried de novo in Arkansas Supreme Court, but the trial is upon evidence as abstracted by the parties and not upon the original record. The abstract must comply with Rule 9(d), to wit:

"Abstract. —The appellant's abstract or abridgment of the record should consist of an impartial condensation, without comment, or emphasis, of only such material parts of the pleadings, proceedings, facts, documents, and other matters in the record as are necessary to an understanding of all questions presented to this court for decision. No more than two pages of the record shall in any instance be abstracted without a page reference to the record. In the abstracting of testimony, the first person rather than the third person shall be used. The Clerk will refuse to accept a brief that is not abstracted in the first person or that does not contain the required references to the record. In the abstracting of depositions taken on interrogatories, requests for admissions and the responses thereto, and interrogatories to parties and the responses thereto, the abstract of each answer must immediately follow the abstract of the question . . . . If the appellee considers the appellant's abstract to be defective he may, at his option, submit with his brief a supplemental abstract. When the case is considered on its merits the court may impose or withhold costs to compensate either party for the other party's noncompliance with this rule. The court may also affirm the judgment or decree for noncompliance with this rule."

3. Fatality to Appeal, if Non-Compliance with Abstract Rules.

Filing the abstract of record is considered mandatory. In civil cases, it must be filed by appellant within rule time; otherwise, the appeal may be dismissed or judgment affirmed [Arkansas #10].

In the case of *Holleman et al. v. Fowler,* 45 S.W. 2d 100 (1970), Justice George Rose Smith presiding, Arkansas Supreme Court held:

"This appears to be a suit by appellee to recover judgment upon a $30,000 note and to impress a constructive trust upon certain land. The Chancellor granted the money judgment but refused to enforce the asserted trust. The appellants gave notice of appeal and filed a two-volume record in this court, but they have not submitted an abstract or a brief. As to them the decree must be affirmed under our rule 10. The appellee filed notice of cross appeal and has submitted a brief urging that the Chancellor erred in refusing to declare a constructive trust. The appellee, however, has not abstracted that part of the record pertinent to her cross appeal, as she should have done. It being impossible for all the seven judges to examine the record, we have no choice except to affirm the decree on cross appeal as well. *Insured Lloyds v. Ahrend* 431 S.W. 2d 740 (1968). AFFIRMED."

In the case of *Webb v. City of Little Rock,* 486 S.W. 2d 29 (1972), the Supreme Court of Arkansas, Justice Conley Bird Presiding, stated in part: "The record contains in excess of 20 exhibits, including officer's reports and photographs about which officers testified, none of which appellants have abstracted . . . . Consequently, we affirm this appeal because of appellant's failure to comply with Rule 9(d)."

H. CHECK LIST ON VITAL ISSUES FOR DOCKETING THE APPEAL.

Deliberate attempt has been made in the foregoing pages to bring into focus as many state illustrations of rules, cases, and forms as our time and space could allow. Some of these examples, case summaries, and opinions may serve as a deterrent to prevent fatality of your next appeal. We suggest the following self-interrogation:

1. Is your record properly certified by clerk of trial court?
2. Is it likely you may encounter unavoidable delay in certification?
3. Are you keeping in touch with the clerk's office in preparation for avoiding a "last day" request for extension of time?
4. If the court reporter has died or some parts are missing from the transcript, are you prepared to follow appellate rules for evidence admission by statement or other available means?
5. Have you made positive arrangements for physical delivery of the record and all essential exhibits several days before time expires?
6. If there are stipulations filed that designated parts of the record may not be transmitted to appellate court, can you locate these parts immediately upon court request?
7. Have you paid all fees to court reporter, trial court clerk, and printer or transmitting agent, prior to expiration date?
8. Are you prepared for docketing the appeal and paying the appellate clerk fees prior to expiration date?
9. Are you keeping in touch with opposing counsel's office to assure his timely availability for record stipulation or other notice service?

5

How to Write the Brief for Appellate Court

In British law practice, the interpretation of the term "brief" might be more frequently applied to that document prepared by the Solicitor and given to the Barrister for his instruction and guidance in conducting their client's case in trial court. His brief would include statement of facts, summary of pleadings, names of witnesses, outline of anticipated evidence, and proposed sequence.

In American law practice, as applicable to state appellate court procedures, it is one prepared by counsel to serve as the basis for an argument upon a cause which has been carried from a lower court to the appellate court. As we consider the term in this chapter, we apply it to court of last resort at the state level. The document is filed for information of the court. It embodies points of law which the lawyer desires to establish. These points are developed by arguments based upon authorities in support of the contention of appellate advocate on behalf of his client. It is a conduit which the lawyer uses to convey to appellate court the essential facts of his client's case. He includes questions of law, applicable prior case decisions in point, statutory law to be applied, and the specific application of said law to his case. As partial answer to the question "How-to-Write-the-Brief," statutory requirements must be foremost. After applicable rules are thoroughly studied by appellate advocate, the question is further answered in the more recent trend toward clinical legal guidance in the "show and tell" learning arena of studying samples.

A. FOLLOW A MODEL EXAMPLE.

With resources of 50 state courts of last resort, and thousands of well-written briefs by outstanding lawyers, the search for model American law briefs proved to be a rewarding experience. The various geographic areas and the wide variety of case decisions offered a maze of potentialities for a thrust of interest applicable to the over-all picture.

Recent trend of the wanderlust in a growing mobile society has created great demand for more uniform laws in all states. It has also created interest in individual rights and responsibilities for the citizen on the move. Big companies are opening new factories and expanding operations into new areas where supervisory people are being transferred. It is not the more restless individual who seeks employment or home planting in another state. It is frequently the experienced, highly skilled technical employee, or the professional income producer and his family, who face legal complications in the transplant of domicile.

Therefore, from the Alaska Supreme Court, we have selected as a model the appellee brief written on behalf of a new resident who successfully sustained the Superior Court of First Judicial District. The appeal was styled: *State of Alaska, Joseph R. Henri, Patrick L. Hunt, Joe Franich, Willett J. Marshall, and Clarence Hafling, Appellants v. Susan K. Wylie, Appellee,* Alaska Supreme Court File No. 1836, OPINION No. 963, 516 P. 2d 142 (November 23, 1973). Appellee was represented by William B. Rozell of the Juneau Law Firm, FAULKNER, BANFIELD, DOOGAN, GROSS & HOLMES. With our annotations to direct reader's attention to exemplary points in form, content, and organization, his brief follows:

B. STUDY SAMPLE BRIEF: ALASKA ILLUSTRATION*

FORM #9

COVER PAGE FORMAT①

THE SUPREME COURT OF THE STATE OF ALASKA

STATE OF ALASKA, JOSEPH R.	)
	)
HENRI, PATRICK L. HUNT, JOE	)
	)

Note: The encircled numerals are added by the author to refer to final pages of this chapter where reader will find more detailed "Footnotes and Comments" on indicated points of merit or demerit observed in this model brief.

FRANICH, WILLETT J. MARSHALL)
)
and CLARENCE HAFLING,)
)
Appellants,)
)
vs.)
)
SUSAN K. WYLIE,)
)
Appellee.)   No. 1836
_____)

Appeal from the Superior Court
of the State of Alaska, First Judicial District

BRIEF OF APPELLEE

FILED February 2, 1973   FAULKNER, BANFIELD, DOOGAN,
In the Supreme Court of   GROSS & HOLMES
the State of Alaska   By   WILLIAM B. ROZELL
                                       311 North Franklin Street
___J. M. McPHETRES___   Juneau, Alaska 99801
Clerk
                                 Attorney for Appellee
___Betty H. Bailey___
Chief Deputy Clerk

[1] SUBJECT INDEX ②

[2.]   TABLE OF AUTHORITIES CITED ③
CASES

[3]   STATUTES AND CONSTITUTIONAL PROVISIONS ④

[4]   RULES

CONSTITUTIONAL PROVISIONS AND
STATUTES INVOLVED IN THE CASE ⑤

Constitution of the United States, Article I, Section 8:
The Congress shall have power ... to regulate commerce with foreign nations, and among the several states, and with the Indian tribes . . . . .

Constitution of the United States, Article IV, Section 2:
The citizens of each state shall be entitled to all privileges and immunities of citizens in the several states . . . . . .

Constitution of the United States, Fourteenth Amendment, Section 1:
All persons born or naturalized in the United States, and subject to the jurisdiction thereof, are citizens of the United States and of the state wherein they reside. No state shall make or enforce any law which shall abridge the privileges or immunities of citizens of the United States; nor shall any state deprive any person of life, liberty, or property, without due process of law; nor deny to any person within its jurisdiction the equal protection of the laws.

Alaska Constitution, Article I, Section 1: *Inherent Rights.*
This constitution is dedicated to the principles that all persons have a natural right to life, liberty, the pursuit of happiness, and the enjoyment of the rewards of their own industry; that all persons are equal and entitled to equal rights, opportunities, and protection under the law; and that all persons have corresponding obligations to the people and to the State.

Alaska Constitution, Article I, Section 7: *Due Process.*
No person shall be deprived of life, liberty, or property, without due process . . . .

Alaska Constitution, Article XII, Section 6: *Merit System.*
The legislature shall establish a system under which the merit principle will govern the employment of persons by the State.

Personnel Rules of the State of Alaska, *Rule 1: "Alaska Resident."*
"Alaska Resident" means a person who has been domiciled in the State for the twelve months immediately prior to making application for State employment.

Personnel Rules of the State of Alaska, *Rule 3 09.0:*
3 09.1. Alaska residence, for purposes of employment preference, shall be established when a person has been domiciled in the State of Alaska for the twelve months immediately prior to his making application for employment.

3 09.3. Residence status for employment shall be re-established on return to Alaska when the individual has maintained Alaska residence for the major part of his life; or, the major part of his adult life. The method of determining residence by either major part of life or major part of adult life shall be that one which is most advantageous to the applicant.

3 09.4. The preference provided Alaska residents shall be within the framework of the merit system as specified by Rule 4 01.1 and 5 03.0 wherein Alaska residents shall be certified from the open competitive list in rank order ahead of any non-Alaskans on the register.

Rule 4 01.0:

The Director shall establish and maintain eligible lists necessary to carry out the purpose of the personnel law and Rules ... provided Alaska residents shall be listed in rank order above non-residents ....

THE SUPREME COURT OF THE STATE OF ALASKA

STATE OF ALASKA, JOSEPH R. HENRI, PATRICK L. HUNT, JOE FRANICH, WILLETT J. MARSHALL, and CLARENCE HAFLING, Appellants, vs. SUSAN K. WYLIE, Appellee.	No. 1836

Appeal from the Superior Court
of the State of Alaska, First Judicial District

BRIEF OF APPELLEE

SUSAN K. WYLIE

[5]   **STATEMENT OF JURISDICTION** ⑥

Appellants have appealed from a decision of the Superior Court for the State of Alaska, First Judicial District, filed on October 30, 1972, entering summary judgment in favor of the plaintiff-appellee, Susan K. Wylie. Notice of appeal was filed by appellants on November 1, 1972. The preparation of the Record on Appeal was completed on November 13, 1972.

The jurisdiction of this Court is based on Article IV, §2 of the Alaska

Constitution, AS 22.05.010, and Rule 6 of the Rules of the Supreme Court of the State of Alaska.

[6]   **STATEMENT OF THE CASE**

The plaintiff-appellee, Susan K. Wylie, does not controvert appellants' statement of the case. However, appellee believes that it will be helpful to this Court if appellants' summary is supplemented ⑦ with a more specific statement of appellee's claim.

Susan Wylie has been a resident and domiciliary of the State of Alaska since May 11, 1972. (8)* ⑧ After she had established residence, Ms. Wylie applied for state employment and passed competitive state examinations. (8-9) However, in accordance with Alaska's one-year durational residency rule, she was listed on eligible lists for state employment after all eligible resident applicants who had lived in the state for one year or more, regardless of their competitive examination scores. For some positions the state refused even to consider her application because she had not been a resident for one year. (9)

On July 14, 1972, Wylie ⑨ commenced this action seeking a declaration that the durational residency requirement is unconstitutional. (1-6) Specifically, she sought a declaration that the definition of "Alaska Resident" in Rule 1, Rule 4 01.1 and Rule 3 09.0 of the State of Alaska, Department of Administration, Division of Personnel, Personnel Rules adopted pursuant to AS 39.25.010-220, are invalid and unconstitutional, and further sought a permanent injunction restraining the enforcement of those rules.

Wylie alleged that the rules are invalid under the United States Constitution in that they:⑩

(a) create an invidious and arbitrary discrimination between residents of the State of Alaska who have been residents for one year or more and other residents of the State in contravention of the 14th Amendment;

(b) create a restriction on the right to be considered for state employment which is unrelated to the applicant's ability to work at such employment or to any valid regulatory purpose in further contravention of the 14th Amendment; and

(c) impose an unreasonable burden on interstate commerce and on the right of citizens of the United States to travel freely among the states in violation of Article I, § 8, Article IV, § 2, and the Fourteenth Amendment of the United States Constitution.

She also alleged that they were invalid under the Alaska Constitution in that they: ⑪

(a) create an invidious and arbitrary discrimination between residents

---

* All parenthetical references are to pages in the record on Appeal unless otherwise indicated.

of the State of Alaska who have been residents for one year or more and other residents of the state in contravention of Article I, § 1 of the Alaska Constitution;

(b) deny to persons who have been residents of the state for less than one year the enjoyment of the rewards of their own industry in contravention of Article I, § 1 of the Alaska Constitution;

(c) create a restriction on the right to be considered for state employment which is unrelated to the applicant's ability to work at such employment or to any valid regulatory purpose in contravention of Article I, § 7 of the Alaska Constitution; and

(d) violate the merit principle in the employment of persons by the State in contravention of Article XII, § 6 of the Alaska Constitution.

The Superior Court granted Wylie's motion ⑫ for summary judgment and permanently enjoined the appellants from enforcing any durational residency requirement for state employment. (99-107) The Court held that such a requirement penalizes the fundamental right to travel and denies equal protection of the law to residents of Alaska. (103) In so holding, it applied the compelling state interest test. (103-04) The court below did not find it necessary to rule on Wylie's other alleged bases of invalidity and specifically declined to interpret Article XII, § 6 of the Alaska Constitution which provides that the merit principle will govern the employment of persons by the state. (103)

[7] SUMMARY OF ARGUMENT ⑬

Durational residency requirements are unconstitutional unless they can be shown to serve a compelling state interest. The durational residency requirement in this case, which gives a preference in state employment to persons who have resided in the state for one year or more, does not serve a compelling state interest and is not even rationally related to a legitimate state objective.

The durational residency requirement for state employment unreasonably discriminates in favor of older residents at the expense of residents who have lived in the state for less than a year, thereby denying newer residents equal protection of the laws. The requirement denies newer residents an equal opportunity to be considered for state employment. While there may be no constitutional right to state employment as such, there is a constitutional right to be free from unreasonable discriminatory practices with respect to such employment.

The durational residency requirement also penalizes newer residents for having recently exercised their fundamental right to travel. Any classification serving to penalize the exercise of a fundamental right is unconstitutional unless it can be shown to be necessary to serve a compelling state interest.

The applicable constitutional test in this case is the compelling state interest test. But regardless of which test is applied, the compelling state interest or the rational relationship test, appellants have failed to show that the durational residency requirement is constitutionally permissible. The State has not demonstrated that the requirement actually serves the governmental interests alleged or that the one-year residency rule is even rationally related to such interests.

Even if legitimate state interests are served by the durational residency requirement, such a requirement is too broad and imprecise to be constitutionally permissible. The requirement is not the least drastic means available and is not necessary and essential to serve those interests.

The Superior Court below held the durational residency requirement invalid on the grounds outlined above. Even if appellants are correct in their specification of error, the durational residency requirement is nevertheless invalid on the other grounds alleged in the court below but not considered by the Superior Court in its Memorandum of Decision. The requirement represents an unreasonable burden on interstate commerce, denies new residents the rewards of their own industry and due process of law, and violates the merit principle in state employment.

[8]   ARGUMENT

I.   THE DURATIONAL RESIDENCY REQUIREMENT FOR STATE EMPLOYMENT IS UNCONSTITUTIONAL UNLESS IT CAN BE SHOWN TO BE NECESSARY TO PROMOTE A COMPELLING GOVERNMENTAL INTEREST. ⑭

The durational residency requirement for state employment denies plaintiff-appellee equal protection of the laws and infringes upon her right to travel. In *Dunn v. Blumstein,* 405 U.S. 330, 31 L.Ed. 2d 274 (1972), the United States Supreme Court reaffirmed its holding in *Shapiro v. Thompson,* 394 U.S. 618, 22 L.Ed. 2d 600 (1969), that the right to travel is a fundamental right under the United States Constitution, and any classification serving to penalize this right, unless shown to be necessary to promote a compelling state interest, is unconstitutional. In any case where a fundamental right is infringed upon the applicable test is the compelling state interest test rather than the less stringent rational relationship test.

The court said in *Dunn:*

"In sum, durational residence laws must be measured by a strict equal protection test; they are unconstitutional unless the State can demonstrate that such laws are 'necessary to promote a *compelling* governmental interest.' . . . It is not sufficient for the State to show that durational residence requirements further a very substantial state interest. In pursuing that important interest, the State cannot choose means which unnecessarily burden or restrict constitutionally protected activity. Statutes affecting constitutional rights must be drawn with 'precision,' ... and must be 'tailored' to serve their legitimate objectives .... And if there are other, reasonable ways to achieve those goals with a lesser burden on constitutionally protected activity, a State may not choose the way of greater interference. If it acts at all, it must choose 'less drastic means.' ..." 31 L.Ed. 2d at 284-85 (citations omitted).

Applying this principle in the present case, the Superior Court held that the durational residency requirement for state employment in Alaska penalizes exercise of the right to travel, does not promote any compelling governmental interest, and therefore is unconstitutional. (99-105).

In every case since *Shapiro* where durational residence requirements have been applied as an absolute requirement for public employment or to create a preferred classification for public employment, they have been struck down as unconstitutional. In *Carter v. Gallagher,* 337 F.Supp.626 (D. Minn. 1971), it was held that a durational residency requirement for obtaining a civil service veteran's preference did not serve a compelling state interest and therefore was unconstitutional. A similar decision was reached in *Stevens v. Campbell,* 332 F.Suppl.102 (D. Mass. 1971), where the court held that such a requirement could not meet even the rational relationship test and therefore, *a fortiori,* did not meet the compelling interest test. In *Vazquez v. Solon,* 72 C.179 (N.D. Ill. 1972), the court granted a preliminary injunction enjoining the City of Chicago and Cook County from enforcing a one-year durational residency requirement for civil service employment. The court made preliminary findings that the durational residency requirement penalized plaintiff solely because she had recently moved into the jurisdiction in the exercise of her constitutionally protected right to travel, that the requirement served no compelling governmental interest, and that the plaintiff would suffer irreparable injury if the preliminary injunction were denied. Following the preliminary injunction, Chicago and Cook County voluntarily repealed their one-year durational residency requirements and the case was concluded by consent decree and stipulation to dismiss.

Similar holdings in non-employment cases emphasize that durational residency requirements penalize exercise of the right to travel and are therefore unconstitutional. *State v. Van Dort,* 502 P.2d 453 (Alaska 1972) (durational residency requirement for voting); *King v. New Rochelle Housing Authority,* 314 F.Supp.427 (S.D.N.Y. 1970), *aff'd* 442 F.2d 646 (2d Cir. 1970), *cert. den.* 404 U.S. 863 (1971) (durational residency requirement for public housing); *Cole v. Housing Authority of Newport,* 312 F.Supp.692 (D.R.I. 1970), *aff'd* 435 F.2d 807 (1st Cir. 1970) (durational residency requirement for public housing); *Vaughan v. Bower,* 313 F.Supp.37 (D. Ariz. 1970), *aff'd* 400 U.S. 884 (1970) (statute permitting state hospital to return inmates to state of former residence if they had not resided in the state for one year); *Crapps v. Duval County Hospital Authority,* 314 F.Supp. 181 (M.D. Fla. 1970) (durational residency requirement for free medical care); *Wymelenberg v. Symar,* 328 F.Supp. 1353 (E.D. Wis. 1971) and *Adams v. State,* Civ. No. 72-67 (Super. Ct. at Sitka, Alaska 1973) (durational residency requirements for suing for divorce).

Appellants attempt to confuse the clear holding in *Dunn* by making the argument that any infringement upon the plaintiff-appellee's right to travel is only derivative in nature (Appellants' Brief, P.6), and that the compelling state interest test applies only to classifications which directly penalize fundamental rights as opposed to interests that are concomitant with or accompanying those rights. (Appellants' Brief, P.14.) *Dunn* rules out this theory. In applying the compelling state interest test therein, the Supreme Court said:

> "This exacting test is appropriate for another reason. . .: Tennessee's durational residence laws classify bona fide residents on the basis of recent travel, penalizing those persons, and only those persons, who have gone from one jurisdiction to another during the qualifying period. Thus, the durational residence requirement directly impinges on the exercise of a second fundamental personal right, the right to travel." 31 L.Ed. 2d at 281-82.

The court's discussion of the right to travel is explicit in holding that, independently of the nature or description of any other right or interest involved, a durational residency requirement is unconstitutional if it penalizes recent travelers without being necessary to promote a compelling state interest. 31 L.Ed.2d at 282-85.

The state's assertion that it has not directly interfered with plaintiff-appellee's fundamental right to travel (Appellants' Brief, p.14) is also without foundation or relevance. Plaintiff-appellee has been penalized by being listed on eligible lists for state employment after all residents who have lived in Alaska one year or more, regardless of their scores on competitive examinations. (9) A durational residency requirement need not actually deter a person from traveling; it need only penalize the exercise of the right to travel. *Dunn v. Blumstein, supra,* 31 L.Ed 2d at 283. And:

> "By definition, the imposition of a durational residence requirement operates to penalize those persons, and only those persons, who have exercised their constitutional right of interstate migration." *Oregon v. Mitchell,* 400 U.S. 112, 238, 272, L.Ed. 2d 346 (1970) (opinion of Justices Brennan, White and Marshall), quoted in *Carter v. Gallagher, supra,* 337 F.Supp. at 631.

Furthermore, the durational residency requirement has directly penalized the right to travel of former members of the class plaintiff-appellee represents, forcing them to leave the state (85-94), and has deterred others from moving to Alaska (95-98).

Clearly, where the right to travel is penalized, the compelling state interest test rather than the rational relationship test applies. *Wellford v. Battaglia*, 343 F.Supp.143 (D. Del. 1972); *Krzewinski v. Kugler*, 338 F.Supp.492 (D. N.J. 1972). *Dandridge v. Williams*, 397 U.S. 471 25 L.Ed. 2d 491 (1970), and *Reid v. Reid*, 404 U.S. 71, 30 L.Ed. 2d 225 (1971), the only recent United States Supreme Court cases cited by appellants, did not involve the right to travel. (See Appellants' Brief, pp.7, 9, 10, 16.)

The recent opinions of this court in *State v. Van Dort, supra,* and *Breese v. Smith*__P.2d__(Alaska, Opinion No.827, pp. 26-31, 1972), require that the compelling state interest test be applied under the Alaska Constitution as well. Indeed, the Superior Court in *Adams v. State, supra,* has held that an even more stringent test must be applied to durational residency requirements in Alaska.

> "The State of Alaska may discriminate among residents on the basis of their length of residency if the discrimination is absolutely necessary for administrative purposes. *State v. Van Dort,* 502 P.2d 453, 454 (Alaska 1972). This is a stricter standard than the United States Supreme Court enunciated in *Dunn* for interfering with the right to travel, that the statute serves a compelling state interest and that the statutory provision is necessary to protect that interest." (Memorandum of Decision, p.3.)

Article I, § 1 of the Alaska Constitution is also broader than the equal protection clause of the United States Constitution, guaranteeing not only equal protection but equal rights and opportunities under the law—including the right of all Alaska residents to be considered for state employment on an equal basis without regard to duration of residence.

Appellants attempt to minimize the importance of equal opportunity for employment, and particularly the opportunity for employment with the state. (See Appellants' Brief, pp. 11-13.) In *Keenan v. Board of Law Examiners of the State of North Carolina,* 317 F. Supp. 1350 (E.D.N.C. 1970), the court said:

> "The right to travel and the right not to be arbitrarily excluded [footnote omitted] from the legal profession, as pronounced in *Schware,* are here entwined. The right to work for a living in one's chosen occupation is for most people a prerequisite to the pursuit of happiness. If a man may be arbitrarily made to give up his life-time endeavor—even for a year—in order to move his residence, it is idle to talk about Fourteenth Amendment protection of personal freedom." 317 F.Supp. at 1361-62.

See also *Potts v. Honorable Justices of the Supreme Court of Hawaii.* 332 F.Supp. 1392 (D. Hawaii, 1971); *Lipman v. Van Zant,* 329 F.Supp.391 (N.D. Miss. 1971); *Webster v. Wofford,* 321 F.Supp.1259 (N.D. Ga. 1970).

In *Whitner v. Davis,* 410 F.2d 24 (9th Cir. 1969), the Ninth Circuit said:

> "While there may be no constitutional right to public employment as such, there is a constitutional right to be free from unreasonably discriminatory practices with respect to such employment." 410 F.2d at 30.

In *Perry v. Sinderman,*__U.S.__33 L.Ed. 2d 570 (1972), Mr. Justice Stewart said:

> "For at least a quarter century, this Court has made clear that even though a person has no 'right' to a valuable governmental benefit and even though the government may deny him the benefit for any number of reasons, there are some reasons upon which the government may not act. It may not deny a benefit to a person on a basis that infringes upon his constitutionally protected interests—especially, his interest in freedom of speech. For if the government could deny a benefit to a person because of his constitutionally protected speech or associations, his exercise of those freedoms would in effect be penalized and inhibited. This would allow the government to 'produce a result which [it] could not command directly'. . . .Such interference with constitutional rights is impermissible. We have applied this general principle to denials of tax exemptions, . . . unemployment benefits, . . . and welfare payments, . . .But, most often, we have applied the principle to denials of public employment. . . .We have applied the principle regardless of the public employee's contractual or other claim to a job. . . ." 33 L.Ed. 2d at 577 (extensive citations omitted).

See also *Truax v. Raich,* 239 U.S. 33, 42, 60 L.Ed. 131, 135 (1915); *Dougall v. Sugerman,* 330 F.Supp. 265 (S.D.N.Y. 1971); *Cohen v. City of Miami,* 54 F.R.D. 274 (S.D. Fla. 1972); *Hsieh v. Civil Service Commission of the City of Seattle,* 79 Wash. 2d 529, 488 P.2d 515 (1971); *Purdy & Fitzpatrick v. State,* 71 Cal. 2d 566, 456 P.2d 645, 79 Cal. Rptr.77 (1969); and see *Toomer v. Witsell,* 334 U.S. 385, 92 L.Ed. 60 (1948); *City of New Brunswick, N.J. v. Zimmerman,* 79 F.2d 428 (3d Cir.1935)(privileges and immunities).

Appellants' position that the state, when acting as an employer, acts as a private party not subject to the equal protection clauses of the federal and Alaska constitutions, and its assertion that residents have no right to be considered for state employment (Appellants' Brief, pp. 11-13), are without legal foundation. Whatever support those theories might once have found in such cases as *Heim v. McCall,* 239 U.S. 175, 60 L.Ed. 206 (1915), and *Atkin v. Kansas,* 191 U.S. 207, 48 L.Ed. 148 (1903), is no longer of any relevance. Those cases have been severely restricted or entirely overruled by modern case law. See, e.g., *Graham v. Richardson,* 403 U.S. 365, 29 L.Ed. 2d 534 (1971); *Dougall v. Sugerman,* 339 F.Supp. 906, 909-10 (S.D.N.Y. 1971); *Krzewinski v. Kugler,* 338 F.Supp. 492 (D.N.J. 1972); *Leger v. Sailer,* 321

F.Supp. 250, 254-55 n. 10 (E.D.Pa. 1970), *aff'd* 403 U.S. 365, 29 L.Ed. 2d 534 (1971); *Gonzales v. Shea,* 318 F.Supp. 572, 578 n. 15, *vacated* 403 U.S. 927, 29 L.Ed .2d 706 (1971); *Purdy & Fitzpatrick v. State,* 71 Cal. 2d 566, 79 Cal. Rptr. 77, 456 P.2d 645, 657 (1967); *Herriott v. City of Seattle,* 81 Wash. 2d 48, 500 P.2d 101 (1972).

II. THE DURATIONAL RESIDENCY REQUIREMENT FOR STATE EMPLOYMENT FAILS TO MEET EITHER THE COMPELLING STATE INTEREST TEST OR THE RATIONAL RELATIONSHIP TEST.

Appellants contend that the durational residency requirement for state employment serves a compelling legitimate state interest because it (1) upgrades and utilizes more fully Alaska's human resources, (2) helps reduce chronic unemployment, primarily among its native residents, and (3) improves the efficiency of state government by reducing personnel turnover and promoting an atmosphere of careerism and professionalism in state employees. (Appellants' Brief, pp. 6-7, 16-23.) The state's data and conclusions are subject to serious question. But even if it is conceded for purposes of this argument that those interests actually are served, the durational residency requirement is nevertheless invalid because it is *too broad and imprecise,* it is not the *least drastic* means available to serve these interests, and it is not *necessary and essential* to promote a compelling state interest as opposed to merely a very substantial state interest. See *Dunn v. Blumstein, supra,* 31 L.Ed. 2d at 284-85. Indeed, a durational residency requirement for public employment fails to meet either the compelling state interest test or the rational relationship test. *Carter v. Gallagher* and *Stevens v. Campbell, supra.*

The state argues that it must educate, train and integrate its natives, and argues that it must keep jobs open while training is carried on. But the durational residency requirement provides no education, no training and no access to job opportunities from remote areas. It is not comparable, for example, to the Alaska Plan, an affirmative action plan for minority hire presently being implemented by the state which is specifically designed to help eliminate the effects of past discrimination toward natives. Furthermore, the durational residency requirement does not keep jobs open for natives or the unskilled. The state positions affected by the durational residency requirement are immediately filled on a competitive basis by the most highly skilled applicants chosen from among all residents who have lived in the state one year or more.

Nor is the durational residency requirement rationally related to combatting unemployment. It creates no new jobs and merely serves to shift the burden of unemployment to newer residents. As the appellants point out (Appellants' Brief, p. 18): ⑮

"[The ability of in-migrants and seasonal workers] to command jobs in Alaska is a *symptom of, rather than a cause of conditions in high unemployment ratios,* particularly among Alaska Natives. Those who need jobs the most tend to be under-educated, untrained, or living in areas of the State remote from job opportunities." (Emphasis added.) The United States Supreme Court in *Shapiro v. Thompson, supra,* explicitly held:

> "A state purpose to encourage employment provides no rational basis for imposing a one-year waiting-period restriction on new residents only." 394 U.S. at 637-38, 22 L.Ed. 2d at 617.

The one-year residence rule here is specifically intended to discriminate in favor of older residents at the expense of bona fide residents who have recently exercised their right to travel, whereas the unemployment statistics cited by the state are illustrative of a problem faced by all residents, old and new alike. (See Appellants' Brief, pp. 20-21.) To the extent the requirement lowers unemployment by keeping people from moving to Alaska, the requirement serves a constitutionally impermissible purpose. E.g., *Shapiro v. Thompson, supra; Edwards v. California,* 314 U.S. 160, 86 L.Ed. 119(1941).

Appellants also contend that the durational residency requirement improves the efficiency of state government by reducing employee turnover and promoting an atmosphere of careerism and professionalism. Even if this is true, the Superior Court below correctly held that such a requirement is too drastic and infringes upon the equal protection clauses of both the United States and Alaska constitutions. If it is the state's goal to encourage new residents to remain at their jobs for a minimally desirable period of time, such longevity can be achieved by much more direct and less drastic methods. For example, the Attorney General's office hires out-of-state attorneys without requiring one ⑮ year's prior residence in Alaska. However, new attorneys are encouraged to remain with the Attorney General's office for at least two years by an agreement whereby the state pays their moving expenses up to $1,500 provided they remain on the job for two years; otherwise the attorneys must pay all or a pro-rated part of this expense themselves.

Furthermore, the state has shown no causal connection between length of residence and employee efficiency. Such a causal relationship must be demonstrated in order for the state to show that the durational residency requirement meets either the rational relationship or the compelling state interest test. *Breese v. Smith, supra,* Opinion No. 827 at 31-37.

The state's argument vaguely outlines the theory that persons who have resided in Alaska for a year or more have a lower turnover rate than persons who have not met the residency requirement, and that employee efficiency is increased by reducing personnel turnover because the employee does not maintain maximum performance until he or she has been on the job for a period of time varying from a few days to a year. (Appellants' Brief, pp. 22-23.) The state's statistics and conclusions are of questionable validity, but are accepted as accurate for purposes of this argument. However, the state has made no statistical showing that residents of less than one year's duration have a lower turnover rate *in the same state jobs* than persons who have been residents for a shorter time and no such showing can be made, because the durational residency rule has precluded residents of less than one year from obtaining most state jobs, presumably including the most desirable state jobs which would normally have a lower rate of personnel turnover.

The real purpose of the durational residency law is also outlined in the state's brief. ⑤ The state "shudders" at being "beset" by "in-migrants" intent on "usurping" state jobs.[1] (Appellants' Brief, especially pp. 17-21.) Appellants' desire to prevent in-migration and protect state jobs is constitutionally impermissible and cannot be allowed regardless of the state's other goals.

> "Thus, the purpose of deterring the in-migration of indigents cannot serve as justification for the classification created by the one-year waiting period, since that purpose is constitutionally impermissible. If a law has 'no other purpose . . . than to chill the assertion of constitutional rights by penalizing those who choose to exercise them, then it [is] patently unconstitutional.' . . ." *Shapiro v. Thompson, supra*, 394 U.S. at 631, 22 L.Ed. 2d at 613.

The goal of promoting provincial prejudices toward long-time residents is not cognizable under the United States Constitution. *Cole v. Housing Authority of the City of Newport, supra; Baldwin v. G.A.F. Seeling, Inc.*, 294 U.S. 511, 523, 79 L. 1032, 1038 (1935). A more precise method can be devised for keeping non-residents from obtaining state employment.

III. THE DURATIONAL RESIDENCY REQUIREMENT IS ALSO INVALID FOR REASONS ALLEGED AND BRIEFED IN THE COURT BELOW BUT NOT CONSIDERED IN THAT COURT'S MEMORANDUM OF DECISION.

Plaintiff-appellee argued in the Superior Court below that the durational residency requirement is also invalid because it denies Susan Wylie the rewards of her own industry and due process of law, and because it violates the merit principle in state employment. Since the Superior Court found the requirement invalid on equal protection grounds and because it penalizes exercise of the right to travel, the court did not consider the other reasons advanced by plaintiff-appellee in its Memorandum of Decision. The Superior Court expressly declined to interpret Article XII, §6 of the Alaska Constitution which requires that state employment be governed by the merit principle. (103)

Appellee believes the Superior Court was correct in holding that the durational residency requirement is invalid because it denies equal protection

---

[1] It should also be noted that plaintiff does not represent a class of in-migrants or seasonal workers. She represents a class of bona fide residents and domiciliaries who have lived in the state less than one year.

of the laws and infringes upon the right to travel. If, however, this court should find that the court below erred on those grounds, the Supreme Court nevertheless should affirm for the reasons set forth in the memoranda filed with the court below and included as part of the Record on Appeal. (18-20, 68-72, 83) In the alternative, this court should remand the cause to the Superior Court for a ruling on the points not covered in that court's Memorandum of Decision. (99-105)

IV.   CONCLUSION ⑯

The one-year durational residency requirement for state employment should be declared invalid and the decision of the Superior Court at Juneau should be affirmed.

>Respectfully submitted, [February 2, 1973]
>FAULKNER, BANFIELD, DOOGAN, GROSS & HOLMES
>BY
>WILLIAM B. ROZELL
>Attorney for Appellee, Susan K. Wylie

C. OPINION

The Alaska Supreme Court on November 23, 1973, Chief Justice Rabinowitz, presiding, issued a 16-page "OPINION," which stated, in part, as follows:

>The State of Alaska and certain officials of the state, appeal from a decision of the superior court holding unconstitutional those personnel regulations of the State of Alaska which give an absolute hiring preference to persons who have resided in Alaska for at least one year. For the reasons stated herein we affirm the decision of the superior court.
>
>. . . We are unable to conclude that the durational residence requirements for state employment are tailored with sufficient precision to satisfy the compelling state interest test. For the foregoing reasons, we conclude that the durational residence hiring preference embodied in Alaska Personnel Rules, 1, 3 09.0, and 4 01.0, is inconsistent with the equal protection of the laws afforded by the Alaska Constitution, Art. I, §1, and by the Fourteenth Amendment to the United States Constitution; [2] and, therefore, we affirm the judgment of the superior court.
>
>   *AFFIRMED.*

---

[2] We note that in a recent case, *York v. State*, 498 P.2d 644 (Hawaii 1972), the Supreme Court of Hawaii, ⑰ employing a rational basis standard of review, held that Hawaii's three-year durational residency ⑱ requirement for state employment violated the Equal Protection clause of the United States Constitution.

FOOTNOTES AND COMMENTS ON MODEL BRIEF:
Alaska Supreme Court Case

①Cover page is in the blue color to identify it from appellant brief in a white color, as required by Alaska Supreme Court rules. Many states now are beginning to use identifying colors for brief covers both in the printed and typewritten forms, as time savers for jurists.

②"Subject Index" of this brief is positioned at the preface location for good directive in reader's attention to organization and pagination.

③"Authorities cited" is also well positioned at the beginning of brief content which appears more readily accessible than at the end as an appendix. The extensive citations of recent case decisions are commendable as taken from similar case decisions. No two cases are entirely alike, and it is unwise for appellate advocate to refer to any citation as a case exactly in point. The pompous attitude could be disfavored.

④It is good form to identify in separate categories the references to statutes, constitutional provisions, and court rules.

⑤If brief is not running an overlength, it is a merited consideration to quote the applicable constitutional provisions, statutes, and court rules specifically applicable in the case, although it may be assumed that they are thoroughly familiar to the Supreme Court Justices.

⑥The opening paragraph setting forth "Statement of Jurisdiction" does bring forth a vital issue at the outset of brief.

⑦In the "Statement of the Case," note the courteous referral to appellant's brief. It may be advisable to supplement appellant's summary with a more specific statement of appellee's claim. Note this model states that there is no controversion of appellant's statement, but "appellee believes that it will be helpful to the court if appellant's summary is supplemented. . . ."

⑧The use of parenthetically enclosed numerals for reference to pages in the record does appear to be a fine plan for avoiding repetition of "Tr-8" for transcript, or "R-2" for record page referrals.

⑨Note the clarity in party identification with first paragraph using "the plaintiff-appellee, Susan K. Wylie"; the second paragraph shortened to "Susan Wylie"; and beginning with third paragraph and throughout the brief said party is merely "Wylie." This avoids any confusion in repetition of words "appellee" with reference to party of prime concern in this brief.

⑩ Note the clarity in position wherein Wylie alleges Alaska State employment rules invalid under U.S. Constitution "in that they. . ." [three specific points of approach listed].

⑪ The same convincing approach is made in support of the allegations of contravention of Articles in Alaska State Constitution.

⑫ Note the clear language in the last paragraph of statement of the case in which the brief writer presents the decision of lower court: "The Superior Court granted Wylie's motion for summary judgment and permanently enjoined the appellants from enforcing any durational residency requirement for state employment. The court held that such a requirement penalizes the fundamental right to travel and denies equal protection of the law to residents of Alaska. In so holding, it applied the compelling state interest test. . . ." Here the main contention of appellant's "compelling state interest test" is very skillfully recognized and presented in a light of fairness and frankness. This is a good point in appellee's image.

⑬ The use of a prefatory two-page "Summary of Argument" focuses attention on the main points. This gives a bird's-eye view to the Justices before the more lengthy complete development of "Argument."

⑭ The "Argument" includes many pertinent references and quotes from similar case situations. Three points are emphasized by all capital letters for eye attention of tired readers in easy scanning.

⑮ Note the courteous yet skillful use of adversary's points which, from different vantage point, appear favorable to Wylie's side.

⑯ Appellee has made a commendable statement of conclusion in one sentence of 25 words and has kept the entire brief very concise yet thorough with only 25 pages in length.

⑰ The court in its 16-page opinion affirming the judgment of the Alaska Superior Court makes a further note that the Supreme Court of Hawaii in 498 P. 2d 644 (1972) had held that "Hawaii's three-year durational residency requirement for state employment violated the Equal Protection Clause of U.S. Constitution." This contention was upheld by the Supreme Court of United States in subsequent ruling (Docket #72-842) on February 26, 1974, striking down durational residency requirement in Arizona, *Memorial Hospital et al v. Maricopa County*, 498 P. 2d 46.

⑱ The case subject and brief format make this a good model. Census report of 1970-73 reveals 32 per cent of all U.S. citizens changed their residence, 60 per cent of whom were in their twenties. The South and West gained 1.2 million migrants, while the North and East lost.

6

How to Proceed in Certiorari Appeals

Certiorari is an appellate proceeding which has increased in volume during recent years of crowded dockets and delayed hearings. The remedy of certiorari is available in all states of USA; however some states term the process a "writ of review." Expediency is the basic thrust for re-examination of lower court action. Brevity is an essential element for this review; and oral argument is frequently waived.

A. SCOPE AND LOCAL INTERPRETATIONS.

In the case decided on October 22, 1973, cited as *McKenzie et al. v. Burris et al.*, 500 S.W. 2d 357, the Arkansas Supreme Court, Justice John Fogleman presiding, in denying the writ, stated at page 363:

"The narrow question presented here, then, is whether the Circuit Court of Pope County had authority to permit a non-resident attorney, not licensed to practice in this state, to participate in the trial of this case in that court but associated with a resident attorney, licensed and regularly engaged in the practice of law in this state, even though the non-resident attorney has, in similar circumstances, engaged in trials or preparation for trial, or settlement negotiations of numerous other cases in Arkansas. We hold that it did. . . ."

Other interpretations as selected from various states are reflected in Table 7 on the following pages.

TABLE #7

CERTIORARI APPELLATE PRACTICES
Selected U.S.A. Local State Citations

STATE	INTERPRETATIONS[1] AND CASE DECISIONS
ARKANSAS	Certiorari cannot ordinarily be used as a substitute for Appeal. *McKenzie v. Burris,* 500 S.W.2d 357, October 1973.
ARKANSAS	Writ of Certiorari used where applicant for writ lost right of appeal through no fault of his own. *McCain v. Collins,* 204 Ark. 521, 164 S.W.2d 448, 451.
CALIFORNIA	It is a writ directed only to an inferior tribunal, *Stewart v. Johnson,* C.C.A. Cal., 97 F.2d 548.
FLORIDA	It is a writ to review erroneous or unwarranted acts or proceedings, *State ex rel Allen v. Rose,* 123 Fla. 544 167 So. 21, 24.
FLORIDA	The writs of "Certiorari" in use are the common-law writs, statutory writ to review judgments of civil courts of record, the rule certiorari for supplying omitted parts of records on appeals or writs or error, and to review interlocutory appeals in equity; and writs of certiorari issued to review judgments or orders of quasi judicial bodies or officers. *Kilgore v. Bird,* 149 Fla. 570, So.2d 541, 544, 545.
FLORIDA	To determine whether judgment is a miscarriage of justice or will result in substantial injury to legal rights. *Goodkind v. Wolkowsky,* 151 Fla. 62, 9 So.2d 553, 562.
FLORIDA	To determine whether judgment is prejudicial and materially harmful. *American Pub. Co. v. Jacksonville Paper Co.* 143 Fla. 835, 197 So. 672, 674.
	To determine whether inferior tribunal acted within, or abused, or exceeded jurisdiction. *Brundage v. O'Berry,* 101 Fla. 320, 134 So. 520, 521.
ILLINOIS	It brings into superior court the record of the administrative or inferior judicial tribunal for inspection. *Murphy v. Cuesta,* Rey & Co., 381 Ill. 162, 45 N.E.2d 26, 28.
IOWA	To determine whether inferior tribunal acted within or abused discretion. *Pierce v. Green,* 229 Iowa, 294 N.W. 237, 253.
MASS.	A writ by supreme judicial court commanding inferior tribunal to certify and return records for correction of

---

[1] See Black's Law Dictionary, Revised Fourth Edition by Publisher's Editorial Staff, West Publishing Co., St. Paul, Minn. 1968, p. 288.

STATE	INTERPRETATIONS AND CASE DECISIONS
	errors or irregularities which appear in the proceedings of any particular case. Pub. St. Mass. 1882 P. 1288, *Coolidge v. Bruce*, 249 Mass. 465, 144 N.E. 397.
MASS.	To correct errors of Law. *Dube v. Mayor of City of Fall River*, 308 Mass. 12, 30 N.E.2d 817, 818. To restrain excesses of jurisdiction. *Stacy v. Mayor of City of Haverhill*, 317 Mass. 188, 57 N.E.2d 564.
MICHIGAN	To review questions of law. *Public Welfare Commission v. Civil Service Commission*, 289 Mich. 101, 286 N.W. 175.
MINNESOTA	It is available for review of official judicial, or quasi judicial actions. *State v. Canfield*, 166 Minn. 414, 208 N.W. 181.
MISSISSIPPI	Certiorari is an appellate proceeding for re-examination of action of interior tribunal or auxiliary process to enable appellate court to obtain information in pending cause. *Shapleigh Hardwood Co. v Brumfield*, 159 Miss. 175, 130 So. 98.
MISSOURI	Used where quashal of record or proceeding is the only relief available. *State ex rel St. Louis County v Evans*, 346 Mo. 209, 139 S.W.2d 967, 969.
MISSOURI	In Missouri, office of writ of certiorari is same as at common law, and courts may properly adopt the usages and principles applicable to issuance of writ as developed under common-law system, consistent with letter and spirit of existing statutes (1972). *State ex rel Hill v. Davis*, 488 S.W.2d 305.
NEW JERSEY	It performs the office of the common-law writ of error. *Berry v. Recorder's Court of Town of West Orange*, 124 N.J. 385, 11 A.2d 743, 745.
NORTH CAROLINA	Issued only for good cause on showing negativing laches in prosecuting appeal. *In re Snelgrove*, 208 N.C. 670, 182 S.E. 335. Lies as substitute for appeal. *Pue v. Hood*, 222 N.C. 310, 22 S.E.2d 896, 898.
PENN.	It lies to determine whether inferior tribunal proceeded regularly. *In re Revocation of Restaurant Liquor License, No. R-8981, Issued to John Mami*, 144 Pa. Super 285, 19 A.2d 549, 552.
RHODE ISLAND	To review questions of law, where circumstances are so exceptional that an immediate review is in interest of justice. *Vingi v. Read*, 68 R.I. 484, 29 A.2d 637, 639.
TENNESSEE	On review of action of board or commission by certiorari, reviewing court is limited to questions of exceeding jurisdiction, or illegal action. T.C.A. §27-801 (1972). *Houston*

STATE	INTERPRETATIONS AND CASE DECISIONS
	v. Memphis and Shelby County Bd. of Adjustment, 488 S.W. 2d 387.
TEXAS	The ordinary office of writ of "certiorari" is to perfect the record on appeal. *Zamora v. Garza,* Tex. Civ. App. 117 S.W.2d 165. Some states preserve the remedy under new name "writ of review." *SW Tel & Tel Co. v. Robinson,* Tex. 1 C.C.A.91, 48 F 771.
VERMONT	Certiorari . . . to be made certain in regard to writ of review. *Leonard v. Wilcox,* 101 Vt. 195, 142 A 762, 766.
WEST VIRGINIA	Originally, as in English practice, certiorari was an original writ commanding judges or officers of inferior courts to certify or return records in a cause for review. *Ashworth v. Hatcher,* 98 W.Va. 323, 128 S.E. 93.

B. OBSERVE REVISED PROCEDURES: FLORIDA EXAMPLE.

From the preceding table, it will be noted that some states have made use of very limited applications which have held practical case use to a minimum of certiorari writs. Other states like Florida and Arkansas have made broader interpretations to facilitate certiorari proceedings by specific Supreme Court guideline rules and forms.

1. Expanded Use of Certiorari

The Florida Appellate Rules appear to provide three specific applicable situations for Writ of Certiorari as set forth in Rule 4.5, "Extraordinary Writs . . . (c) Certiorari," stating in part as follows:

From District Court to Supreme Court. Where any decision of a district court of appeal (1) affects a class of constitutional or state officers, or (2) passes upon a question certified by such district court to be of great public interest, or (3) is in direct conflict with a decision of another district court of appeal or of the Supreme Court on the same point of law, petition may be filed with the Supreme Court to issue a writ of certiorari to review such decision.

The Supreme Court shall consider the petition, supporting record or portions thereof and the briefs on jurisdiction, without oral argument unless otherwise directed, and if the Court determines that it has jurisdiction, the said petition shall be granted; otherwise the same shall be denied or dismissed.

2. Petition for Writ of Certiorari.

The Petition Form is set forth under Florida Supreme Court Rule #7.2 (i) *In Re: Florida Appellate Rules,* No. 37079 (1968) as amended July 15, 1973. This form is as follows:

FORM#10

PETITION FOR WRIT OF CERTIORARI: FLORIDA ILLUSTRATION

IN THE SUPREME COURT OF FLORIDA

_____ Petitioner	)	PETITION FOR A WRIT OF CERTIORARI TO
	)	
vs.	)	THE DISTRICT COURT OF APPEAL, SECOND
	)	
_____ Respondent	)	DISTRICT

TO THE SUPREME COURT OF THE STATE OF FLORIDA:

Petitioner,_____,presents this, his petition for a writ of certiorari and states:

1. Petitioner seeks to have reviewed an order (or decision) of the District Court of Appeal, Second District, dated the___day of_____, 19__, and filed in the records of said District Court on the___day of_____, 19__, in_____Book___, Page___.

2. This petition is presented under and pursuant to Article 5, Section 4, of the Florida Constitution, and Rule 4.5c of the Florida Appellate Rules.

3. This petition is accompanied by a certified transcript of the record of the proceedings, including the decision petitioner seeks to have reviewed, and a supporting brief.

4. The following are the facts of the case:

[Give in lettered sub-paragraphs and support statements by reference to the transcript.]

5. On the foregoing facts the Court was presented with the following point of law: [Here state point of law involved.]

On this point of law the District Court of Appeal, Second District, rendered the following decision or holding:

[Here give ruling or holding of the district court of appeal whose decision is sought to be reviewed.]

6. The same point of law was involved in the case of_____vs._____, decided by the District Court of Appeal, First District, on the___day of____, 19__. This decision was reported in__So.2d, page___, and a copy of the

decision is attached to this petition as Exhibit 1. The facts involved in____vs.____were as follows:

[Here state facts involved in the case from the other appellate district.]

On these facts the District Court of Appeal, First District rules as follows: [Here set forth ruling.]

7. The decision of the District Court of Appeal, Second District, which petitioner seeks to have reviewed is in direct conflict with the above-mentioned decision of the District Court of Appeal, First District. Because of the reasons and authorities set forth in petitioner's brief, it is believed that the decision hereby sought to be reviewed is erroneous and that the conflicting decision of the District Court of Appeal, First District, is correct and should be approved by this Court as the controlling law for the State of Florida.

WHEREFORE, petitioner requests this Court to grant a writ of certiorari and enter its order quashing the decision and order hereby sought to be reviewed, approving the decision of the District Court of Appeal, First District, as the correct decision, and granting such other and further relief as shall seem right and proper to the Court.

_____
Attorney for Petitioner

(CERTIFICATE OF SERVICE)

Address

C. REVIEW IMPLEMENTATION IN APPLICABLE STATE.

Observation of statutory directives for certiorari use in one state may be of general assistance and stimulation in your applicable case.

1. Procedure Guidelines: Arkansas Supreme Court Rule 16 [certiorari]

(a) *Pleadings—Number of copies* —In cases in which the jurisdiction of this court is in fact appellate although in form original, such as petitions for writs of prohibition, certiorari, or mandamus, the pleadings with their exhibits are treated as the record, and the pleader is required to file only the original typewritten copy, with evidence of service of copy upon the adverse party or his counsel of record in the trial court. . . .

(b) *Response* —A response to all such petitions shall be filed within 10 days after service of petition on respondent, unless, for good cause shown, the Court shall grant additional time upon request within 10 days.

(c) *Abstracts and Briefs—Time for Filing* —Printed abstracts and briefs are required as in other cases, the parties' time under Rule 7 for filing abstract and brief to be calculated from the date on which the petition is filed.

(d) *Applications for Temporary Relief* —When the petitioner intends to apply to the full court for temporary relief pending the consideration of the petition upon its merits, eight clearly legible copies of the petition must be filed, and reasonable notice of the application for temporary relief must be served upon the other party or his counsel of record in the trial court.

2. Recent Case Illustration: Certiorari Procedure Steps

TABLE #8

FILING DATE	ITEMIZED PAPERS AS FILED
3-2-1972	1. Original Petition for Writ of Certiorari
3-2-72	2. Verification of Petition
3-2-72	3. Certificate of Service on Respondent Counsel
3-2-72	4. Exhibits attached to Original Petition
	A. Divorce Decree of 3-18-71 as granted to plaintiff (Pulaski Chancery Court #150620: Baxter v. Baxter)
	B. Petition for Contempt of Court Citation: 12-8-71
	C. Response of Defendant
	D. Order for jail confinement for Contempt of Court signed by Chancellor Kay Matthews on 2-25-72
3-2-72	5. Memorandum in Support of Petition for Certiorari
3-3-72	6. Amended Petition for Writ of Certiorari
3-3-72	7. Certified Copies of Exhibits "A", "B", "C", and "D" (filed as executed by Clerk of trial court)
5-22-72	8. Abstract and Brief of Petitioner—Defendant
6-27-72	9. Abstract and Brief of Respondent*—Plaintiff
8-18-72	10. Reply Brief of Petitoner—Defendant
9-25-72	11. OPINION OF SUPREME COURT: WRIT DENIED.

The above procedure steps are taken from Arkansas Supreme Court case #5973 (1972) from which *Respondent's Brief is presented on following pages with permission of the writer, Attorney Dale Price of Little Rock, Arkansas, said case cited as *Baxter v. Matthews et al.* 484 S.W.2d 702 (1972).

FORM #11

D. SAMPLE BRIEF OF RESPONDENTS IN CERTIORARI: Cover Page*
SUPREME COURT OF ARKANSAS

BILLIE JAMES BAXTER .... Petitioner
     v. No. 5-5973

---

*Encircled numerals are added throughout this model brief to identify author's footnote references to annotations at last page of this chapter wherein merits and demerits of this sample brief are discussed.

HONORABLE KAY L. MATTHEWS,
   CHANCELLOR AND WILLA ANN
   BAXTER .... Respondents

PETITION FOR WRIT OF CERTIORARI
HON. KAY MATTHEWS, Chancellor

ABSTRACT AND BRIEF OF
RESPONDENTS ①

HOWELL, PRICE, HOWELL
BY DALE PRICE
Attorney for Respondent Willa Ann Baxter
211 Spring Street
Little Rock, Arkansas 72201

F I L E D
June 27 1972
JIMMY H. HAWKINS
   Clerk

1. Table of Contents ②

ABSTRACT AND BRIEF
of
RESPONDENTS

b.   **STATEMENT OF CASE**

SUPREME COURT OF ARKANSAS

BILLIE JAMES BAXTER .... Petitioner
   v.   No. 5-5973
HONORABLE KAY L. MATTHEWS,
   CHANCELLOR AND WILLA ANN
   BAXTER .... Respondents

PETITION FOR WRIT OF CERTIORARI
Hon. Kay Matthews, Chancellor

ABSTRACT AND BRIEF OF RESPONDENTS

STATEMENT OF CASE ③

This matter arose out of a domestic relations suit in the Third Division of the Chancery Court of Pulaski County, Arkansas, wherein respondent Willa Ann Baxter sought and was granted a decree of absolute divorce from petitioner Billie James Baxter, a dentist, on March 18, 1971. In that decree respondent was granted custody of the parties' four minor children, and petitioner was ordered to pay $200.00 per week as child support until May 1, 1971, and then to pay $250.00 per week thereafter as child support.

Subsequently, respondent filed a Petition for a Citation for Contempt alleging non-payment of child support by the petitioner. At a hearing on December 22, 1971, an Order was rendered by the Court finding petitioner in open and willful contempt for failing to make support payments as ordered by the Decree, and the Court found that petitioner had the ability to pay. The Order for contempt ordered petitioner committed in the Pulaski County Jail for ninety days, this being conditioned that if petitioner would pay the sum of $2,000.00 in cash he could secure his immediate release. Petitioner paid the $2,000.00 in cash and was released.

Thereafter, respondent was again caused to file another Petition for Citation for non-payment of child support by the petitioner. At a hearing on February 23, 1972, the Court entered an Order finding petitioner in willful, disrespectful contempt in failing, without just cause or excuse, to pay support payments. Petitioner was ordered confined for six months, with the stipulation that he could gain his release by posting $2,000.00 in cash with the Sheriff.

Petitioner has appealed to this Court from this Order of the Chancery Court, Third Division, of Pulaski County, Arkansas, entered on February 24, 1972.

c.   **POINTS TO BE RELIED UPON**

The Court did not err nor abuse its discretion ④ in finding petitioner in contempt and finding that changed conditions did not exist that would render petitioner unable to comply with the Order of the Court.

d.   SUPPLEMENTAL
                                          ABSTRACT OF RECORD

(For the purpose of this appeal, respondents respectfully refer the Court to the abstract of record in the brief of petitioner, but respondents present the following supplemental abstract ⑤ of testimony as necessary to an understanding of all questions presented in this Court for decision.)

(1) *PROCEEDINGS, DECEMBER 22, 1971, (R.49)*
[Under Arkansas Supreme Court Rule abstracted
testimony is in first person] ⑥
CROSS EXAMINATION
OF BILLIE JAMES BAXTER
$(R^2.85)$

I am sure some of these judgments that have been discussed here were outstanding at the time I entered the agreed decree. I don't know what my gross income is for this year (R.85). ⑦

I have told my fourteen-year-old son that if I get custody of him today we were going to Florida this afternoon. The people that I am going to see is paying my way and my son's way. I have been out on Asher Avenue to One-Eyed Jack's and I run a liquor tab out there. I have not been there but about four times. I eat there, too. I do have drinks out there. I have been to Steak and Ale two times, and I eat at Hank's all the time. I don't believe I have been drinking in Peck's (R.86, 87).

I have not made a payment on the pickup truck I am obligated on for two years (R.88).

It has been two months, I believe, since I made a payment on the horse trailer. That payment is roughly sixty a month, I believe (R.89).

I put Pyramid Life's name on the checks I have given to Mrs. Baxter. I did it so she could not spend it for food. Regardless of whether there was food in the house I knew she would have to take that particular check and take it to Pyramid Life (R.91).

THE COURT:

Counselor, he has admitted being in contempt. He has been treating patients and does not know how much he earned, and he has not been abiding by the Court's order. This is contempt. The Court will have two or three questions (R.91).

THE COURT:

It is correct that you led the youngster to believe instead of you going out with the sheriff you might be going with him to Florida?

---

[2] [The letter "R" followed by numerals herein makes reference to pages of transcribed "Record" of proceedings as certified from the trial court.]

Yes. I did not talk with his mother about taking him to Florida (R.93).

I did not have any insurance on my car and I ran off the side of the road and wrecked it (R.93).

I have not paid Ted Mueller this year on the debt I owe him. I paid him last year a thousand dollars (R.95).

I am practicing dentistry, and I am in my office four days per week (R.96).

It is correct that under the court order since September 1, 1971, I have advanced a total of about $788.00 to Mrs. Baxter or to she and the mortgageholder of the house note. During that same period of time from September 1st until today I don't know what sums I have taken in at my clinic. Well, from 11/1 to 11/30 my clinic income was $5,072.00 during the month of November. For September, $5,015.00. It would be approximately that, I suppose, for October. Aside from my overhead at the clinic I recall making a six-hundred-dollar payment last week on one of my debts (R.99, 100).

I don't recall any other sizable payments on any other debts over these three months (R.101).

The week-end of December 11th I had the children. I took them to my place on Saturday afternoon at Devonshire Apartments at 8401 1-30. I was away from the children from twelve o'clock at night until about four a.m. I got a call, a lady, and she said she wanted to talk to me about the children. She said, "We are having a party and I think it would be interesting." I was downstairs sitting in a car (R.102-104).

I told my oldest son Nick that if my former wife would let him live with me that I would give her a car (R.116).

(2) PROCEEDINGS, FEBRUARY 23, 1972 (R.131)
CROSS EXAMINATION ⑧
OF BILLIE JAMES BAXTER
(R.182)

I have not owned a car since last September. I got three or four people whose car I drive. On December 30th I paid Kelly Springfield Tire Company $83.01 for some tires on a girl's car I was using. (Plaintiff's Exhibit I—R.240.) She gave me a check for it but it is not deposited (R.182, 183).

I had occasion to pick up a dinner check at Hank's one time. I can identify that as my check and my signature. (Plaintiff's Exhibit 2—R.240.) I did not pay a forty-dollar dinner check at Hank's on January 20th of this year (R.183, 184).

I did not make a contribution to McClellan High School Athletic Department. It is payment for an ad put in last year for the children which I think she put in. It might have been through the office. That is a year old. That is my check. (Plaintiff's Exhibit 4—R.241.) (R.185-186.)

I paid Fountain Products of Arkansas, a coffee vending service, for coffee on January 10th. That is my check for $45.00. (Plaintiff's Exhibit 5–R.241.) That is my check to *Photoplay* for magazines for the office. (Plaintiff's Exhibit 6–R.242.) I don't read them. I still spend time at Peck's Drive-In. That is my check. (Plaintiff's Exhibit 7–R.242.) (R.186, 187.)

During the month of January, January 1st to January 17th, I deposited $3,296.50 to my account. From January 17th to January 31st I deposited an additional $3,012.15. In January I deposited in excess of $6,300.00. At the end of January my bank balance was $590.68. (Plaintiff's Exhibits 8 and 9–R.243, 244.) (R.188, 189.)

I have only given my wife fifty dollars since I was ordered to be either placed in jail or put two thousand dollars in. (9) That was the week before Christmas. Since that time I have not paid any funds to her other than fifty dollars (R.189, 190). . . .

I deposited about sixty-three hundred dollars in the bank account during the month of January. During that month I sent fifty dollars to Mrs. Baxter to support my four children. I have not sent any sums during this month of February, 1972 (R. 201).

THE COURT: The Court will then make a finding that about forty-five hundred dollars is pressing in keeping the office door open for expenses (R.201).

e.   BRIEF AND ARGUMENT

I

The Court did not err nor abuse its discretion in finding petitioner in contempt and finding that changed conditions did not exist that would render petitioner unable to comply with the Order of the Court.

Respondent Willa Ann Baxter was granted an uncontested decree of divorce on March 18, 1971, wherein petitioner Billie James Baxter agreed to and was ordered to pay $250.00 per week as child support for the parties' four minor children (R.8). At the time of the divorce decree, as well as at the time of all subsequent hearings, petitioner was and remains a licensed dentist with a full-time office and practice in Pulaski County, Arkansas. Petitioner was found in willful contempt for failure to make child support payments, and was found to have the ability to make such payments in a contempt hearing on December 22, 1971 (R.30, 31). After this hearing respondent was again forced to petition for a Citation for Contempt hearing. On February 23, 1972, petitioner was again found to be in willful, disrespectful contempt in failing and refusing, without just cause or excuse, to make child support payments as ordered by the Court below (R.40, 41).

Petitioner, in his Brief and Argument, states that Arkansas case law has told us that imprisonment for failure to pay an allowance for a child's maintenance can only be justified on the grounds of willful (10) disobedience to the order of the court. Respondent emphatically agrees on this point and would point out that the case at bar falls directly under such case law. Respondent would argue that petitioner, as the chancellor below correctly found, is admittedly, by his own testimony, in willful disobedience and contempt of the court's order without just cause or excuse.

The facts as revealed by the testimony ⓘ of the petitioner himself before the Court below, are most enlightening in this matter. He states that he is in his dentistry office four days a week, with Thursdays off (R.96). Although petitioner owns no car himself, he can afford to buy tires for a car belonging to some girl (R.182, 183, 240). He admits that he has written a forty-dollar check to Hank's for dinner for two on at least one occasion (R.183, 184, 240). He can afford to purchase coffee for everyone at his office for $45.00 (R.186, 241). He still can afford to spend his time at Peck's Drive-In (R.187, 242). During the month of January, 1972, he deposited in excess of $6,300.00 in his bank account, and had a bank balance at the end of January of $590.60 (R.188, 189, 243, 244).

The Court found from the testimony of the petitioner, that his office expenses required to operate his dental office were $4,500.00 (R.201). With his deposit of $6,300.00 during the month of January, this would leave approximately some $1,800.00 unaccounted for by petitioner. Out of this amount, petitioner openly admitted that during the month of January he paid respondent exactly $50.00 to support and feed his four children (R.201). He admitted that during the month of February, 1972, he sent no sums whatever for child support (R.201).

In view of the testimony of the petitioner himself, respondent would strongly argue that there can be no question that petitioner was and is in willful disobedience of the Court's order.

This Court has held that it is well-settled law that the decision of the chancellor will not be disturbed unless it is against a preponderance of the evidence. See *Ex Parte Johnson*, 221 Ark. 77, 251 S.W.2d 1012 (1952). Respondent would argue that the clear preponderance of the evidence and testimony reflect that the chancellor below clearly did not abuse his discretion in finding petitioner in contempt. In *Hervey v. Hervey*, 186 Ark. 179, 52 S.W. 2d 963 (1932), this Court said at page 964: "Whether or not the failure of the appellant to pay was in willful disobedience of the order of the court or from inability to meet the payments was a question of fact. . . ." Being a question of fact, respondent would argue that the chancellor was in the best position to determine contempt, without a showing that the preponderance of the evidence is against his finding. Respondent would further argue that petitioner has wholly failed to show a preponderance of evidence which would be contra to the finding of the chancellor below.

This Court has said, in *Ex Parte Johnson, Supra*, at page 1013 that: ⓘ ". . . the enforcement by contempt of a court's orders in respect to the payment of a child's support by its father is a matter that rests in the sound discretion of the chancellor, just as it is in his sound discretion either to relieve altogether or in part or compel payment of an accumulation of unpaid allowances." The chancellor below clearly has not abused his discretion in view of the evidence.

Petitioner seems to place great reliance on the case of *Peters v. Peters,* 238 Ark. 361, 381 S.W. 2d 748 (1964). However, that case can be easily contrasted to the fact situation before this court. The court in the *Peters* case was faced with an alimony payment which a wage earner was to make. In the instant case we are talking about child support payments, not alimony. Additionally, the *Peters* case reflected a situation where a man had, at least temporarily, no earning capacity at all. In the instant case, petitioner admits working four days a week and depositing $6,300.00 during the month of January, a situation wholly unlike the Court faced in the *Peters* case. Finally, this Court held, in *Peters,* that the reduction was temporary only, and that upon a showing that the appellant could resume full employment, the chancellor was ordered to resume full compliance with the orders in the divorce decree. In the instant case, petitioner has never ceased his full practice of dentistry.

There has been absolutely *no* showing of changed conditions which could justify the relief sought by petitioner. "The changed conditions mentioned in the decree must be construed to mean conditions that, in good conscience, would justify the relief." See *Tennison v. Tennison,* 216 Ark. 784, 227 S.W. 2d 138 (1950). In view of petitioner's income, station in the professional community of dentistry, and his admission of paying only $50.00 for the support of his four minor children from January 1, 1972, to February 23, 1972, there can be no doubt that petitioner was properly found to be in willful and disobedient contempt of the Court's orders. As recognized in the *Hervey* case, *supra,* and the *Tennison* case, *supra,* chancery courts have inherent powers to punish for such contempt for disobedience to their orders. Respondent could plead no more eloquently ⑬ than this Court in *Ex Parte Johnson, supra,* at page 1014, when it said:

"It seems to us that this power is especially important if chancery courts, with their limited means, are to guard the rights of dependent children in cases like this." ⑭

f.   CONCLUSION

Respondent would respectfully argue that, based on the evidence and testimony, the chancellor below did not abuse his discretion in finding petitioner in willful contempt, and he did not err in finding that no changed conditions existed which would justify petitioner's refusal to comply with the order of the court.

Therefore, respondent would ask this Court to affirm the finding ⑮ of contempt made by the chancellor below.

Respectfully submitted,
HOWELL, PRICE, HOWELL & BARRON
BY DALE PRICE ⑯
Attorneys for Respondent
Willa Ann Baxter

2. Opinion.

In the foregoing matter, Arkansas State Supreme Court, Justice Lyle Brown presiding on September 25, 1972, stated in part, as follows:

"... Unquestionably petitioner is heavily in debt. Much of the indebtedness was accumulated for the purchase of luxuries, some of which have been replevied. On the other hand, these four children constitute a serious financial burden on the mother. . .

"The chancellor found that petitioner had been in willful disobedience of the court's order and we do not reverse such finding unless we can say that the decision was against the preponderance of evidence. We do not so find. Writ of Certiorari *Denied.*"

FOOTNOTES AND COMMENTS

Author's Annotations on Respondent's Brief in Certiorari Procedure Before Arkansas Supreme Court (1972):

① The 7 x 9-inch printed booklet combines abstract, brief and argument. It has cover page of no particular identifying color to signify petitioner or respondent's brief. All pertinent information is properly given and filing date stamped by Supreme Court Clerk on this cover page.

② Citations are paged for quick reference and placed with table of contents. This also serves as index for statement of case, points to be relied upon, supplemental abstract of record, argument, and conclusion.

③ The statement of the case is clearly presented to set forth the background developments which precipitated the order finding petitioner in "willful and disrespectful contempt" of court by his failing without just cause or excuse, to pay support payments for four minor children, under prior order of the court.

④ Only one point is relied upon in this defense against the petition for writ of certiorari, to wit: "The court did not err nor abuse its discretion in finding petitioner in contempt . . ." Brevity is one of the commendable aspects of this brief.

⑤ The respondent's supplemental abstract of testimony is properly and respectfully presented as necessary to an understanding of all questions for appellate court decision.

⑥ The abstract of testimony fully complies with Arkansas Supreme Court Rule that testimony be abstracted in first person.

⑦ Page references to the record are indicated by "R" preceding the numeral. It would appear that "R" is unnecessary if the footnote explanation merely stated that numerals in parenthesis make reference to pages of transcribed "Record" of proceedings from the trial court.

⑧ The supplemental abstract of testimony is concise. Also, it has well-selected quotes from testimony of petitioner in the two cross-examination hearings on December 22, 1971, and on February 23, 1972.

⑨ Note the frank but respectful revealing of trial court's patience prior to issuing final contempt order bearing punishment by jail confinement with alternate cash bond payment to be applied in lump sum on arrearages due for his four children.

⑩ The respondent's brief and argument makes good use of petitioner's statement of grounds for imprisonment for failure to pay child maintenance as being justified only on "willful disobedience of the order of the court." Respondent agrees with this point and alleges the case at bar has proved willful disobedience.

⑪ Respondent's argument is based upon petitioner's own testimony of his earnings and ability to pay, plus his making no excuse for failure to do so.

⑫ Respondent makes pertinent case citations and applicable quotations from prior decisions of this same appellate court under similar case situations on routine appeal procedures.

⑬ Respondent pays tribute to appellate jurisdiction and its "eloquence" in quoting from a prior ruling on a similar point emphasizing the court's importance in guarding "the rights of dependent children in cases like this."

⑭ Note the respondent's clear and careful analysis of contrast in cases relied upon by petitioner.

⑮ Conclusion makes a concise request of appellate court to affirm the finding of contempt made by the chancellor in trial court and to deny the writ of certiorari.

⑯ It is commendable that this senior partner handles "his" case, from client's employment in lower court, to final conclusion in appellate levels. He has first-hand knowledge of pertinent testimony to be abstracted and parts of record to be designated. It is unwise to delete any unfavorable portions of evidence, lest opponent make issue of said omission, regardless of how irrelevant it may appear to new counsel.

The introductory summary in this model brief makes a frank but fair approach to the partisan position of his client. It begins with the strongest point of argument favoring sustaining lower court decision. It anticipates, and converts to good use, opponent's argument regarding willful and deliberate failure to abide by trial court orders for children's support. It cites cases appearing to hold contrary to argument, but directs court attention to points of difference. It answers charges and courteously exposes opponent's weak points. For these, and many other reasons, we have selected this model appellee brief from recent successes in defense of certiorari proceeding in a State Supreme Court, considering a subject of universal concern—enforcing support for dependent children.

7

How to Proceed from Prohibition Writs Throughout Appellate Rehearing and Brief Amicus Curiae

For our last illustration of good brief writing, we have selected an Oklahoma State Supreme Court Rehearing and the filing therein of *Amicus Curiae Brief* by American Bar Association under counsel leadership of its current President James D. Fellers of Oklahoma City, Oklahoma.

The case originated from three cases consolidated in Supreme Court of Oklahoma. Defendants had filed application with said court for writs of prohibition to the district judges before whom the matters were pending. The three separate cases were filed by individual county bar associations and the Oklahoma Bar Association in proceedings against municipal bond marketeers and their agents. The purpose was to enjoin defendants from alleged unlawful practice of law by persons who were not members of the Bar. After the first hearing, the Supreme Court held in a four-to-five decision that the repeal of legislation regulating the practice of law had left a vacuum so that there was no valid restriction against the non-forensic practice of law by unlicensed persons in Oklahoma. Motions for Rehearing were filed and granted, and the matter was briefed further by American Bar Association in *amicus curiae* and reargued. Final Opinion was filed on November 23, 1972, in said case cited as *R.J. Edwards Inc., et al. v. R.L. Hurt, District Judge, et al.* (Okl. 1972), 504 P.2d 407. Because of extensive analysis of basic problem and importance of issues in unauthorized practice of law, excerpts of principal opinion and brief amicus curiae are by permission included in this chapter.

A. WRIT OF PROHIBITION AS AN APPELLATE REMEDY.

The case selected for review in this chapter is significant in the fact that three matters of appellate remedies were sought during the processing of the various hearings: writ of prohibition, motion for rehearing, and application for permission to enter and file brief as amicus curiae. Actions for injunctions were separately filed in the District Courts of Payne, Major, and Canadian Counties, by the respective County Bar Associations and the Oklahoma Bar Association. Thereafter petitions for writs of prohibition were filed requesting the Supreme Court of Oklahoma to prohibit the judges of the respective District Courts from proceeding further. This Court then ordered the cases transferred to said Supreme Court for final disposition. The injunctive relief was denied, and prohibition was granted.

1. Definitions of "Prohibition."

Black's Law Dictionary[1] defines prohibition as the name of a writ issued by a superior court, directed to the judge and parties of a suit in inferior court. . . .

Among various supreme court definitions, we find an early landmark case from Oklahoma cited, *State v. Stanfield,* 11 Okl. Cr. 147; 143 P. 519, 522, which states, in part: "An extraordinary judicial writ issuing out of a court of superior jurisdiction, directed to an inferior court or tribunal exercising judicial powers, for the purpose of preventing the inferior tribunal from usurping a jurisdiction with which it is not lawfully vested."

TABLE #9

2. Writ of Prohibition Usage.

Selected U.S.A. Local State Citations

STATE	INTERPRETATIONS AND CASE DECISIONS
ARKANSAS	Prohibition does not lie unless court is wholly without jurisdiction of subject matter, or there is no adequate remedy by

---

[1]*Black's Law Dictionary,* Revised Fourth Edition by the Publisher's Editorial Staff. West Publishing Company, St. Paul, Minnesota (1968, p. 1377).

STATE	INTERPRETATIONS AND CASE DECISIONS
	appeal or otherwise. *Slitter vs. Ponder,* 252 Ark. 414, 479 S.W.2d 567, (1972). Writ of Prohibition will not lie where jurisdiction of trial court depends upon determination of fact. *Arkansas State Highway Commission vs. Roberts,* 248 Ark. 1005, 455 S.W.2d 125 (1970).
GEORGIA	Prohibition is an extraordinary judicial writ issuing out of court of superior jurisdiction for the purpose of preventing the inferior tribunal from assuming or exceeding jurisdiction over matters beyond its cognizance. *Jackson vs. Calhoun,* 156 Ga. 756, 20 S.E. 114, 115.
MISSOURI	Generally, where court has once acquired jurisdiction in case, either in personam or in rem, other courts may and should be prohibited from exercising any jurisdiction over the case. *State ex rel. Catholic Charities of St. Louis vs. Hoester,* 494 S.W.2d 70 (1973).
	Where realtor properly pleaded cause of action and prayer for damages which trial court said he would strike unless prohibited from doing so, prohibition was proper remedy. *State ex rel. Smith vs. Green,* 494 S.W.2d 55 (1973).
MISSOURI	Prohibition—To prevent court from action in excess of its jurisdiction. *State ex rel. Pruitt v. Adams,* 500 S.W.2d 742.
NEW YORK	Writ of Prohibition is only issued in cases of extreme necessity where the grievance cannot be redressed by ordinary proceedings at law or in equity or by appeal. *Niagara Falls Power Co. vs. Halpin,* 45 N.Y.S. 2d 421, 424, 181 Misc. 13.
NORTH DAKOTA	The writ of prohibition arrests the proceedings of any tribunal, corporation, board, or person, when such proceedings are without or in excess of jurisdiction of such tribunal. *State vs. Packard,* 32 N.D. 301; 155 N.W. 666.
TEXAS	A writ of prohibition is that process by which a superior court prevents inferior courts, tribunals, officers, or persons from usurping or exercising jurisdiction with which they have not been vested. Vernon's Ann. St. Const. art. 5 §5.—*State ex rel. Smith v. Blackwell,* 500 S.W.2d 97 (1973).
KENTUCKY	*Prohibition* would not lie after litigant had forfeited his right of appeal from Circuit Court, therefore by losing his right of appeal, *mandamus* was inappropriate. *Barnes et al. v. Ashcraft,* 490 S.W.2d 485 (1973).
OKLAHOMA	Writ of Prohibition is an extraordinary judicial writ or superior jurisdiction issued to inferior court.... *State v. Stanfield,* 11 Okl. Cr. 147, 143 P. 519, 522.

B. APPELLATE RIGHTS AND POTENTIALITIES IN REHEARINGS.

At all times you must keep your client informed of his case status. Immediately upon decision being reached by appellate court, a copy of the Opinion should be secured and time scheduled for a full conference with the client. Whether you have won or lost, the immediate person-to-person communication with your client is mandatory for extension of best attorney-client relationship. All state supreme courts have very brief time limits within which petition for rehearings may be filed. Usually a certificate must be signed stating that motion for rehearing is not filed for purpose of delay. Courts are reluctant to grant rehearings, and the increasing caseload of recent years has lessened permission grantings to less than one percent. Chances of reversal of original opinion are much less than one percent. Specific rules of court may limit the grounds for petition rehearings. Sometimes new counsel will spot issues overlooked by the court. Furthermore amicus curiae may appear as belated but influential counsel for rehearings.

1. Counsel Obligation to Accept Amicus Curiae.

It is counsel's duty and obligation to the client to pursue every possible remedy. Your Latin appellate client will readily understand and define your *amicus curiae* term as "a friend of the court." Your trial colleague will join you in interpreting the term as a counsellor bystander who interposes and volunteers information upon some matter of law in regard to which the court is doubtful or mistaken. This interpretation has been accepted and handed down from early case decisions to date.

TABLE #10

2. Amicus Curiae Definitions and Case Usage

Selected U.S.A. Local State Citations

STATE	INTERPRETATIONS AND CASE DECISIONS
INDIANA	Amicus Curiae is a counsellor who interposes and volunteers information upon some matter of which the court may take judicial cognizance. *In re Perry,* 83 Ind. App. 456, 148 N.E. 163, 165.
MISSOURI	Amicus curiae cannot inject new issues into case and court will not pass on contentions argued by amicus curiae but not presented by parties. *Robert Williams & Co., Inc. v.*

STATE	INTERPRETATIONS AND CASE DECISIONS
	State Tax Commission, 498 S.W.2d 527 (Missouri 1973).
NEW HAMPSHIRE	Amicus curiae implies friendly intervention of counsel to remind court of legal matter which has escaped its notice, and regarding which it appears to be in danger of going wrong. *Blanchard v. Boston & M.R.* 86 N.H. 263, 167 A. 158, 160.
NEW YORK	Amicus curiae is a person who has no right to appear in a suit but is allowed to introduce argument, authority, or evidence to protect his interests. *Ladue v. Goodhead,* 181 Misc. 807, 44 N.Y.S.2d 783, 787.
MISSOURI	*Universal C.I.T. Credit Corp. v. State Farm Mut. Auto Ins. Co. 493 S.W.2d 385.* (1973)
TEXAS	Counsel employed by defendant during trial could not properly assume office of amicus curiae on appeal. Office of amicus curiae is to aid court, and cannot be subverted to litigant use in case, *Booth v. State,* 499 S.W.2d 129 (1973).

C. BRIEF AMICUS CURIAE: Oklahoma Illustration.

From case cited as *R.J. Edwards, Inc., et al. v. R.L. Hurt et al.,* 504 P.2d 407 (1972).

(Ref.): *Unauthorized Practice News,* MAY 1973, American Bar Association, vol. xxxvii, No. 1, (Chicago, Illinois).[2]

Oklahoma Supreme Court Upholds
Inherent Power of the Courts
to Control Unauthorized Practice of Law
in Oklahoma

On November 28, 1972, the Supreme Court of the State of Oklahoma decided that, under the Oklahoma Constitution, the Judicial Department of the State is vested with full and complete authority, independent of the power of the legislature, to control and regulate the practice of law in all its forms and to prevent the intrusion of unlicensed persons into the practice, without regard to whether their acts are "forensic" (relating to representation in court) or "non-forensic" in nature. In light of the extensive analysis of the basic problem and the importance of the issue in the field of unauthorized practice of the law, the complete texts of the principal opinion in *R.J.*

---

[2] Special permission for use herein was granted by C. Russell Twist, Staff Director, Professional Standards, American Bar Association, Chicago, Illinois, by letter dated October 29, 1973.

Edwards, Inc., et al. v. R.L. Hurt, District Judge, et al. and related cases, a separate concurring opinion and a separate opinion concurring in part and dissenting in part are published below.

The three cases, consolidated in the Supreme Court of Oklahoma, were filed by individual county bar associations and the Oklahoma Bar Association against municipal bond marketers and their agents to enjoin practices of the defendants alleged to constitute the unlawful practice of law by persons who were not members of the Bar. The defendants took the position that their acts did not constitute the practice of law and that, if their activities could be considered law practice, they were of a "non-forensic" variety over which the judicial branch of the government has no jurisdiction, that the legislature alone can determine who may and who may not engage in the non-forensic practice of law, and that the law did not prohibit them from the non-forensic practice of the law. The defendants filed applications with the Supreme Court of Oklahoma for writs of prohibition to the district judges before whom the matters were pending, and the Supreme Court ordered the cases transferred to it for hearing and determination.

After hearing, the court first held in a five to four decision that the repeal of legislation regulating the practice of law had left a vacuum so that there was no valid restriction against the non-forensic practice of law by unlicensed persons in Oklahoma. Inherent in the decision was a determination that the court did not have inherent constitutional power to prohibit the non-forensic practice of law, but that this was a matter for legislative control.

Motions for rehearing were filed and granted, and the matter was briefed further and reargued. The American Bar Association, acting through Robert W. Meserve, then President elect, James D. Fellers of Oklahoma City, Oklahoma and the members of the Standing Committee on Unauthorized Practice of Law filed a brief as amicus curiae in support of the inherent power of the judiciary to regulate the practice of law, both of a forensic and non-forensic nature.

FORM #12

1. Petition for Permission to File Brief Amicus Curiae*

IN THE SUPREME COURT OF THE STATE OF OKLAHOMA

R.J. Edwards, Inc., et al., Petitioners,	)
vs.	) No. 40,338
R.L. *Hurt,* District Judge, et al., Respondents	)
Milburn, Cochran & Company, Inc., Petitioners	)

*[Encircled numerals are added hereto as reference to author's annotations at close of this chapter.]

vs.	) No. 42,166
F.B.H. Spellman, District Judge, et al., Respondents	)
Stifel, Nicholaus & Company, Inc., et al., Petitioners	)
vs.	) No. 43,254
Hon. Jack R. Parr, Special Dist. Judge, et al., Respondents	)

APPLICATION OF AMERICAN BAR ASSOCIATION [1]
FOR LEAVE TO FILE BRIEF AMICUS CURIAE

The American Bar Association respectfully shows:

1. It is a national organization of lawyers and judges with more than 153,000 members. It exists for the purpose, among other things, of promoting the orderly administration of justice and to that end recognizes its obligation to assist the courts in important cases involving substantial public interest.

2. Captioned cases involve substantial public interests and vitally concern the administration of justice. Applicant has been directed by its Board of Governors to seek leave of this Court to file brief *amicus curiae*.

WHEREFORE, the American Bar Association requests that it be granted leave to file a brief amicus curiae in typewritten form within 15 days of this date, or within such time as the Court may direct.

Respectfully submitted,

Robert W. Meserve	Andrew Hourigan, Jr.
James D. Fellers	Warren H. Resh
John D. Lane	Oglesby H. Young
Edward I. Cutler	Fred Beck
Robert O. Hetlage	

Attorneys for the American Bar Association,

Amicus Curiae

By: s/ J A M E S D. F E L L E R S

t/ James D. Fellers

Fellers, Snider, Baggett, Blankenship & Bailey
2700 First National Center, Oklahoma City, Okla.

CERTIFICATE OF SERVICE

I certify that I mailed a copy of the foregoing application for leave to file brief amicus curiae on February 1, 1972, to the following attorneys for petitioners:

Leon S. Hirsch, Esq.	George J. Fagin, Esq.
Paul Johanning, Esq.	2720 First National Center

David Hudson, Esq.   Oklahoma City, Okla.
                                            73102

1208 Concord Bldg., Oklahoma City, Okla.

s/ J A M E S D. F E L L E R S

t/ JAMES D. FELLERS

[Original stamped: "FILED, Supreme Court of Oklahoma,
February 1, 1972, ANDY PAYNE, CLERK."]

Brief Amicus Curiae

FORM #13

PROCEEDINGS RELATIVE TO PETITION
FOR REHEARING BY THE
OKLAHOMA BAR ASSOCIATION

BRIEF OF AMERICAN BAR ASSOCIATION[3]
AMICUS CURIAE

Robert W. Meserve, Boston, Massachusetts, President-Elect

Members of the Standing Committee on the
          Unauthorized Practice of Law:

John D. Lane, Washington, D.C., Chairman
Edward I. Cutler, Tampa, Florida
Robert O. Hetlage, St. Louis, Missouri
Andrew Hourigan, Jr., Wilkes-Barre, Pennsylvania
Warren H. Resh, Madison, Wisconsin
Preble Stolz, Berkeley, California
Oglesby H. Young, Portland, Oregon
Frederick W. Beck, Chicago, Illinois, Counsel

Presented by: James D. Fellers, 2700 First Nat'l. Center,
          Oklahoma City, Oklahoma 73102

          Attorneys for the American Bar Association

          Filed February 18, 1972

---

[3]"Resource Materials," *Unauthorized Practice News,* Vol. xxxvi, No. 3, Standing Committee on Unauthorized Practice of Law, American Bar Association, Chicago, Illinois 60637, (June 1972) pp. 15-34. [Published herein by permission of American Bar Association, Chicago, Illinois and by permission of its local counsel, James D. Fellers, Oklahoma City, Oklahoma, President of American Bar Association 1974-75.]

TABLE OF CONTENTS

CITATIONS ②
Cases

Miscellaneous

Nature of Case

This brief is filed on behalf of the American Bar Association as *amicus curiae* pursuant to direction of its Board of Governors and upon leave of this court.

The nature of the action, the pleadings, and other facts are set forth in the Petitioners' and Respondents' briefs and the Respondents' petition for rehearing, ③ and accordingly we shall not undertake more than a brief outline.

These proceedings were commenced in the District Court as actions seeking injunctions against the Petitioners for alleged unauthorized practice of law; upon the filing herein of petitions for Writs of Prohibition, this court ordered the respective causes pending in the lower court to be transferred to this court for hearing and determination.

Since this dispute was not heard by the lower court, there is no record or recitation of facts available for examination by the Supreme Court of the State of Oklahoma. Instead, this issue is jurisdictional in nature.

In the Supreme Court's decision of October 26, 1971, attention is focused upon the State Bar Act of 1929, and its repeal in 1939. The court reports that the repeal provided "that the Oklahoma Supreme Court shall have exclusive power and authority to pass upon the qualifications and fitness of all applicants for admission to the practice of law in the State of Oklahoma. We are cited to no statute authorizing the courts to enjoin the non-forensic practice of law by laymen."

Thus, the court has defined its power narrowly, and stated that it lacks inherent power to control, regulate or prohibit laymen from giving legal advice and preparing legal instruments. This is tantamount to assuming that even if the petitioners were engaging in the practice of law, the court lacks authority to supervise petitioners' activities since the petitioners are laymen operating outside of the courtroom.

The petitions in the district courts (transferred to the Supreme Court) separately alleged that R.J. Edwards, Inc., and Paul Nieto, its agent; Milburn, Cochran & Company, Inc., et al.; and Stifel, Nicolaus & Company, Inc., et al., were each engaged in selling and marketing municipal bonds and other types of securities, and gave legal advice to municipal authorities and boards of education. It was further alleged that these corporations prepared resolutions, election proclamations, contracts, transcripts of bond proceedings, and negotiable coupon bonds. Respondents concluded that this constituted an unauthorized practice of law, and prayed for injunctions.

An opinion rendered by a majority of the Oklahoma Supreme Court on October 26, 1971 denied the injunctive relief sought by the County Bar Associations and the Oklahoma Bar Association, and the respondent judges were prohibited from proceeding further in the actions filed in their courts.

Interests of Amicus Curiae

The American Bar Association was organized August 21, 1878. It is a national organization of lawyers and judges with more than 153,000 members at the present time. The current objectives of the Association are stated in Article 1.2 of its constitution, as follows:

§ 1.2 Purposes. The purposes of the Association are to uphold and defend the Constitution of the United States and maintain representative government; to advance the science of jurisprudence; to promote throughout the nation the administration of justice and the uniformity of legislation and of judicial decisions; to uphold the honor of the profession of law; to apply the knowledge and experience of the profession to the promotion of the public good; to encourage cordial intercourse among the members of the American bar; and to correlate and promote the activities of the bar organizations in the nation within these purposes and in the interests of the profession and of the public.

The American Bar Association is organized and exists for the purpose, among other things, of promoting the orderly administration of justice throughout the nation and to that end recognizes its obligation to assist the courts in important cases involving substantial public interests and the efficient practice of law. For that reason, it requests and is granted leave from time to time to render such assistance as it can in cases which vitally concern the administration of justice.

Question to Which This Brief Is Addressed

The questions presented are correctly set forth at length in the Respondents' brief and petition for rehearing, and will not be repeated in detail here.

In the majority decision of October 26, 1971 the Supreme Court of the State of Oklahoma did not discuss factual circumstances, since the court denied that it had jurisdiction over the disputed practices.

The basic question is whether the judicial branch of government has the inherent power to regulate the non-forensic practice of law by laymen.

Summary of Argument ④

The concept that an attorney is an officer of the court is universally recognized. Whether he shall be admitted, or whether he shall be disbarred, has been held to be a judicial and not a legislative question. The inherent, if not exclusive, power of the court in the disciplinary process has been affirmed in numerous cases.

It would be an anomaly if the power of the courts to protect the public from the improper or unlawful practice of law were limited to licensed attorneys and did not extend or apply to incompetent and unqualified laymen and lay intermediaries attempting to perform the duties of lawyers. Such a limitation of the power of the courts would reduce the legal profession to an unskilled vocation, destroy the usefulness of licensed attorneys as officers of the court, and substantially impair and disrupt the orderly and effective administration of justice by the judicial department of the government.

ARGUMENT ⑤

I. The Inherent Power of the Judiciary

Article IV, Section 1, of the Oklahoma Constitution provides for the distribution of governmental powers:

"The powers of the government of the State of Oklahoma shall be divided into three separate departments: The Legislative, Executive and Judicial; and except as provided in this Constitution, the Legislative, Executive and Judicial departments of government shall be separate and distinct, and neither shall exercise the powers properly belonging to either of the others."

Since Article VII, Section 1, of the Oklahoma Constitution vests the judicial power in the Supreme Court and other enumerated courts, the legislature cannot, by any action on its part, acquire the judicial function.

What is the scope of constitutional powers granted to the judiciary? It is undisputed that the grant of constitutional powers is accompanied by reasonable and suitable means to carry out such powers. "The rule of constitutional interpretation announced in *McCullock* v. *Maryland,* 4 Wheat. 316 4 L. Ed. 579, that that which was reasonably appropriate and relevant to the exercise of a granted power was to be considered as accompanying the grant, has been so universally applied that it suffices merely to state it..." See *In re Morse,* 98 Vt. 85, 126 A.550 (1924).

In its opinion of October 26, 1971 the majority of the Supreme Court of the State of Oklahoma stated: "Our 'inherent powers,' or implied powers, should be used when necessary to the judicial function. When unnecessary to the judicial function the power is vested in the legislature under Art. 4, Sec. 1, Oklahoma Const., and prior decisions of this court."

It is postulated that an apt definition of "inherent authority" should include matters which are essential to the existence, dignity and functions of the court as a constitutional tribunal. Inherent powers which have been claimed by the judiciary are not dominant above constitutions. Rather, as one of the three branches of government, the judiciary asserts independence under the constitutions. Inherent powers have been exercised in a variety of instances, such as power to establish procedures, the physical surroundings of courtrooms, contempt citations and *pro hac vice* admissions to out-of-state attorneys.

The concept that an attorney is an officer of the court is universally recognized. Whether he shall be admitted, or whether he shall be disbarred has been held to be a judicial, not a legislative, question. *In re Splane,* 123 Pa. 527, 16 A. 481 (1889). The inherent, if not exclusive, power of the court in the disciplinary process has been affirmed in numerous cases. Courts often have been called on to consider the constitutionality of a statute seeking to supervise the conduct of attorneys against a challenge that the legislation is an unconstitutional interference with the powers of the judiciary. Faced with these challenges, courts either have struck down the legislation as an unconstitutional interference with their inherent power or have held that, while the legislature might properly set minimum standards, the courts could not be prevented from requiring their own and more stringent standards. *In re Bailey,* 30 Ariz. 407, 248 P. 29 (1926); *In re Lavine,* 2 Cal. 2d 324, 41 P. 2 161 (1935); *Ruckenbrod* v. *Mullins,* 102 Utah 548, 133 P. 2d 325 (1943); *Re Cannon,* 206 Wis. 374, 240 N.W. 373 (1932). Inherent power to regulate the practice of law and to supervise the admission and disbarment of attorneys would be meaningless without power to protect and enforce rules against offenders, even though they have never been licensed by the courts. The dilemma is posed in *In re Baker,* 8 N.J. 321, 85 A. 2d 505, 512 (1951): "In the absence of power to control or punish unauthorized persons who presume to practice as attorneys and officers of this court, the power to control admissions to the bar would be nugatory."

II. The Evolution of Judicial Regulation of Access to the Practice of Law

A. The Historical Background

An early treatment of the problem was when Kosho, Mikado of Japan, in 457 B.C. rounded up and beheaded the leaders of an association formed to settle the estates of wealthy subjects. This drastic action was founded on the premise that such a group could not have the conscience and responsibility essential to the discharge of such a confidential trust. See 3 *Unauthorized Practice News* 70 (June 1937).

The legal profession, as we now know it, originally grew up around the courts. After Henry II appointed five clerks in 1178 to devote full time to the business of acting as judges in litigation, the central courts of England began to develop and, within the next 100 years, the legal profession began to develop around them. See 1 Pollock and Maitland, *History of English Law,* p. 133 (1st Ed. 1895).

It has been frequently suggested, and particularly by lay individuals and agencies attempting to engage in the unlawful practice of law, that the Bar originated as a kind of selfish monopoly, greedily exploiting a valuable franchise for the benefit of its favored members. Such selfish monopolies are unjust, or so the argument goes, and any member of the public ought to be permitted to do anything the lawyers do.

Nothing could be further from the truth. Experience suggests that errors brought about by laymen have led to disappointed expectations and complex entanglements, thus leading to more, rather than less, work for lawyers. Significantly, the Bar did not come first in legal history; it was a result, and not a cause. It was precisely the practice of law by unqualified persons—and that is the definition of unauthorized practice—which came first. The Bar came into existence later, as a result of the serious damage which was inflicted upon the public by virtue of the inexpert and often unscrupulous practices of unqualified and unregulated lay practitioners. The public would not stand for it; and it was the public which demanded the calling into existence of *a trained body of men and women, learned and skilled in the law, their character attested by official scrutiny, and their practices supervised by the court, as a necessary safeguard to public interest.* And this demand, as the historical record shows, took place only a little over a hundred years after the creation of the central courts of England in 1178, and the concomitant beginning of the legal profession. For the first Unauthorized Practice Statute was passed in 1292.

In that year Edward I authorized John Metingham, then Lord Chief Justice of the Court of Common Pleas, and the other justices of that court to appoint a certain number of "Attornies and Lawyers of the most apt for their learning and skill, who might do service to his court and people; and that those so chosen only, and no other" should practice. The king and his council then deemed "the number of seven score to be sufficient for that employment," although the number was henceforth left to the discretion of the justices. See Herbert, *Antiquities of the Inns of Court and Chancery*, 165-67 (1804). 1 Pollock and Maitland, *History of English Law*, 194 (1st Ed. 1895).

In *Rhode Island Bar Ass'n.* v. *Automobile Serv. Ass'n.*, 55 R.I. 122, 179 A. 139 (1935), Justice Condon carefully reviewed the 1292 ordinance of Edward I and the statute, 4 Henry IV, c. 18 (1402), which provided "that all the attornies shall be examined by the justices, and by their discretions their names put in the roll, and they that be good and virtuous, and of good fame, shall be received and sworn well and truly to serve in their offices . . . and the other attornies shall be put out . . ." He concluded: "This statute . . . is of interest to us here, however, only to illustrate that *the bar arose out of a public demand for the exclusion of those who assumed to practice law without adequate qualifications therefor.* It is also of importance because it shows beyond question that *the duty of excluding unauthorized persons was left to the discretion of the justices."* (p. 144) 55 R.I. at 133-34, 179 Atl. 144. Similar limitations were placed on membership in the bar in ancient Rome. See Pound, *The Lawyer from Antiquity to Modern Times* 51 (1953).

III. Protecting the Public

Acting as an independent branch of government, and utilizing inherent powers, courts have declared what constitutes the unauthorized practice of law and punished for contempt those who practiced without authority; the judicial power is generalized as a power to regulate the "practice of law."

The *amicus* endorses and republishes that portion of the dissent which includes the following:

"Insofar as I have researched the problem of whether under a constitutional provision similar to our Art. IV, Sec. 1, the power to declare unlawful the practice of non-forensic law by unauthorized persons does not 'properly belong' to the courts but 'only belongs' to the Legislature, under the exercise of its police powers, I have been unable to find a case from any jurisdiction so holding."

The courts in numerous decisions in different jurisdictions have undertaken to define and designate what constitutes the practice of law; but it is generally recognized that it is extremely difficult, perhaps impossible, to formulate a precise and completely comprehensive definition of the practice of law or to prescribe limits to the scope of that activity. *Bump* v. *District Court of Polk County*, 232 Iowa 623, 5 N.W. 2d 914 (1914); *Clark* v. *Austin*, 340 Mo. 467, 101 S.W. 2d 977 (1937); *State ex rel. Johnson* v. *Childe*, 147 Neb. 527, 23 N.W. 2d 720 (1946); *State ex rel. Johnson* v. *Childe*, 139 Neb. 91, 295 N.W. 381 (1941); *Auerbacher* v. *Wood*, 142 N.J. Eq. 484, 59 A. 2d 863 (1948); *Shortz* v. *Farrell*, 327 Pa. 81, 193 A. 20 (1937).

In this court's opinion of October 26, 1971 it is noted that petitioners were engaged in selling and marketing municipal bonds and other types of securities, and giving legal advice to municipal authorities and boards of education.

In Informative Opinion A of 1967 (see Appendix B) the American Bar Association Standing Committee on the Unauthorized Practice of Law discussed the rendering of legal services by lay agencies in the issuance and sale of municipal bonds. After reviewing decisions by several courts and unauthorized practice committees it was concluded that:

"Such activities inevitably lead to several undesirable results. Without the benefit of counsel, these lay agencies prepare forms from their files which have been used in other bond transactions which may, or may not, meet the specific needs of the current situation. There have been numerous complaints about the inadequacy of some of these forms from commercial bond counsel, who are later called upon to issue an opinion on the validity and marketability of the bond issues. On occasions, these lay agencies supply the municipality with forms and suggest to the municipality that they can prepare these forms themselves without the benefit of counsel. On other occasions, the lay agencies retain counsel to prepare these forms for the municipality and suggest to the municipality that since its attorney has prepared these forms, there is no need for the municipality to seek independent counsel. Since there obviously is no attorney-client relationship present between the retained counsel and the municipality, this is a clear violation of Canons 35 and 47 . . .

A lay agency engages in the unauthorized practice of law when it furnishes or prepares forms which must be prepared with legal skill and knowledge, and when it directs the proceedings of municipalities issuing bonds in a manner requiring the exercise of legal skill and knowledge. This is true whether or not the lay agency retains counsel to prepare such forms and to direct the proceedings for it. The relationship of attorney and client is a direct relationship between the municipality and its attorney. The primary interest of the lay agency is not always the protection of the municipality and therein lies the danger."

A licensed attorney at law in the practice of his profession generally engages in three principal types of professional activity. These are, first, legal advice and instructions to clients to inform them of their rights and obligations; second, preparation for clients of documents requiring knowledge of legal principles which is not possessed by an ordinary layman; and, third, appearance for clients before public tribunals, which possess the power and authority to determine rights of life, liberty and property according to law, in order to assist in the proper interpretation and enforcement of law. *Clark* v. *Austin*, 340 Mo. 467, 101 S.W. 2d 977 (1937); *Shortz* v. *Farrell*, 327 Pa. 81, 193 A. 20 (1937).

In *People* v. *Alfani*, 227 N.Y. 334, 125 N.E. 671 (1919), and *Land Title*

Abstract and Trust Company v. *Dworken,* 129 Ohio St. 23, 193 N.E. 650 (1934), the practice of law was discussed in these terms: "The practice of law is not limited to the conduct of cases in courts. It embraces the preparation of pleadings and other papers incident to actions and special proceedings and the management of such actions and proceedings on behalf of clients before judges and courts, and in addition conveyancing, the preparation of legal instruments of all kinds, and in general all advice to clients and all action taken for them in matters connected with the law." See *Tumulty* v. *Rosenblum,* 134 N.J.L. 514, 48 A. 2d 850 (1946). In *Richmond Association of Credit Men* v. *Bar Association of City of Richmond,* 167 Va. 327, 189 S.E. 153 (1937), quoting from *People* v. *Merchants' Protective Corporation,* 189 Cal. 531, 209 P. 363 (1922), the court said: "The phrase 'practicing law,' or its equivalent, 'the practice of law,' has long had a sufficiently definite meaning throughout this country to be given a place in both constitutional and statutory law without further definition."

The courts consider primarily the protection of the public in determining whether a particular activity is the "practice of law" and should be limited to members of the bar. That is, the courts ask whether the activity, if undertaken by laymen, will harm the public.

A. Examples In Which the Judicial Department Has Exercised Inherent Power to Define and Regulate the Non-Forensic Practice of Law

The scope of the problem of unauthorized practice of law is enormous and by no means restricted to a few isolated areas. It is fairly universal throughout all phases of the practice of law outside the courtroom. The range of the efforts of laymen and corporations to practice law is partially illustrated by the variety of cases which have been before the courts, and in which the judicial department has exercised its inherent power to define and regulate the practice of law.

A striking illustration is provided by the case of *In re Baker,* 8 N.J. 321, 85 A. 2d 505 (1951), a case involving two laymen who prepared a will for an 80 year old farmer, naming themselves as residuary legatees. In holding them guilty of contempt of court for the unauthorized practice of the law, Chief Justice Vanderbilt expressed the continuing rationale of the unauthorized practice of law effort in the following terms:

"It is generally conceded throughout the country that the power to control admissions to the Bar and to discipline members of the Bar is inherent in the judiciary . . . but whether inherent or expressed, these powers over the admission and discipline of members of the Bar would be meaningless and futile if laymen might practice law with impunity. The damage which would overtake the public from permitting such unauthorized practice of law is strikingly illustrated in the present case. The reason for prohibiting the unauthorized practice of the law by laymen is not to aid the legal profession but to safeguard the public from the disastrous results that are bound to flow from the activities of untrained and incompetent individuals, assuming to practice a learned profession which entails years of preparation and without being bound by the high standards of professional conduct and integrity which are imposed on members of the Bar by the Canons of Professional Ethics, which are zealously enforced by the court for the public good." 85 A. 2d 511-512.

It is submitted that the public requires protection from abuses outside the courtroom, even more than protection inside the courtroom for the reasons enunciated in *People* v. *Alfani,* 27 N.Y. 334, 125 N.E. 671 (1919):

"Is it only in courts or in legal proceedings that danger lies from such evils? On the contrary, the danger there is at a minimum for very little can go wrong in a court where the proceedings are public and the presiding officer is generally a man of judgment and experience. Any judge of much active work on the bench has had frequent occasion to guide the young practitioner or protect the client from the haste or folly of an older one. Not so in the office. Here the client is with his attorney alone, without the impartial supervision of a judge. Ignorance and stupidity may here create damage which the courts of the land cannot thereafter undo. Did the legislature mean to leave this field to any person out of which to make a living? Reason says no. Practicing law as an attorney likewise covers the drawing of legal instruments as a business."

Many other examples can be cited. ⑥

1. Title Companies

These corporations illustrate the typical example of how unauthorized practice gets started. A corporation is chartered for the purpose of insuring titles and issuing title policies. The next step is to invite the public to bring the entire real estate transaction to the company. Its salaried officers then draw the contract of sale between the buyer and seller, prepare all necessary instruments to put title in the purchaser, give legal advice concerning the effect of various instruments involved in the sale of the real estate and in general take all steps necessary to close the entire transaction. All this is done under the claim that it is "incidental" to the business of the corporation in issuing the title policy. One of the best opinions in this field is *Hexter Title & Abstract Co.* v. *Grievance Committee,* 142 Tex. 506, 179 S.W. 2d 946 (1944). We quote a portion of the opinion as illustrative of the practices of some title companies:

"Had the title companies in Texas limited their operations to insuring titles, there would have been no serious quarrel. But, instead they proceeded to take over all the services formerly performed by lawyers, short of actual litigation. They not only examined the title, but they drew papers for both vendor and purchaser, mortgagor and mortgagee, and when title requirements had been met, notified all parties to come up and close. In closing, they had the papers signed, interpreted the contract of sale, if any, and advised all parties right and left on such questions of law as might be asked, in addition to computing the prorations. Some closings were handled by salaried attorneys and some by lay employees."

However, Texas was not the only state in which title companies were persistent for they had to be taken to the highest court in quite a number of other jurisdictions before the practices were stopped. *Land Title Abstract and Trust Co.* v. *Dworken,* 129 Ohio St. 23, 193 N.E. 650 (1934), *People* v. *Lawyers Title Corp.,* 282, N.Y. 513, 27 N.E. 2d 30 (1940), *Title Guaranty Co.* v. *Denver Bar Association,* 135 Colo. 423, 312 P. 2d 1011 (1957), and *Pioneer Title Insurance and Trust Company* v. *State Bar of Nevada,* 74 Nev. 186, 326 P. 2d 408 (1958).

Title companies, without success, have attempted to carry on their activities through attorneys in an affiliated law firm. *In Re L.R.,* 7 N.J. 390, 81 A 2d 725 (1951), and *In Re Rothman,* 12 N.J. 528, 97 A 2d 621 (1953).

2. Real Estate Brokers—Drawing Legal Instruments and Giving Legal Advice to Others

The real estate brokers have not been slow to enter the practice of law by drawing the instruments which are necessary to complete a real estate transaction by putting title in the buyer, including the preparation ,of contracts, mortgages, releases and other real estate documents. A typical case is *Paul* v. *Stanley,* 168 Wash. 371, 12 P. 2d 401 (1932), where the defendant, a real estate broker, was enjoined from drawing legal instruments including so-called "simple instruments"—deeds, mortgages, contracts and other documents—in the real estate field as constituting the unauthorized practice of law. A very strong case is that of *Arkansas Bar Ass'n.* v. *Sam Block,* 323 S.W. 2d 912 (1959). See also *Washington State Bar Association* v. *Washington Association of Realtors,* 41 Wash. 2d 697, 251 P. 2d 619 (1952), *People* v. *Schafer,* 404 Ill. 45, 87 N.E. 2d 773 (1949), *Conway-Bogue Realty Investment Co.* v. *Denver Bar Association,* 135 Colo. 398, 312 P. 2d 998 (1957), *In Re Gore,* 58 Ohio App. 79, 15 N.E. 2d 968 (1937), *People* v. *Sipper,* 61 Cal. App. 2d 844, 142 P. 2d 960 (1943).

In *Howton* v. *Morrow,* 269 Ky. 1, 106 S.W. 2d 81 (1937), an attorney was held to have been a licensed practicing lawyer for two years to qualify as candidate for the office of County Attorney. In so holding the court among other things said "practicing law is not confined to performing services in actions or proceedings in courts of justice but includes giving title, preparing wills, contracts, deeds, mortgages and other instruments of a legal nature."

3. Automobile Clubs

It would seem that a corporation or other agency whose primary object is or should be to furnish travel information to its members and to tow their automobiles in when disabled and to furnish other services in connection with travel ought to be able to stay out of the practice of law; but not so. In the case of *In Re Maclub of America,* 295 Mass. 45, 3 N.E. 2d 272 (1936), the respondent in connection with its legitimate business activities furnished the services of attorneys to its members who may have fallen afoul of the law while on the road. The court among other things said:

> "The respondent buys and pays for legal services in behalf of all its members. It could not furnish those services in conformity to its contracts with its members unless it was dealing in the purchase and sale of legal services to be rendered by lawyers in its behalf and upon its credit. This method of conducting its business conclusively stamps the activities of the respondent as the unauthorized practice of the law. *It busy and sells practice of the law on a commercial basis as essentially as a merchant buys and sells his wares.*"

Other similar cases are *People ex rel. Chicago Bar Association* v. *Motorists Association,* 354 Ill. 595, 188 N.E. 827 (1933), *State ex rel Seawell* v. *Carolina Motor Club,* 209 N.C. 624, 184 S.E. 540 (1936), *Rhode Island Bar Association* v. *Automobile Service Association,* 55 R.I. 122, 179 A. 139 (1935).

4. Collection Agencies

Collection agencies have attempted to practice law by the maintenance of a legal department through which they would collect their principals' claims in courts or by hiring and controlling an attorney for the same purpose. *State ex rel Freebourn* v. *Merchants Credit Service,* 104 Mont. 72, 66 Pac. 2d 337 (1937), *Richmond Ass'n of Credit Men, Inc.* v. *Bar Ass'n,* 167 Va. 327, 189 S.E. 153 (1937).

5. Tax Counsel

Lay agencies and particularly accountants have heavily invaded the tax field. The leading cases on this subject as illustrating the attempts by laymen to take over this field are *Lowell Bar Association* v. *Loeb,* 315 Mass. 176, 52 N.E. 2d 27 (1943), where a layman was permitted to fill out short tax forms for others but was not permitted to examine statutes, judicial decisions and departmental rulings and advise a client concerning the same; *Gardner* v. *Conway,* 234 Minn. 468, 48 N.W. 2d (1951), where a layman was resolving difficult questions of law in preparing tax returns and also advised concerning the legal effect of the taxpayers' marital and business status in connection with the return; and *Agran* v. *Shapiro,* 128 Cal. App. 2d 807, 273 P. 2d 619 (1954), where an accountant resolved difficult questions of law concerning a net loss carry over after examining and interpreting applicable statutes.

6. Appearance Before Administrative Agencies

Some of the most persistent unauthorized practitioners are those who attempt to represent others before administrative agencies of various kinds claiming that it is in the public interest to do so, and that appearance before such agencies is not the practice of law.

Illustrative cases of this type are: *Hoffmeister* v. *Faerber,* Mo. 293 S.W. 2d 554 (1955), (representing claimants in unemployment compensation matters); *Clark* v. *Austin,* 340 Mo. 477, 101 S.W. 2d 977 (1937), (representing parties before Public Service Commission); *Curry* v. *Dahlberg,* 341 Mo. 897, 110 S.W. 2d 741 (1937), ("commerce" or "rate" "expert" acquiring contracts for refunds exacted in violation of Maximum Freight Rate Acts); *West Virginia State Bar* v. *Early,* W. Va., 109 S.E. 2d 240 (1959), (representing claimants before State Workmen's Compensation Commission); *Johnson* v. *Childe,* 147 Neb. 527, 23 N.W. 2d 720 (1946), (representing parties before State Railroad Commission); and *Stack* v. *P.G. Garage, Inc.,* 7 N.J. 118, 80 Atl. 2d 545 (1951), (representing parties before County Tax Board); and *People ex rel Chicago Bar Association* v. *Goodman,* 366 Ill. 346, 8 N.E. 2d 941 (1937).

7. Adjustors

Independent adjustors who hold themselves out to the public as being engaged in the business of adjusting, settling and collecting claims for personal injuries are unlawful practitioners. *Fitchette* v. *Taylor,* 191 Minn. 582, 254 N.W. 910 (1934), and *Meunier* v. *Bernich,* La. App., 170 So. 567 (1936). In the course of their work such adjustors have improperly attempted to give legal advice. *Liberty Mutual Insurance Co.* v. *Jones,* 334 Mo. 932, 130 S.W. 2d 945 (1939).

8. Banks and Trust Companies

In *People ex rel* v. *Denver Clearing House Banks,* 99 Colo. 50, 59 P. 2d 468 (1936), the defendant banks as a general practice drafted wills where they were named executors or trustees and gave legal advice to testators regarding the same and drew living trusts and life insurance trust agreements where they were named executors, all without the testator having any independent legal advice. These acts were performed by trust officers, "regular salaried employees, integral and essential parts of the banks' organization, generally members of the Bar but practically limited, by custom on contract, to the bank's business," and hence in all their acts they were as much a part of the corporation as the president or cashier. These acts obviously were the practice of law and were held so to be by the court.

In *Cain, et al* v. *Merchants National Bank and Trust Company of Fargo,* 66 N.D. 746, 268 N.W. 719 (1936), three wills were drawn by an assistant trust officer who was a licensed attorney, which the court said constituted an isolated instance of the practice of law; and the bank further stepped out of its lawful field of activity when it drew chattel mortgages for the accommodation of customers in transactions in which the bank had no interest.

The case of *State* v. *St. Louis Union Trust Company,* 335 Mo. 845, 74 S.W. 2d 348 (1934), involved a similar situation where trust officers were drawing wills, living trusts and life insurance trusts where the defendant bank was named fiduciary and giving advice regarding the same claiming that its acts were legal as being "incident to its trust business." The court again held that these acts were unauthorized practice of law.

Re Eastern Idaho Loan and Trust Company v. *Hawley,* 49 Idaho 280, 288 P. 157 (1930), presented a factual situation where the bank advertised that it was competent to draw wills and trusts and stated that "we make a specialty of drawing contracts, deeds and mortgages . . . It will pay you to see us about this important matter. We can help you arrange your affairs . . ." The court held that this was a solicitation of law business and stated that the statute permitting banks to act as executor or administrator or in other fiduciary capacities did not confer upon trust companies the power to draft wills, trusts, trust declarations or other similar instruments.

In *Judd* v. *City Trust and Savings Bank,* 133 Ohio St. 81, 12 N.E. 2d 288 (1937), the defendant's trust officers undertook to prepare and draft wills, trust agreements and other legal instruments for its customers. The court said: "a salaried trust officer or employee of a bank or trust company, regularly employed, whether a member of the Bar or not, is as much an integral and essential part of its organization as the president or cashier. Corporations may not practice law. Therefore, when a trust company through its attorney employee performs services for customers or patrons in drawing wills, trust agreements, or contracts and other instruments requiring the exercise of legal skill, such corporation must be held to be practicing law."

IV. Professional Responsibility

Not only is the public entitled to the advice and services of those who have prepared themselves for the profession by completing required courses of study, but to the further protection of the *Code of Professional Responsibility* by which the licensed attorney is governed, the violation of which may cause his disbarment, which indeed could deprive him of his means of earning a livelihood.

In 1908 the American Bar Association first adopted Canons of Ethics; thereafter these Canons were amended from time to time in order to provide standards of integrity for the legal profession. The various states of the union were urged by the American Bar Association to adopt these Canons of Ethics as a step toward providing such standards for lawyers.

In 1965 a Special Committee was appointed to make a study of the Canons of Ethics and to determine whether extensive revision was necessary, and if so, what form such revision should take. The Committee submitted a new *Code of Professional Responsibility* which was adopted by the House of Delegates* on August 12, 1969 to become effective for American Bar Association members on January 1, 1970.

Implementation followed quickly. The new *Code of Professional Responsibility* has been adopted in the District of Columbia, and forty states, including Oklahoma, 5 O.S. 1971, Ch. 1, App. 3. (In Oklahoma, the *Code* was adopted by rule of the Supreme Court on December 16, 1969 in SCBD No. 2212.) In seven other jurisdictions the state bar association has approved the Code and transmitted it to the highest court in the state with a recommendation for adoption. This list of states which have adopted the *Code* continues to grow.

It is apparent that in a relatively short period of time, the *Code* will be recognized by the bench and bar as the accepted standard for the ethical conduct of lawyers throughout the country.

The *Code of Professional Responsibility* consists of nine canons [7] or axiomatic norms, a substantial number of interpretive ethical considerations, and disciplinary rules which articulate minimum standards of conduct for the profession enforceable by sanctions imposed by local disciplinary agencies.

Relevant canons include the following:

Canon 3—A Lawyer Should Assist in Preventing the Unauthorized Practice of Law. The Ethical Considerations following Canon 3 articulate the rationale for concern about the shortcomings of unauthorized practice of law. See EC 3-1, 3-2, 3-3, 3-4 and 3-5, Appendix A.

Canon 4—A Lawyer Should Preserve the Confidences and Secrets of a Client.

Canon 5—A Lawyer Should Exercise Independent Professional Judgment on Behalf of a Client.

Canon 6—A Lawyer Should Represent a Client Competently.

Underlying the *Code of Professional Responsibility* is the principle that the lawyer must represent his client with undivided loyalty, and must have no conflicting interests to interfere with this undivided allegiance. Every man is entitled to receive legal advice from men skilled in law, and to be served by one who is his lawyer, rather than a person motivated or controlled by a divided or outside interest. No employee of a corporation, or layman pursuing a private business objective, can qualify to give disinterested advice, however expert he may represent himself to be in any specialized field.

The relation between attorney and client is confidential. An attorney may not disclose confidential communications, or the advice given. When a

---

*The House of Delegates, which is designed to be representative of the legal profession in the United States is not only the governing body of the American Bar Association; because of the presence of representatives of all state bar associations, the largest and most important local bar associations, and of other important national professional groups, it is in fact a broadly representative policy forum for the profession as a whole.

commercial corporation gives legal advice or renders other legal services, uninfluenced devotion to the client's interests does not exist. There exists along with, and necessarily influencing, the devotion to the client, the duty which the employee owes to the general employer. And nowhere more than in the practice of law is it true that no man can serve two masters.

Violations of the Disciplinary Rules of the *Code* are enforceable by sanctions imposed by appropriate disciplinary authorities.

The adoption of ethical standards reinforced by disciplinary procedures assure the public of confidential, loyal, competent service based upon the independent judgment of a trained professional.

Significantly, the *Code of Professional Responsibility* requires high standards of conduct from lawyers both inside and outside of the courtroom. For example, after explaining factual circumstances in the privacy of his lawyer's office, the client may ask for an opinion as to whether or not a dispute should be litigated. The decision to be made is one which requires independence, and legal skill and competence untarnished by conflicts of interest. The lawyer's advice and conduct must be consistent with the concepts of the *Code* even though he is not comporting himself within the confines of the courtroom.

The *Code of Professional Responsibility* recognizes no dichotomy between forensic and non-forensic practice of law. A lawyer must report misconduct to authorities, whether or not the misconduct occurred in a courtroom (See DR 2-103). The prohibitions against advertising and solicitation, rooted in a desire to protect the public from misleading, extravagant, artful, self-laudatory brashness (See DR 2-102, 3, 4), apply with equal force both inside and outside of the courtroom.

It would be anomalous to establish high standards of conduct for lawyers [8] practicing law, and then to fail to protect the public from laymen practicing law outside the courtroom. The result would encourage incompetent and unethical laymen to give legal advice and to complete legal documents for clients for compensation. In addition, disbarred attorneys would have a market in which to compete and this would be detrimental to the public interest.

V. It May Be Presumed That the Legislature Did Not Intend to Leave a Void in This Vital Area

Section 4255 O.S. 1931 (State Bar Act 1929) provided that:
"No person shall practice law in the State subsequent to the first meeting of The State Bar unless he shall be an active member thereof as hereinbefore defined."

That Act was applied in *State Bar* v. *Retail Credit Association,* 170 Okl. 246, 37 P. 2d 954 (1935). That Act (Sec. 4210-4258, O.S. 1931) was repealed in 1939 (Session Laws 1939, page 70). 5 O.S. 1961, Sec. 12 (enacted 1939), provides that the Oklahoma Supreme Court shall have exclusive power and authority to pass upon the qualifications and fitness of *all applicants for admission* to the practice of law in the State of Oklahoma.

In view of the fact that thirty-three years have passed since the State Bar Act of 1929 has been repealed, and the legislature has not adopted legislation (if, and to the extent, that it would do so) to supervise laymen who give legal advice and prepare legal instruments for compensation, it may be presumed that the legislature assents to the inherent jurisdiction of the judiciary to act in this vital area.

Because of the potential for abuse and neglect of the public interest, it is unthinkable that the legislature intended that non-forensic acts constituting the practice of law by laymen should go unregulated. After thirty-three years of inaction, it may be presumed that the legislature did not intend to leave a void. Rather, the legislature intended that the judicial branch of government would exercise its constitutional prerogatives to supervise the practice of law when engaged in by lawyers or laymen, both inside and outside the courtroom.

CONCLUSION ⑨

FOR THE REASONS STATED, IT IS RESPECTFULLY SUBMITTED THAT THIS MATTER WOULD BE REHEARD, AND THAT PETITIONERS' REQUEST THAT THIS COURT ISSUE WRITS OF PROHIBITION SHOULD BE DENIED.

Presented by:

James D. Fellers
2700 First Nat'l. Center
Oklahoma City, Oklahoma 73102
Telephone (405) 232-0621
A Member of the Bar of
the State of Oklahoma

Respectfully submitted,
Robert W. Meserve
John D. Lane
Edward I. Cutler
Robert O. Hetlage
Andrew Hourigan, Jr.
Warren H. Resh
Oglesby H. Young
Frederick W. Beck
  Attorneys for the American
  Bar Association
    Amicus Curiae

D. OPINION.

After full hearing, the Supreme Court of Oklahoma withdrew its prior opinion and promulgated the present opinion upholding the inherent judicial power to regulate the practice of law in all its forms and to prevent the intrusion of unlicensed persons into the practice.

OPINIONS OF SUPREME COURT [4]

Prepared for Publication by Office of the Chief Justice of Supreme Court . . .

(For Official Publication) ⑩
(Syllabus)

Under the Oklahoma Constitution, the Judicial Department was vested with full and complete authority, independent of the power of the Legislative Department, to control and regulate the practice of law in all its forms and to prevent the intrusion of unlicensed persons into the practice, without regard to whether their acts are "forensic" or "non-forensic."

Original proceedings for writs of prohibition.

Actions for injunctions were separately filed in the District Courts of Payne, Major and Canadian Counties by the respective County Bar Associations and the Oklahoma Bar Association. Thereafter, petitions for writs of prohibition were filed in this Court to prohibit the judges of the respective District Courts from proceeding further. This Court then ordered the cases transferred to this Court for final disposition. Injunctive relief denied; prohibition granted. . . . .

BARNES, J. We shall refer to the parties by the characters in which they appeared in the courts of first instance, namely, as plaintiffs and as defendants.

These cases originated in the district courts of Payne, Major and Canadian Counties. Each was initiated by a petition against the respective defendants, municipal bond marketers and their agents, filed by the individual county bar associations, together with the Oklahoma Bar Association, to enjoin certain practices of the defendants, alleged to constitute the unlawful practice of law, by these defendants who were not members of the bar. The charges, in brief, were that the defendant corporations, who are engaged in negotiating for marketing, and also, themselves, in selling municipal bond issues and other types of securities, undertake, in that connection, to give legal advice to municipal authorities, to school boards, and to other representatives of entities who may be contemplating borrowing money through the issuance of bonds. It also is alleged that the corporate defendants, acting through their agents, the individual defendants, or through others, prepare resolutions, election proclamations, contracts, transcripts of bond proceedings and negotiable coupon bonds, all of which acts also are asserted to constitute the illegal practice of law by the defendants.

The defendants took the position that their acts did not amount to the practice of law in that they were merely assisting in filling out forms

---

[4] "Oklahoma Supreme Court Upholds Inherent Power of Courts to Control Unauthorized Practice of Law in Oklahoma," *Unauthorized Practice News,* Vol. xxxvii, No. 1 American Bar Association, Chicago, Ill. 60637 (May 1973) pp. 1-21.

prescribed by the Attorney General according to his direction, and that, if this could be considered law practice, it was of the non-forensic variety, over which (it was asserted) the judicial branch of the government has no jurisdiction, on the theory that the Legislature alone may wield the police power in that regard. Subsidiarily, the defendants also raised the proposition that, in any event, the respective bar associations were without standing to maintain the actions, asserting that this Court has retained for itself exclusive jurisdiction in that regard.

Before these matters proceeded to hearing on the merits upon the issues raised in the district courts, the defendants filed with us applications for writs of prohibition to the respective district judges before whom the matters were pending, by which route defendants sought to achieve a prompt resolution, in their favor, of the contentions which they had urged in the district courts. We ordered the case to be transferred here for hearing and determination. We shall resolve the several issues in accordance with the applicable legal principles. . . . . . . The Oklahoma Bar Association is unique among other associations of attorneys in this State in that it is the only one this Court, in the exercise of the power herein discussed, has created to protect the public against the unauthorized practice of law, and it is the one organized bar association that is in a position to speak and act in such matters throughout the State, generally.

We recognize that strong arguments have been made for affording individual attorneys and local or county bar associations the right to be heard in an action like the present one, as evidenced by the cases cited and discussed in the annotation at 90 A.L.R.2d 7, 64-77, both inclusive, and the footnotes to 7 Am. Jur. 2d, "Attorneys at Law," § 89. However, in the present cases the plaintiffs' petition made no distinction between the injury they, or either of them would suffer from the defendants' alleged unauthorized practice and the injury the public might suffer. (Plaintiffs' petitions merely alleged that they *and the public* will suffer irreparable damage unless defendants are enjoined from engaging in the unauthorized practice of law.) Consequently, in view of what is herein indicated concerning the Court's delegation of duties to the Oklahoma Bar Association as its "arm," in the regulation of the practice of law in the State and of the "confusion, if not chaos" that might result "from independent proceedings of this sort" by individual lawyers and local and or county bar associations of this State (see *Dade-Commonwealth Title Ins. Co. v. North Dade Bar Ass'n.,* Fla., 152 So. 2d 723), we hold that the Oklahoma Bar Association is the only proper party to bring an action of this character. Accordingly, it is our opinion that the trial court, in the Payne County case, erred in not sustaining, as to the County Bar Association that appeared as a plaintiff in that action, the defendants' challenge to the plaintiffs' capacities to sue therein.

As it is our opinion that no cause of action has been shown therefor, the injunctive relief that plaintiffs sought against the defendants in the three actions here involved is denied and the respondent judges are prohibited from proceeding further therein.

BERRY, C.M., and WILLIAMS, HODGES, LAVENDER and SIMMS, JJ., concur. DAVISON, V.C.J., and IRWIN, J., concur in result. JACKSON, J., concurs in part, dissents in part.

E. CONCLUDING VIEWS: COURT HAS INHERENT POWER TO CONTROL UNAUTHORIZED PRACTICE OF LAW.

From a mere cursory glance at the preceding excerpts, it might appear that both sides to the original controversy were winners in the "Opinion" on rehearing. Every lawyer will find profitable time spent in reading the full opinions, including the concurring in part and dissenting in part, as written by Mr. Justice Jackson, Mr. Justice Irwin, and Mr. Vice Chief Justice Davison, excerpts from which are as follows: [5]

> *Justice Jackson:* I concur in the view that injunctive relief should be denied and that prohibition should be granted .... I am well aware that most other states have held that the court may prohibit the practice of law by unlicensed practitioners .... Some have done so by statutory authorization. I do agree that this court may lawfully suppress the preparation of pleadings and wills and other documents by unlicensed practitioners that are destined for consideration in the courts ..... I would not authorize the Oklahoma Bar Association to file any action in a district court for the suppression of an unlicensed practitioner without the prior approval of this court.
>
> *Justice Irwin (views concurred by Mr. Vice Chief Justice Davison):* I concur in the results reached by the majority of my associates that the Judicial Department is vested with the power and authority to control and regulate the practice of law and to prevent the intrusion of unlicensed persons into the practice without regard to whether their acts are "forensic" or "non-forensic."

F. AUTHOR'S ANNOTATIONS: FOOTNOTES AND COMMENTS ON EXEMPLARY POINTS IN AMICUS CURIAE MODEL BRIEF.

① Note the commendable use of a clear, concise statement covering less than one page in the application on February 1, 1972 by the American Bar Association for leave to file brief amicus curiae. It identifies the amicus curiae, its purpose before this court, and its allegation that captioned cases involve substantial public interests and vital concerns for the administration of justice.

② Citations of cases are taken from Supreme Court rulings of thirty different states in United States of America. This legal brief writer has breadth of vision to see the need

---

[5] "Oklahoma Court Upholds Control," *Unauthorized Practice News,* Vol. xxxvii, No. 1, American Bar Association, 1155 E. 60th, Chicago, Ill. (May 1973), pp. 18-19.

of an all-out pitch to arouse interest in as many general practitioners as possible. Appellate advocates in the broad legal arena of remote state areas have vital concerns for the administration of justice. Likewise in this handbook, it has been the author's persistent effort to take examples, illustrations, definitions, rules, forms, and case citations from as many different states as possible. To make this out-reach to the up-state, down-state, and state-line appellate advocates of the lesser metropolitan areas, many tables have been compiled herein for brevity.

In the administration of justice, the appellate advocate is to be commended for seeing the need and taking the time to proceed as amicus curiae on behalf of local, state and American Bar Association. Mr. Feller's brief, on which permission was granted to use as model herein, exemplifies a dedicated professional alert on behalf of leading lawyers to right the wrongs of unethical practice of law.

③ Note the very courteous and professional acknowledgment of the existence of prior Petitioners' and Respondents' briefs, and Respondents' Petition for Rehearing. The amicus curiae makes his supplement by a brief outline of one page. For the court's information, he rapidly covers the case development from inception before the lower courts to the majority decision when the Oklahoma Supreme Court denied the injunctive relief sought by County Bar Associations and Oklahoma Bar Association, from which petition for rehearing was filed and Amicus Curiae appearance was sought.

④ "Summary of the Argument" gives a succinct preview encompassed within five very clearly written sentences covering less than half a page. This brevity reflects great merit considering the extensive involvement and consolidation of cases from different lower court jurisdictions.

⑤ The expanded "Argument" is well developed within proper space under five major headings. These are indicated by Roman numerals and heavy black type to direct busy reader's quick focus of attention on these high points for consideration:

    I. The Inherent Power of the Judiciary
    II. The Evolution of Judicial Regulation to the Practice of Law
    III. Protecting the Public
    IV. Professional Responsibility
    V. [Summary] It May Be Presumed that the Legislature Did Not Leave a Void in this Vital Area.

⑥ Note that the persuasive argument in this brief makes an outreach to direct attention of the Court to prior commendable decisions of its peers from many other State Supreme Court decisions in protecting the public against unauthorized, non-forensic practice of law in the following other professions:

    1. Title Companies
    2. Real Estate Brokers
    3. Automobile Clubs
    4. Collection Agencies
    5. Tax Counsel
    6. Appearance Before Administrative Agencies
    7. Adjusters
    8. Banks and Trust Companies

⑦ A strong argument is developed with basic conclusion drawn from implementation of new Code of Professional Responsibility adopted by most of the states in the early seventies. This pamphlet is available through American Bar Association, and should be on the desk of every appellate advocate. Six of the Nine Canons were quoted as applicable in this rehearing matter.

⑧ The amicus curiae brief writer makes a very impressive point when he states near the conclusion of his argument: "It would be anomolous to establish high standards of conduct for lawyers, and then fail to protect the public from laymen practicing law outside the court."

⑨ The Conclusion is clearly and respectfully worded in one impressive sentence as set forth in all caps, to wit:

FOR THE REASONS STATED, IT IS RESPECTFULLY SUBMITTED THAT THIS MATTER SHOULD BE REHEARD AND THAT PETI-TIONERS' REQUEST SHOULD BE DENIED.

⑩ The OPINION of the Oklahoma Supreme Court as reached on November 28, 1972, is set forth from the syllabus released for official publication. Every appellate advocate has a paramount interest in the control of law practice and its adherence to all phases of the Code of Professional Responsibility in protecting the public from illegal, unauthorized, and unethical practices.

The result of this appeal, as gained upon rehearing, is certainly convincing proof that this brief was well written. It is a rare occasion for any State Supreme Court to grant a rehearing and be persuaded to reverse its original decision. It would appear that no winning Amicus Curiae Brief of the mid-1970 period, before any of the 50 State Supreme Courts, could have a more universal interest or serve as a better model than that written by James D. Fellers of Oklahoma City, President of American Bar Association [1974-75], whose appearance as amicus curiae was in public spirited defense of the legal profession and its obligation to promote justice in the courts and to protect the public against unauthorized practice of law.

8

Final Argument and Format of Brief in State Court Jurisdiction

For the wrap-up of appellate activity before state court of last resort, we summarize and emphasize the litigant's best points. The precision, the courtesy, and the professional role of the advocate will enhance the persuasive factors of evidence and justice on behalf of the client. The lawyer's fair play and personal conduct in consideration for others are always important final impressions in the law suit. The format and rule-adherence of your printed briefs remain with each Supreme Court Justice. He has a copy of your written argument for reference when the final decision is being crystalized. Write it well, and crown it with a finale of persuasive oral argument.

A. ACQUIRE GOOD PUBLIC IMAGE VIA APPELLATE FINALE.

Active practitioners can expect increasing future demands upon time and patience in civil appellate procedures for state court systems. The volume will be greater. The client will be more communicative with anticipation of a common bond for attorney-client personal conferences pertaining to appeal procedures. He will be apprehensive and eager for information. He will look forward to scheduled appointments for regular progress reports on the work you are doing in his behalf. News media with audio visual programs have brought forth a more informed and more inquisitive breed of litigants at all levels of state court processing. When your office is contacted, the appellate client's focal attention will be on the one track of his case. In his world of concern he has the only lawsuit, and there are all kinds of adverse circumstances which could make him skeptical. He deserves to be able to reach you for conferences, regardless of the fact that there is really no news to report to him at the moment. He is your emissary of good will and your primary source for procreation of bigger and better potential case solutions.

B. EXPECT MORE RIGID CONTROLS ON ORAL ARGUMENT SCHEDULES.

It will be unfair to you as a skilled advocate and unfair to your client in final case result if you delay until the last day for requesting and scheduling of oral argument. This is your final opportunity to enhance your brief with your personal persuasion. Although there is a growing trend toward shorter time allotment, the opportunity to present a few brief climactical statements should not be waived. It is true that the oral argument may be your constitutional or statutory right, but you will likewise want to make sure you have the indulgence of the specific appellate forum.

The crowded dockets of recent years have necessitated specific rules of court to be issued in order that time may be scheduled for the court to hear oral argument. It is mandatory that each instance of appellate planning be prefaced by careful study of the latest rules. No waivers or special privileges should be requested for bending those rules. Effort is being exerted in all states toward best use of docket time as a means of reducing backlog of pending cases. To avail oneself of the right to argue orally, we direct reader's attention to examples of "how-to" rules in selected states:

1. Arkansas (1973) Supreme Court Rule 18—Oral Arguments:

"(a) *Request Made in Time.*—Where either side petitioning desires to make an oral argument in any case, counsel shall notify the Court and opposing counsel of such intention, not less than two weeks before the case will be reached for submission. Argument will be set for the earliest practicable date and all necessary parties given notice thereof.

"Counsel not requesting oral argument are not required to be present, but when such counsel do not intend to appear, notice of that fact shall be given to the Clerk at least five days before the date set for oral argument.

"(b) *Counsel Limited—Time.*—Only two of counsel will be heard for each side, and not more than 30 minutes will be allowed to each side for argument, without special leave of Court, granted before the argument begins. Applications for additional time for argument must be by written motion, filed not less than one week before the case will be reached for submission and setting forth the reasons why additional time is thought to be necessary.

"(c) *Apportionment of Time.*—The time allowed may be apportioned between the counsel on the same side at their discretion; provided, always, that a fair presentation of the case shall be made by the party having the opening and closing argument.

"(d) *Reading from Books.*—Counsel are not permitted to read from books, briefs or records, except short extracts which they consider necessary to properly emphasize some point.

"(e) *Substance of Authorities Stated.*—Instead of reading authorities, counsel are expected to cite them in their briefs and to state the substance in argument.

"(f) *Interruptions Not Permitted.*—Counsel will not be permitted to interrupt opposing counsel with questions or otherwise, except by leave of the Court.

"(g) *Oral Argument Not Permitted, When.*—Oral arguments are not permitted in support of or in opposition to petitions for rehearing.

"(h) *Amici Curiae Counsel.*—Will not be permitted to participate in the oral argument.

"(i) *Argument Date Fixed.*—Where a case has once been set for oral argument and notice given, argument and submission will be on the date fixed unless otherwise ordered by the Court.

"(j) *Citing Cases Outside the Brief.*—If a case outside the brief is to be cited, the citation must be furnished opposing counsel in advance as soon as possible."

2. Florida (1973) Rule 3.10—Oral Arguments:

"(a) *Application For.* Oral arguments may be allowed in any case appealed, or presented, to the Court if applied for at the time the applicant's first brief is filed. The application for oral argument shall not be incorporated in the briefs or other bound papers but shall be filed on a separate paper. The application shall be filed with the clerk and a copy thereof shall be served on the opposite party in the same manner that briefs are required to be served.

"(b) *Time Allowed.* Not more than 30 minutes to the side will be allowed for arguments in the Supreme Court."

3. Idaho (1973) Rule 30—Oral Argument:

"No appeal shall be assigned for argument unless written request is made by separate instrument for such argument by counsel within five days after filing respondent's brief. Causes in which no request for oral argument is received will be deemed submitted on the briefs filed pursuant to these rules. However, the court may in its discretion order argument on both sides."

4. Illinois (1971) Rule 352—Conduct of Oral Arguments:

"A party shall request oral argument by stating at the bottom of the cover page of his brief that oral argument is requested.... No party may argue unless he has filed his brief as required by the rule and paid any fee required by law."

5. Indiana (1972) Appellate Rule 10—Oral Argument:

"(a) *When Granted.* Under separate petition filed in writing by either party within the time allowed for filing briefs, a party may request oral argument. However, oral argument will not be granted except at the court's discretion. The Court will order, without application, oral argument in such cases as it deems proper....

"(b) *Time Allowed for Argument.* Each side will be allowed 30 minutes for argument...a party is not obliged to use all of the time allowed, and the court may terminate the argument whenever in its judgment further argument is unnecessary."

6. Missouri (1974) Special Rule 1 Missouri Court of Appeals, Springfield District—Oral Argument: . . .

"(b) Any party desiring to orally argue his cause shall serve notice thereof upon the other parties and the clerk of this Court within 10 days after respondent's brief is due to be filed under Supreme Court Rule 84.05 (a) or as extended by order of the Court. Such notice may be endorsed upon the brief of the party and may be withdrawn at any time.

"(c) The time allowed for oral argument shall be 25 minutes for the appellant and 20 minutes for the respondent, unless the Court, for good cause shown not less than 5 days before the date upon which the case is set for argument, shall otherwise order...not more than five minutes of the total allowed and reserved time shall be consumed by reply argument."

C. CONCENTRATE ON THE COHESIVENESS OF WRITTEN AND ORAL ARGUMENT.

The finale of your appellate success will likely rest upon the coherent persuasion of your oral presentation, written argument, and impressive brief format. Take cognizance of today's preferences for brevity in all procedures.

1. Restricted Lengths of Briefs.

New rules of appellate procedure indicate strong trends toward page limitations of brief contents. This will mean that the advocate must give more time to the preparation of his final written document. It is more difficult to confine persuasive thoughts within a few impressive words than it is to ramble. Brevity in page count, however, will focus attention on critical issues. Supreme Court Justices will appreciate the shorter lengths which may aid in reducing case backlog.

Many distinguished jurists have taken the time to admonish members of the bar toward brevity. For illustration, in the case of *Davis v. Johnson,* decided February 28, 1973, cited as 479 S.W. 2d 525, 251 Ark. 1078, Justice George Rose Smith, presiding, the Opinion states [in part]:

> . . . The appellants, however, have not seen fit to abstract the testimony heard by the chancellor; so we are unable to say that he was mistaken upon issues of fact.
>
> . . . Without reference to the merits of the case, we are impelled by the appellants' statement of the case to remind the members of the bar of our rule requiring the appellants' statement of the case to be short. "This statement, ordinarily not exceeding two pages in length, should be sufficient to enable the court to read the abstract with an understanding of the nature of the case, the general fact situation, and the action taken by the trial court." Rule 9(b). In the case at bar the appellant's opening statement, comprising eleven printed pages, is actually longer than this opinion. While there is no penalty for an infraction of this particular rule, we do expect appellate advocates to familiarize themselves with our rules and to observe them. *AFFIRMED.*

Selected State rulings on page limitations are as follows:

a. FLORIDA (1973) Rule 3.7 e (5)—*Length of Briefs:* "Briefs shall contain not more than 50 pages, whether printed or typewritten, exclusive of appendices herein required, unless the court permits enlargement of the brief."

b. HAWAII (1972) Rule 3—*Briefs:* "Except after leave granted, the clerk will not receive an opening or answering brief of more than 80 typewritten pages, or a reply brief of more than 20 typewritten pages, exclusive of indices and appendices . . . ."

c. NEBRASKA (1971) Rule 9—*Briefs:*

a. *How Printed.* "All briefs shall be printed unless otherwise allowed by the court on good cause shown. Briefs shall be printed on unglazed white book paper on pages 6½ inches wide and 9½ inches long, trimmed size. . . ."

c. *Length of Briefs.* "The total content of all briefs filed on behalf of any party to a cause pending in this court on its original submission shall not exceed 100 pages, unless otherwise ordered by the court."

d. NEVADA (1973) Rule 28 (g)—*Length of Briefs:* "Except by permission of the court, briefs shall not exceed 30 pages of standard typographic printing, or 50 pages of printing by any other process of duplicating or copying, exclusive of pages containing the table of contents, table of citations, and any addendum containing statutes, rules, regulations, etc."

e. RHODE ISLAND (1972) Rule 16 (d)—*Form of Briefs:* "If briefs are typewritten, they shall be on good paper of sufficient opacity to be distinctly legible . . . . Unless authorized by Court order, briefs shall not exceed a total of 50 pages."

2. Brief Covers Require Identifying Colors.

In further attention to expediency and time-saving devices, many of the states require identifying colors to be used for brief covers, as indicated by the following illustrations and revision dates:

a. COLORADO (1970) Rule 32 (a): "If briefs are produced by commercial printing or duplicating firms, or, if produced otherwise and the covers to be described are available, the cover of the brief of the appellant should be blue; that of appellee, red; that of an intervenor or amicus curiae, green; that of any reply brief, gray." These identifying colors have gained some uniformity as reflected in same designation for several other states, to wit: Iowa (1973) Rule 344.2; Indiana (1971) Rule 8.2 A(3); Nevada (1973) Rule 32(a).

Another group of states in the early seventies began requiring white cover page for appellant, and blue for appellee brief identification, to wit: Alaska (1973), and Virginia (1972) Rule 5:34.

3. "County Lawyer" Gives Legal Guidance to Local Printer.

Appellate advocate in non-metropolitan centers must check current printing and format rules applicable to each appeal case. This includes all minute details bearing final impression on the appellate court, including compliance with any rules or customary colors expected for printed brief covers. A New York City advocate might consider this precaution as almost frivolous in admonition, but his competent specialized legal printer may not be available in all localities of today's suburban demands for on-the-spot appellate advocates. The local printer of a remote state-line county seat can not be expected to keep abreast of most recent rules of his state supreme court. The entire responsibility for success of the appeal and rule compliances must rest squarely on the shoulders of appellate advocate. The finality of case decision should not be jeopardized by any color frustration caused by appellate advocate's failure to see that his printer uses the right color paperback for your brief's identification.

D. A CHALLENGE TO THE LAWYERS IN REMOTE AREAS.

The following pages, in Part II of this book, are intended to encourage motivation for every lawyer to accept new challenges afforded in further upper levels of appellate practice.

Advocate entry into the meticulous framework of various state supreme court appellate details will indeed produce more courage and less awe for participation in the federal court appellate arena.

PART TWO

Appellate Civil Practice and Procedure in Federal Court Jurisdictions

9

How to Take Federal Court Appeals as of Right
(Know Your Rules, How and Where to Find Them)

Specific directives and case illustrations are provided in many publications for implementation of Federal Rules of Appellate Procedure. The United States Supreme Court Advisory Committee on Appellate Rules prepares intensive notes covering various aspects and provisions of the rules. These notes may be found at pertinent sections of Title 28, United States Code, as applicable to the particular rule to which they relate. Appellate advocates will refresh memory and keep abreast of revisions which are being made from time to time. Continuing legal education seminars and workshops are available in all sections of the country. It is the lawyer's responsibility to take advantage of these enlightening and updating opportunities. The professional who expects services to be marketable for today's clientele must up-date his legal education with the same diligence as that demanded of the medical profession.

Outstanding leaders of the legal profession are expressing concern over the growing complacency of lawyers. Perhaps the recent crises of political scandal, energy depletion, population explosion, escalating inflation, and burgeoning caseloads will shock all appellate advocates into a rebound of diligence, alertness, enlightenment, and ethical endeavors. Time has come for the general practitioner to take greater participation in federal court practice at all levels and specifically at appellate level. The clientele is waiting!

A. COLLECT APPELLATE RULE BOOKLETS FOR DESK-SIDE REFERENCE.

In accepting the challenge from distinguished members of the Judiciary, every appellate advocate can establish schedules which will provide "homework" routines toward self-education in a renewed vigor for learning and applying rules of procedure. It is only by new efforts that better teamwork can be accomplished to meet the common goal of relieving court congestion and over-crowded dockets.

Regardless of local pressures from clientele, the remote area of the law practice, increasing overhead expense, inadequate or outmoded library, every lawyer has a professional responsibility to keep informed on rules of court. For ready reference in desk-side handbooks, the inexpensive paperback pamphlets are available with condensed listing of the most recent appellate court rules. Each case must be prepared by the advocate at court of original jurisdiction with such expertise as to be prepared for appellate procedures. Local court rules are priorities.

1. Keep files of Latest U.S. Government Pamphlets on Rules.

U.S. Government Printing Office distributes, at a nominal cost, many valuable rule books in pamphlet form for Federal Court Advocates.

a. FRAP Pamphlet.

Revised editions are timely issued under the Title *Federal Rules of Appellate Procedure,* which includes 46 rules. This booklet, "Printed for the Use of the Committee on the Judiciary, House of Representatives,"[1] is available for desk-side use of every lawyer. It has only 33 pages and is easily adaptable for desk top storage, or for carrying in coat pocket as commuter accessory. Reading time can be grasped while waiting for that late bus, or that late-arriving client. This can lead the way to the more detailed reference in U.S. Code.

The rules of civil procedure are prescribed as authorized in § 2072, Title 28, United States Code, which states:

> The Supreme Court shall have the power to prescribe by general rules, the forms of process, writs, pleadings, and motions, and the practice and procedure of the district courts and courts of appeals of the United States in

---

[1] Superintendent of Documents, *Federal Rules of Appellate Procedure.* Document #82-974-0-72-3, U.S. Government Printing Office, Washington, D.C. 20402 (October 1, 1972).

civil actions, including admiralty and maritime cases, and appeals therein, and the practice and procedure in proceedings for the review by the courts of appeals of decisions of the Tax Court of the United States, and for judicial review or enforcement of orders of administrative agencies, boards, commissions, and officers. . . .

b. Rules of Procedure, U.S. District Court Pamphlet.

For best background preparation toward appellate practice, the updated rules of procedure in U.S. District Court are also essential for desk-side reference. The new pamphlet entitled "Rules of Civil Procedure for the United States District Courts"[2] as amended in 1974 will be very essential because of the many changes made in rules as adopted by U.S. Supreme Court in 1973, and approved, as amended by 93D Congress, 2D Session # H.R. 5463, in 1974. The new pamphlet 0-1974 is a Revision of U.S. Government Printing Office booklet #65 558-0 of 1971, indicating also that it was "printed for use of the Committee on the Judiciary."

These U.S. Government Printing Office booklets provide excellent guidelines and many suggested forms. A reference table is compiled below (in Table #11) to convey an itemized list of the 32 suggested forms in the U.S. District Court document on civil procedure.

TABLE # 11

ITEMIZED FORMS IMPLEMENTING RULES OF CIVIL PROCEDURE IN U.S. DISTRICTS

Form No.	TITLE	Referred Rule No.	Pamphlet Page No.
1	SUMMONS	4	69
2	ALLEGATION OF JURISDICTION	9(h)	70
3	COMPLAINT ON A PROMISSORY NOTE	8(e), 18	71
4	COMPLAINT ON AN ACCOUNT		71
5	COMPLAINT–GOODS SOLD AND DELIVERED		72
6	COMPLAINT FOR MONEY LENT		72
7	COMPLAINT–MONEY PAID BY MISTAKE		72
8	COMPLAINT–MONEY HAD AND RECEIVED		72
9	COMPLAINT FOR NEGLIGENCE		72

2 Superintendent of Documents, *Rules of Civil Procedure for the U.S. District Courts (with Forms),* Document #476-253-0-72-2 (rev. 1974), U.S. Government Printing Office, Washington, D.C. 20402.

TABLE # 11 (*continued*)

Form No.	TITLE	Referred Rule No.	Pamphlet Page No.
10	COMPLAINT FOR NEGLIGENCE WHERE PLAINTIFF UNABLE TO DETERMINE DEFINITELY PERSON RESPONSIBLE AND WHERE HIS EVIDENCE MAY JUSTIFY FINDING OF WILLFULNESS, RECKLESSNESS OR NEGLIGENCE		73
11	COMPLAINT FOR CONVERSION		73
12	COMPLAINT–SPECIFIC PERFORMANCE OF CONTRACT TO CONVEY LAND		73
13	COMPLAINT–CLAIM FOR DEBT AND TO SET ASIDE FRAUDULENT CONVEYANCE	18(b)	74
14	COMPLAINT–NEGLIGENCE UNDER FEDERAL EMPLOYER'S LIABILITY ACT		74
15	COMPLAINT–DAMAGES–MERCHANT MARINE ACT		75
16	COMPLAINT–INFRINGEMENT OF PATENT		75
17	COMPLAINT–INFRINGEMENT OF COPYRIGHT		76
18	COMPLAINT FOR INTERPLEADER AND DECLARATORY RELIEF		77
19	MOTION TO DISMISS, PRESENTING DEFENSE OF FAILURE TO STATE A CLAIM, LACK OF SERVICE, IMPROPER VENUE, OR LACK OF JURISDICTION	7(b),12(b)	78
20	ANSWER, PRESENTING DEFENSE	12(b)	79
21	ANSWER TO COMPLAINT IN FORM 8		80
22	MOTION (Abrogated–1963)		80
22-A	SUMMONS AND COMPLAINT AGAINST THIRD PARTY DEFENDANT		80
22-B	MOTION TO BRING IN THIRD PARTY		81
23	MOTION TO INTERVENE AS DEFENDANT	24	82
24	REQUEST FOR DOCUMENT PRODUCTION	34	83
25	REQUEST FOR ADMISSION	36	83
26	ALLEGATION OF REASON–OMITTED PARTY		84
27	NOTICE OF APPEAL	73(b)	84
28	NOTICE: CONDEMNATION		85
29	COMPLAINT–CONDEMNATION		85
30	SUGGESTION OF DEATH UPON RECORD	25(a)(1)	86
31	JUDGMENT ON JURY VERDICT	54(a),58	86
32	JUDGMENT ON COURT DECISION	58	87

c. New Rules of the United States Court of Customs and Patent Appeals.

Pursuant to *28 United States Code, 2071,* new rules were adopted effective January 1, 1974, for the United States Court of Customs and Patent Appeals. The court's existing rules were rescinded as of that date, but this did not affect any action properly taken before these rules became effective. The new issue[3] of 29 pages is likewise available through U.S. Government Printing Office as pamphlet #508-390-0-73-2, at a nominal cost. It is the handy blue-back pocket size, adaptable for carry-along, or for regular desk-top availability. Letter of transmittal from the Clerk of U.S. Court of Customs and Patent Appeals points out some of the significant changes in this 1974 revision. He advises that the clerk will no longer estimate the cost of printing the transcript and transmit record portions to the printer. Under new Rule 5.6, counsel must designate portions of the record which they wish included and the appellant will be responsible for filing 25 copies of a printed transcript with the court and serving an additional 5 copies on opposing counsel within the time specified. The certified record, as transmitted from the Customs Court or the Patent Office, will be available in the clerk's office for this purpose and will be released to counsel for the appellant, or his designee, upon the filing of a written request. The record will be returnable within the time specified for the filing of the transcript. Documentary and physical exhibits will not be released for printing purposes unless ordered by the court pursuant to a motion filed under Rule 5.3. Your attention is also called to the other provisions of Rule 5.6 relative to the contents of the transcript.

Other changes include:

1. Increase in filing fee from $15 to $50 (Rule 5.15)
2. Notice of appearance (Rule 2.2)
3. The format of printed transcripts, briefs, motions, and other papers (Rule 5.8)
4. Correction or modification of the record (Rules 3.3 and 4.2)
5. Briefs—contents, time for filing, service, etc. (Rules 5.9, 5.10)
6. Computation of time for filing of papers (Rule 5.2)
7. Service of papers (Rule 5.1)

---

[3] Superintendent of Documents, *Rules of United States Court of Customs and Patent Appeals,* Document #508-390-0-73-3 (effective January 1, 1974), U.S. Government Printing Office, Washington, D.C. 20402.

8. Admission to the bar (Rule 2.1)
9. Calendar of cases (Rule 5.12)
10. Time allowed for oral argument (Rule 5.13)
11. Visual aids (Rule 5.7)
12. *Amicus Curiae* (Rules 5.11 and 5.13)
13. *In camera* proceeding (Rule 5.13)
14. Typewritten papers (Rule 5.14)

With the announcement of the new rules, effective January 1, 1974, Chief Judge Markey also announced the convocation of a one-day Judicial Conference of the United States Court of Customs and Patent Appeals in April, 1974. This Conference was the first in the history of the court. It will likely be succeeded by similar annual conferences.

d. New Rules of United States Tax Court, Effective January 1, 1974.

The United States Tax Court completely revised its Rules of Practice and Procedure for the first time in its 50-year history, said revisions effective January 1, 1974. The American Bar Association Section of Taxation immediately programmed a "National Institute on Tax Court Practice Under Its New Rules of Procedure."

Topics covered in this Institute[4] and the Code references are included herein for the assistance of those desiring to pursue a "home study" approach for self-enlightenment, or for those registrants who may desire to use this source for refreshing their memory of presentations:

PANEL I: BRINGING A TAX COURT CASE

References: Internal Revenue Code Sections 6212, 6123, and 6503(a)
            Treasury Regulation Sections 601.105 and 601.106
RULES: Title I—Scope of Rules; Title II—The Court
          Title III—Commencement of Case; Title IV—Pleadings
          Title V—Parties; and Title XX Practice Before the Court

PANEL II: DISCOVERY

RULES: Title VII—Discovery Title VIII—Depositions

---

[4] Section of Taxation, American Bar Association *National Institute,* news release flyer. Chicago, Ill. 60637 (February 22, 1974).

Title IX—Admissions & Stipulations;
Title X—General Provisions

PANEL III: PRE-TRIAL AND SETTLEMENTS

RULES: Title V—Motions; Title XI—Pretrial Conferences;
Title XII—Decisions without Trial

PANEL IV: TRIALS AND APPEALS

Title XIII—Calendars and Continuances — IRC §7446
Title XIV—Trials   IRC §7458
Title XV—Decision   IRC §7460(b)
Title XVI—Post Trial Proceedings   IRC §7481
Title XVII—Small Tax Cases   IRC §7463
Title XVIII—Commissioners of the Court   IRC §7456(c)
Title XIX—Appeals   IRC §7482—7486

e. National and Regional Distribution Sources of Government Documents.

Handy rule booklets for appellate advocates are sometimes available for distribution through the Library of Congress, and can be obtained by constituent request directed to your Congressman's office. However, supplies at this source are frequently depleted except for copies which are part of the permanent collections of the Library. Adequate supplies are normally available for purchase by writing directly to one of the following distribution offices:

(1) If the document is a current popular item or a report which has lately been in the news, it might be obtained faster at a regional distribution center.

(a) For residents east of the Mississippi River, the center is:

PUBLIC DOCUMENTS DISTRIBUTION CENTER
5801 Tabor Avenue
Philadelphia, Pennsylvania 19120

(b) For residents west of the Mississippi River, the order should be placed with:

PUEBLO MEMORIAL INDUSTRIAL CENTER
P.O. Box 713
Pueblo, Colorado 81002

(2) If the requested item cannot be considered to be current, popular, or recently newsworthy publication, the order should be sent to:

SUPERINTENDENT OF DOCUMENTS
U.S. GOVERNMENT PRINTING OFFICE
Washington, D.C. 20402

(3) For current *Rules of the Supreme Court of the United States,* including current revisions [a 75-page pamphlet @ 50¢] :

CLB PUBLISHERS, INC., LAW PRINTING CO.
1117-1119 14th Street, NW
Washington, D.C. 20005

2. Contact Clerks in Appellate Courts of Appeals for Current Rule Books.

As provided in Rule 47 of Federal Rules of Procedure, each court of appeals by action of a majority of the current judges in regular active service may, from time to time, make and amend rules governing its practice, not inconsistent with FRAP rules. Copies of rules made by a court of appeals shall upon their promulgation be furnished to the Administrative Office of the United States Courts.

The clerks of each circuit appellate court are burdened with heavy case filing and processing. However, they are most cooperative in responding whenever their aid is sought. They immediately advise the source of distribution for rule books in inexpensive paperbacks, or typewritten copies which have been Xeroxed to meet current requests.

Each of the eleven clerks' offices extended great courtesy in immediate response to this practicing attorney's request for material. These pamphlets are published directly by the courts, by committees appointed by the courts, by bar associations, or by commercial suppliers. Local Federal Bar Associations are instrumental in preparing handy pocket size booklets similar to those released by the Superintendent of Documents in the U.S. Government Printing Office. Table No. 12 has been compiled herein for reader's guidance as to source of specific state and circuit appellate court pamphlets containing local rules.

TABLE #12

U.S. CIRCUIT APPELLATE COURT RULES

SUPPLEMENTING THE FEDERAL RULES OF APPELLATE PROCEDURE

Bibliography of Source Booklets for Lawyers' Information in Each of the
ELEVEN CIRCUITS, U.S. COURTS OF APPEALS

TABLE #12 (*continued*)

CIRCUIT NO.	APPLICABLE STATE OR TER.	DISTRIBUTION SOURCE	PAMPHLET TITLE	REV. DATE
D.C.	1. District of Columbia 20001	Clerk's Office U.S. Circuit Court of Appeals, Washington, D.C.	"Local Rules Supplementing F.R.A.P. for U.S. Courts"	1973
First	2. Maine 3. Massachusetts 4. New Hampshire 5. Rhode Island 6. Puerto Rico	U.S. Clerk's Office, Court of Appeals, Federal Bldg., Boston, Mass. 02109 or— Blanchard Press Inc., Boston, Mass. 02102	"Rules of the U.S. Court of Appeals for the First Circuit"	Nov. 6 1973
Second	7. Connecticut 8. New York 9. Vermont	U.S. Second Circuit Clerk's Office, Court of Appeals, Federal Bldg., New York, N.Y. 10007 or— Record Press Inc., 95 Morton St., New York, N.Y. 10014	"Appeals to the Second Circuit Prepared by the Committee on Federal Courts, Bar Association of the City of New York"	1971
Third	10. Delaware 11. New Jersey 12. Pennsylvania 13. Virgin Islands	U.S. Clerk's Office, Court of Appeals, Federal Courthouse, Philadelphia, Pa. 19107 or— International Printing Co., Philadelphia, Pa., 19102	"Rules of the United States Court of Appeals for the Third Circuit"	Jan. 1 1974

TABLE #12 (continued)

Bibliography of Source Booklets for Lawyers' Information in Each of the
ELEVEN CIRCUITS, U.S. COURT OF APPEALS

CIRCUIT NO.	APPLICABLE STATE OR TER.	DISTRIBUTION SOURCE	PAMPHLET TITLE	REV. DATE
Fourth	14. Maryland 15. North Carolina 16. South Carolina 17. Virginia 18. West Virginia	U.S. Clerk's Office, Court of Appeals, Fourth Circuit, Federal Building, Richmond, Va. 23219 or— Lewis Printing Co., Richmond, Va. 23220	"Federal Rules of Procedure, Including Local Rules of the U.S. Court of Appeals for the Fourth Circuit"	July 1973
Fifth	19. Alabama 20. Florida 21. Georgia 22. Louisiana 23. Mississippi 24. Texas 25. Canal Zone	U.S. Clerk's Office, Court of Appeals, Fifth Circuit Federal Building, New Orleans, La. 70130 or— West Publishing Co., St. Paul, Minn. 55102	"U.S. Court of Appeals for the Fifth Circuit Local Rules Supplementing the Federal Rules of Procedure"	1974
Sixth	26. Kentucky 27. Michigan 28. Ohio 29. Tennessee	U.S. Clerk's Office, Court of Appeals Sixth Circuit, Federal Building, Cincinnati, Ohio 45202 or— Cincinnati Chapter, Federal Bar Assn., Cincinnati, 45202	"Practitioner's Handbook for Appeals to the U.S. Court of Appeals for the Sixth Circuit"	1973
Seventh	30. Illinois 31. Indiana	U.S. Clerk's Office, Court of Appeals, Seventh Circuit, Chicago, 60604 or—	"Practitioner's Handbook for Appeals to the U.S. Court of Appeals for the	Nov. 1973

TABLE #12 (*continued*)

Bibliography of Source Booklets for Lawyers' Information in Each of the
ELEVEN CIRCUITS, U.S. COURT OF APPEALS

CIRCUIT NO.	APPLICABLE STATE OR TER.	DISTRIBUTION SOURCE	PAMPHLET TITLE	REV. DATE
	32. Wisconsin	Gunthrop-Warren Co., 123 N. Wacker Drive, Chicago, Ill. 60606	Seventh Circuit"	
Eighth	33. Arkansas 34. Iowa 35. Minnesota 36. Missouri 37. Nebraska 38. North Dakota 39. South Dakota	U.S. Clerk's Office, Court of Appeals, Eighth Circuit, Federal Building, St. Louis, Mo. 63101 or— St. Louis Law Printing Co. Inc., 812 Olive, St. Louis 63101	"Rules, United States Court of Appeals for the Eighth Circuit"	Aug. 1973
Ninth	40. Alaska 41. Arizona 42. California 43. Hawaii 44. Idaho 45. Montana 46. Nevada 47. Oregon 48. Washington 49. Guam	U.S. Clerk's Office, Court of Appeals, Ninth Circuit, Federal Bldg., P.O. Box 547 San Francisco, Calif. 94101	"Rules of the United States Court of Appeals for the Ninth Circuit"	Jan. 22 1974
Tenth	50. Colorado 51. Kansas 52. New Mexico 53. Oklahoma 54. Utah 55. Wyoming	U.S. Clerk's Office, Court of Appeals, Tenth Circuit, Federal Building, Denver, Colorado 80202	"Rules of Court— United States Court of Appeals for the Tenth Circuit"	Oct. 16 1973
SUPREME COURT OF UNITED STATES		CLB Publishers, Inc. 1117-1119 14th St. NW, Washington, D.C. 20005	"Rules of the Supreme Court of the United States, USA" (paperback, 75 pp)	Dec. 1 1971

B. PROCEDURE STEPS AND TIME LIMITS ON APPEALS AS OF RIGHT.

The busy advocate knows that his first priority in law practice is to fulfill requirements and make application for admission to practice in jurisdictions of anticipated court appearances. Admission before State Supreme Court and before the local United States District Courts is normally followed by the superb highlight for the young lawyer who likely makes his first trip to Washington, D.C., for the admission before U.S. Supreme Court. From these three steps, complacency frequently supplants knowledge and diligence. Some lawyers forget the important step of timely processing admission to practice before the U.S. Circuit Court of Appeals for the jurisdiction of the appellate docket. Neglect to apply for admission is not only professionally embarrassing, but also could lead to loss of client's appellate cause by court dismissal of the appeal.

1. Admission to Bar of Appellate Court: FRAP RULE # 46. Attorneys.

An attorney who has been admitted to practice before the Supreme Court of United States, or highest court of a state, or another U.S. Court of Appeals, or a U.S. District Court (including the district courts for the Canal Zone, Guam and the Virgin Islands), and now is of good moral and professional character, is eligible for admission to the bar of a court of appeals. Applicant shall file with the Clerk of appeals, on form approved by court and furnished by the Clerk, an application for admission containing his personal statement showing eligibility for membership. He shall take and subscribe to the provided form of oath or affirmation. Thereafter, upon written or oral motion of a member of that bar, the court will act upon the application, and applicant pays fee prescribed by Circuits. See Table 13, as follows:

TABLE #13

ATTORNEY ADMISSION RULES TO PRACTICE IN APPELLATE CIRCUITS

CIRCUIT NO.	RULE NO.	LOCAL FEE	SUMMARY OF RULES [Supplementing FRAP #46]
1	3	$10	Admitted in open court on Motion, or as the Court determines.
2	46	$10	Admitted upon written motion, acted upon by a single judge, or oral motion at beginning of any court session without the presence of applicant being required.
3	7, 9	[Court Prescribes]	Each applicant for admission to the bar of this court shall pay a library fee; and at time of case docketing shall file written appearance including address where papers may be mailed or served.
4	6	$20	File written application for admission on form furnished by Clerk. Thereafter Court acts on application upon written or oral motion of a member of the car of the court, upon personal appearance or not.
5	5	$10 or $20	File written application pursuant to FRAP #46, and pay Clerk the admission fee of $10, if practice less than 5 years, and under 30 years of age; fee of $20, if over 5 years' practice, age over 30 years.

TABLE NO. 13 (*continued*)

6	p. 9 [Handbook]	$15	Admitted on oral motion by an attorney who is already authorized to practice before Sixth Circuit. Motion to be presented at any session beginning or by personal appearance before a Judge of the Court.
7	7(a) and (b)	$15	File written application for admission on form furnished by Clerk. Admission may be ordered in open court or by active or senior circuit judge in chambers. In open court applicant must appear in person with sponsor; in chambers, with sponsor's written motion.
8	15	$10	Same procedure for admission as prescribed in FRAP Rule #46. Admission fee waived for attorney appointed to represent a party in forma pauperis without compensation.
9	11	$6	Admitted by personal appearance on oral motion of sponsoring member; or by written motion on court approved form furnished by clerk.
10	4	$15	Admission governed by provisions of Rule #46, FRAP; and further upon written motion filed on Forms furnished by Clerk, immediately upon filing of the case or entering an appearance in a case in court.

2. When to Take Appeals as of Right: FRAP RULE #4.

In a civil case (including a civil action which involves an admiralty or maritime claim and a proceeding in bankruptcy or a controversy arising therein in which an appeal is permitted by law as of right from a district court to a court of appeals), the notice of appeal required by Rule 3 shall be filed with the clerk of the district court as illustrated in the following time schedule:

- 30 days from entry of judgment or order appealed from.
- 60 days from entry of judgment if the United States, or an officer or agency of the United States, is a party.
- 14 days from the date on which first notice of appeal was filed in civil cases for any other party desiring to appeal.
- 30 days' extension may be granted upon showing excusable neglect.

3. Where and How to File Notice of Appeal: FRAP RULE#3.

An appeal permitted by law as of right from a district court to a court of appeals shall be taken by filing a notice of appeal with the clerk of the district court within the time allowed by Rule 4. Failure of appellant to take any step other than the timely filing of notice does not affect the validity of appeal, but is ground only for such action as the court of appeals deems appropriate, *which may include dismissal* of the appeal. The clerk of the district court shall serve notice of the filing of a notice of appeal by mailing a copy thereof to counsel of record of each party other than the appellant, or if a party is not represented by counsel, to the party at his last known address.

4. Content and Form of Appeal Notice.

Form 1 in the FRAP appendix is a suggested form of a notice of appeal, and follows herein.

FORM #14

NOTICE OF APPEAL TO A COURT OF APPEALS FROM A JUDGMENT OR ORDER OF A DISTRICT COURT [FRAP #1]

UNITED STATES DISTRICT COURT FOR THE _____ DISTRICT

OF _____

A. B., PLAINTIFF)
)
)
V.)   FILE NUMBER _____
)
)
)
C. D., DEFENDANT)

NOTICE OF APPEAL

Notice is hereby given that C.D., defendant above named, hereby appeals to the United States Court of Appeals for the _____ Circuit [from the final judgment] [from the order (describing it)]

_____

_____

_____

entered in this action on the _____ day of _____ 19 _____.

(S) _____

_____
(Address)
ATTORNEY FOR C.D.

10

Appeal in Bankruptcy

Increasing backlogs in the bankruptcy courts, and appeals therefrom, have focused concerned inquiries into the procedures and practices under the Federal Bankruptcy Act. Great need of amendments and rules revisions became apparent by the mid-seventies. The spiraling inflation and easy credit of prior decades catapulted many unsuspecting citizens into financial crises with no solution except bankruptcy. In shocking instances the well-meaning creditors likewise were thrown into bankruptcy, and the problem telescoped. The growing volume of the caseload minimized the attention that referees, trustees, and jurists could give to the merits of each case.

A. CRIME INFILTRATION SHOCKS BANKRUPTCY COURTS.

The spread of the crime wave opened doors for organized crime to steal millions of dollars from the public through planned fraudulent bankruptcies or so-called *"scams"* as reported by the Justice Department. To produce a "scam," underworld figures either start a company or infiltrate an existing one, build up an extra large inventory that they sell through "fences," and then declare the company bankrupt. These forms of infiltrating and looting are estimated to produce illegal revenue of billions of dollars per year. The research center of the Law Enforcement Assistance Administration, under the auspices of National Institute of Law Enforcement and Criminal Justice, recently reported hundreds of these case investigations on fraudulent bankruptcies. The biggest, boldest, and most audacious bankruptcy "scam" was a takeover in New York City of a financially troubled firm by loan sharks which caused the meatpacking firm creditors a loss in excess of $1.3 million dollars.

**B. SOLUTIONS FOCUS ON NEW RULES AND FEDERAL
    COURT REDISTRICTING.**

Tightening of the Bankruptcy laws, updating of federal bankruptcy court rules and expansion of federal court services are now being implemented. Unprepared advocates are being called upon to handle bankruptcy cases for the first time in many years of law practice. It is now mandatory that attention of the ethical leaders of the legal profession be focused on the new rules which became effective. An all-out alert in cooperative endeavor will be necessary not only from the viewpoint of the advocates handling criminal cases in the bankruptcy scandals, but also in the appellate advocates handling the civil appeals which have increased from the bankruptcy overload in each of the United States District Courts. An appendix to this chapter with Exhibits "A," "B," and "C" will reflect geographic boundaries of the new locations and expansions made in the federal districts in recent years. This creation of new districts and realignment of old boundary lines is part of the solution to the problems of federal court backlogs and greater attention in bankruptcy appeals.

New rules of procedure took effect for straight bankruptcy and Chapter XIII cases which supersede all conflicting provisions of the Federal Bankruptcy Act and all of the prior local rules in the District Courts. These new rules, as approved by the Judicial Conference of the United States, the U.S. Supreme Court, and Congress, are now being used in bankruptcy courts throughout the nation. It is imperative that practitioners be informed on the nature, extent and meaning of these new rules, in order that greater justice can be administered in this well-meaning vehicle intended to render a legal service to the financially oppressed victims of poor judgment. Our Federal Bankruptcy Act of 1938 was never envisioned to be a vehicle for crime permission or promotion by its very existence.

Motivation and Challenges to Appellate Advocates.

Those who practice law as appellate advocates in the Federal Court realm must light new fires of vigilance to move into their rightful seats as trusted heads of the legal profession. A loud call is issued by the demand of appellate litigants for a new breed of appellate advocates to implement and abide by the new rules for bankruptcy courts.

**C. SUPREME COURT OF UNITED STATES ISSUES REVISED
    BANKRUPTCY PROCEDURES.**

In order that the reader might grasp the sweeping influence of the current innovation we quote the Supreme Court of the United States under its ORDER of 1973, which states [in part]. . .

1. That the rules and forms as approved by the Judicial Conference of the United States, to be known as the Bankruptcy Rules and Official Bankruptcy Forms, be, and they hereby are prescribed pursuant to Section 2075, Title 28, United States Code, to govern the forms of process, writs, pleadings, and motions, and the practice and procedure under the Bankruptcy Act, in the proceedings and to the extent set forth herein, in the United States district courts. . . .

2. That the aforementioned Bankruptcy Rules and Official Bankruptcy Forms . . . shall be applicable to proceedings then pending, except to the extent that in the opinion of the court their application in a particular proceeding then pending would not be feasible or would work injustice, in which event the former procedure applies.

3. That General Orders in Bankruptcy 1 to 7 inclusive, 9 to 12 inclusive, 14 to 26 inclusive, 28 to 40 inclusive, 42 to 45 inclusive, 15 to 20 inclusive, 22 to 47 inclusive, and 70 to 72 inclusive, heretofore prescribed to this Court, be, and they hereby are, abrogated. . . .

This court further ordered:

1. That the rules and forms . . . to be known as Chapter XIII Rules and Official Chapter XIII Forms, be, and they hereby are prescribed pursuant to Section 1075, Title 28, United States Code, to govern the forms of process, writs, pleadings, and motions and the practice and procedure under Chapter XIII of the Bankruptcy Act, in the proceedings and to the extent set forth therein. . . .

D. IMPLEMENTATION OF NEW PROCEDURES IN BANKRUPTCY APPEALS.

Official forms are provided together with all new rules as released by U.S. Government Printing Office, Washington, D.C. 20402 (1973). Paperback pamphlet is available by purchase from Superintendent of Documents at $2.00, domestic postpaid, Stock No. 5271-00343. This pamphlet should be on the desk of every appellate advocate anticipating any client representation in bankruptcy court appeals to U.S. District Courts.

These rules are quite new, and each current appellate advocate will certainly want to give personal interpretation of the "letter of the law" as applicable to his specific case. To summarize these very concise and well written federal court revised rules might make an unfortunate result of diluting the very point on which the reader desires to make his own interpretation in the particular instance of quandary. Our best service at this time appears to be that of motivating studious effort from each individual advocate and of dispelling any reluctance in answering the call of new clientele in bankruptcy appeals. The exact appellate directives are therefore quoted from above reference[1] in order that this handbook might be the sourcebook tool intended herein, as best evidence on bankruptcy appeal implementation and guidance:

PART VIII. APPEAL TO DISTRICT COURT

1. Manner of Taking Appeal (Rule 801).

An appeal from a judgment or order of a referee to a district court shall be taken by filing a notice of appeal with the referee within the time allowed by Rule 802. Failure of an appellant to take any step other than that specified in the first sentence does not affect the validity of the appeal, but is ground only for such action as the district court deems appropriate, which may include dismissal of appeal. The notice of appeal shall conform substantially to Official Form No. 28, shall contain the names of all parties to the judgment or order appealed from and the names and addresses of their respective attorneys, and shall be accompanied by the fee fixed by the Judicial Conference of the United States pursuant to §40c of the Act. Each appellant shall file a sufficient number of copies of the Notice of Appeal to enable the referee to comply promptly with Rule 804.

2. Time for Filing Notice of Appeal (Rule 802).

(a) *Ten-Day Period*. The notice of appeal shall be filed with the referee within 10 days of the date of the entry of the judgment or order appealed from. If a timely notice of appeal is filed by a party, any other party may file a notice of appeal within 10 days of the date on which the first notice of appeal was filed, or within the time otherwise prescribed by this rule, whichever period last expires.

(b) *Effect of Motion on Time for Appeal*. The running of the time for filing a notice of appeal is terminated as to all parties by a timely motion filed with the referee by any party pursuant to the rules hereafter enumerated in this subdivision. The full time for appeal fixed by this rule commences to run and is to be computed from the entry of any of the following orders made upon a timely motion under such rules: (1) granting or denying a motion for judgment notwithstanding the verdict under Rule 115(b)(4); (2) granting or

---

[1]*Rules of Bankruptcy Procedure,* U.S. Government Printing Office #95-205-0. U.S. Superintendent of Documents, Washington, D.C. 20402 (1973).

denying a motion under Rule 752(b) to amend or make additional findings of fact, whether or not alteration of the judgment would be required if the motion is granted; (3) granting or denying a motion under Rule 923 to alter or amend the judgment; or (4) denying a motion for a new trial under Rule 923.

(c) *Extension of Time for Appeal.* The referee may extend the time for filing the notice of appeal by any party for a period not to exceed 20 days from the expiration of the time otherwise prescribed by this rule. A request to extend the time for filing a notice of appeal must be made before such time has expired, except that a request made after the expiration of such time may be granted upon a showing of excusable neglect if the judgment or order does not authorize the sale of any property.

3. Finality of Referee's Judgment or Order (Rule 803).

Unless a notice of appeal is filed as prescribed by Rules 801 and 802, the judgment or order of the referee shall become final.

4. Service of the Notice of Appeal (Rule 804).

The referee shall serve notice of the filing of a notice of appeal by mailing a copy thereof to counsel of record of each party other than the appellant or, if a party is not represented by counsel, to the party at his last known address. Failure to serve notice shall not affect the validity of the appeal. The referee shall note on each copy served the date of the filing of the notice of appeal and shall note in the docket the names of the parties to whom he mails copies and the date of the mailing.

5. Stay Pending Appeal (Rule 805).

A motion for a stay of the judgment or order of a referee, for approval of a supersedeas bond, or for other relief pending appeal must ordinarily be made in the first instance to the referee. Notwithstanding Rule 762 but subject to the power of the district court reserved hereinafter, the referee may suspend or order the continuation of proceedings or make any other appropriate order during the pendency of an appeal upon such terms as will protect the rights of all parties in interest. A motion for such relief, or for modification or termination of relief granted by the referee, may be made to the district court, but the motion shall show why the relief, modification, or termination was not obtained from the referee. The district court may condition the relief it grants under this rule upon the filing of a bond or other appropriate security with the referee. A trustee or receiver may be required to give a supersedeas bond or other appropriate security in order to obtain a stay when taking an appeal.

6. Record and Issues on Appeal (Rule 806).

Within 10 days after filing the notice of appeal the appellant shall file with the referee and serve on the appellee a designation of the contents for inclusion in the record on appeal and a statement of the issues he intends to present on the appeal. The record shall include the contents so designated and the findings of fact, conclusions of law, and orders entered thereon. If the appellee deems any other papers to be necessary, he shall, within 7 days after the service of the statement of the appellant, file and serve on the appellant a designation of additional papers to be included. If the record designated by any party includes a transcript of any proceeding or a part thereof, he shall immediately after the designation order the transcript and make satisfactory arrangements for payment of its costs. All parties shall take any other action necessary to enable the referee to assemble and transmit the record.

7. Transmission of the Record; Docketing of the Appeal (Rule 807).

The record on appeal shall be transmitted by the referee to the clerk of the district court within 30 days after the filing of the statement of the issues unless a different time is prescribed by order of the district court, and the clerk shall thereupon enter the appeal on the docket.

8. Filing and Service of Briefs (Rule 808).

Unless a local rule or court order excuses the filing of briefs or provides for different time limits:
    (1) The appellant shall serve and file his brief within 15 days after entry of the appeal on the docket pursuant to Rule 807.
    (2) The appellee shall serve and file his brief within 15 days after service of the brief of the appellant.
    (3) The appellant may serve and file a reply brief within 5 days after service of the brief of the appellee.

9. Oral Argument (Rule 809).

Unless otherwise provided by local rule or court order the parties shall be given an opportunity to be heard on oral argument.

10. Disposition of Appeal; Weight Accorded Referee's Findings (Rule 810).

Upon an appeal the district court may affirm, modify, or reverse a referee's judgment or order, or remand with instructions for further proceedings. The court shall accept the referee's findings of fact unless they are clearly erroneous, and shall give due regard to the opportunity of the referee to judge of the credibility of the witnesses.

11. Costs (Rule 811).

Except as otherwise provided by law, agreed to by the parties, or ordered by the court, costs shall be taxed against the losing party on an appeal; if a judgment is affirmed or reversed in part or is vacated, costs shall be allowed only as ordered by the court. Costs incurred in the preparation and transmission of the record, the cost of the reporter's transcript, if necessary for the determination of the appeal, the premiums paid for cost of supersedeas bonds or other bonds to preserve rights pending appeal, and the fee for filing the notice of appeal shall be taxed by the referee as costs of the appeal in favor of the party entitled to costs under this rule.

12. Motion for Rehearing (Rule 812).

Unless otherwise provided by local rule or court order, a motion for rehearing may be filed within 10 days after entry of the judgment of the district court.

13. Duties of Clerk on Disposition of Appeal (Rule 813).

Immediately upon the entry of an order or judgment the clerk of the district court shall serve a notice of the entry by mail upon each party to the appeal, together with a copy of any opinion respecting the order or judgment, and shall make a note of the mailing in the docket. Original papers transmitted as the record on appeal shall be returned to the referee upon disposition of the appeal.

14. Suspension of Rules in Part VIII (Rule 814).

In the interest of expediting decision or for other good cause, the district court may, by local rule or order, suspend the requirements or provisions of the rules in Part VIII, except Rules 801, 802, 803, and 810, and may also order proceedings in accordance with its direction.

E. ANNOTATIONS.

Annotations on these new rules are to be found in the Advisory Committee's notes. These notes are set forth in the same U.S. Government Printing Office Release #95-025-0-73-2 of 1973, under the following:

Appendix A: Excerpt from Report of Committee on Rules of Practical Procedure to the Judicial Conference of the United States Re Title I Bankruptcy Rules at pages 201-205, pertaining to Part VIII—Appeals to District Court.

For the guidance of advocates accustomed to former appellate rules on bankruptcy, the committee notes contrast and compare the new rules with prior rules not only as to substance but also as to citations.

FORM #15

F. ILLUSTRATION: NOTICE OF APPEAL TO A DISTRICT COURT FROM A JUDGMENT OR ORDER OF A REFEREE ENTERED IN ADVERSARY PROCEEDING (FORM U.S. 28).[2]

UNITED STATES DISTRICT COURT FOR THE_____ DISTRICT OF_____

In re_____, Bankrupt

_____, PLAINTIFF   Bankruptcy No._____
                v.
_____, DEFENDANT

NOTICE OF APPEAL TO DISTRICT COURT

_____, the plaintiff [or defendant *or other party*] appeals to the district court from the judgment [or order] of the referee entered in this case on_____ [*here described the judgment or order appealed from*] _____

_____

The parties to the judgment [*or* order] appealed from and the names and addresses of their respective attorneys are as follows:

_____

_____

Dated:_____   Signed:_____
                                     Attorney for Appellant
                         Address:_____

                                 _____

G. NEW GEOGRAPHIC BOUNDARIES PENDING FOR BANKRUPTCY APPELLATE CIRCUITS (see Exhibits A, B, and C).

_____

[2]*Rules of Bankruptcy Procedure,* U.S. Government Printing Office #95-205-O. U.S. Superintendent of Documents, Washington, D.C. 20402 (1973), p. 86.

COMMISSION ON REVISION OF THE
FEDERAL COURT APPELLATE SYSTEM
209 COURT OF CLAIMS BUILDING
717 MADISON PLACE, N.W.
WASHINGTON, D.C. 20005
(202) 382-2943

Senator Roman L. Hruska
Chairman

Judge J. Edward Lumbard
Vice Chairman

A. Leo Levin
Executive Director

CONGRESSMAN JACK BROOKS
SENATOR QUENTIN N. BURDICK
EMANUEL CELLER
ROGER C. CRAMTON
CONGRESSMAN WALTER FLOWERS
SENATOR EDWARD J. GURNEY
CONGRESSMAN EDWARD HUTCHINSON
FRANCIS R. KIRKHAM
SENATOR JOHN L. McCLELLAN
JUDGE ROGER ROBB
BERNARD G. SEGAL
JUDGE ALFRED T. SULMONETTI
HERBERT WECHSLER
CONGRESSMAN CHARLES E. WIGGINS

December 18, 1973

Honorable Richard M. Nixon
President of the United States
Washington, D. C.

Honorable Gerald R. Ford
President of the Senate
Washington, D. C.

Honorable Carl B. Albert
Speaker of the House of
    Representatives
Washington, D. C.

Honorable Warren E. Burger
Chief Justice of the United States
Washington, D. C.

Gentlemen:

In accordance with the provisions of section 6, paragraph (1), Public Law No. 489, Ninety-second Congress, the Commission on Revision of the Federal Court Appellate System herewith submits its report of recommendations for change in the geographical boundaries of the federal judicial circuits.

Respectfully yours,

Senator Roman L. Hruska
Chairman

U.S. Government Printing Office Pamphlet
No: 529-173 O - 73 - 2
Superintendent of Documents, Washington, D.C.

EXHIBIT A

5th CIRCUIT

COMMISSION'S RECOMMENDATION

U.S. Government Printing Office Pamphlet
No: = = = 529-173 O - 73 - 3 [December, 1973]
Superintendent of Documents, Washington, D.C.

EXHIBIT B

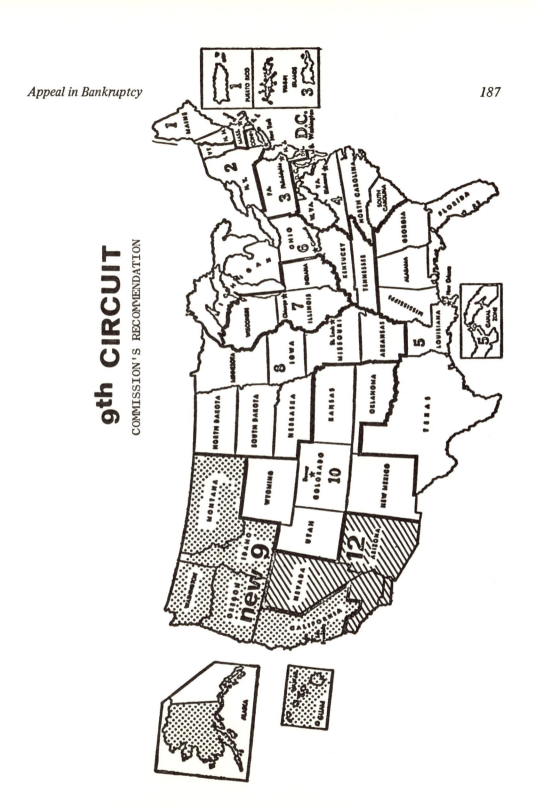

9th CIRCUIT
COMMISSION'S RECOMMENDATION

U. S. GOVERNMENT PRINTING OFFICE: 1973 O - 529-173

[Superintendent of Documents, Washington, D.C.
December 1973]

EXHIBIT C

11

How and When to Seek Review on Writ of Certiorari in the Supreme Court of the United States

The enraged client frequently may be heard to direct his lawyer, "Take my case to the highest court in the land!" The average litigant has no conception of technicalities involved in most appellate procedures. Patience, experience, and legal knowledge on the part of the appellate advocate can administer legal counseling as a soothing balm through articulate communication to bring forth good attorney-client relationship, good image of the legal profession, and faith in justice of an appellate system. More confidence emanates from study of new rules.

Space in this one volume is not ample for discussion of various types of U.S. Supreme Court reviews as a matter of right, or special appeals by permission, or upon reviews by judicial discretion. However, the general practitioner should have a basic knowledge of all processes; and we emphasize the procedures for jurisdiction on writ of certiorari as set forth in U.S. Supreme Court Rules, Numbers 19 through 27.[1] Appraisal of case merit on certiorari can be focused by attention to court rules on jurisdiction, included herein for reader's convenience:

---

[1]*Rules of the Supreme Court of the United States,* including Revisions of Dec. 1, 1971. CLB Publishers, Inc., Law Printing Co. (formerly Thiel Press, Inc.), 1117-1119, 14th Street, NW, Washington, D.C. 20005.

A. CONSIDERATIONS GOVERNING REVIEW ON CERTIORARI: Rule 19.

1. [When Granted]: A review on writ of certiorari is not a matter of right, but of sound judicial discretion, and will be granted only where there are special and important reasons therefor. The following, while neither controlling nor fully measuring the court's discretion, indicate the character of reasons which will be considered:

(a) Where a state court has decided a federal question of substance not theretofore determined by this court, or has decided it in a way probably not in accord with applicable decisions of this court.

(b) Where a court of appeals has rendered a decision in conflict with the decision of another court of appeals on the same matter; or has decided on important state or territorial question in a way in conflict with applicable state or territorial law; or has decided an important question of federal law which has not been, but should be settled by this court; or has decided a federal question in a way in conflict with applicable decisions of this court; or has so far departed from the accepted and usual course of judicial proceedings, or so far sanctioned such departure by a lower court, as to call for an exercise of this court's power of supervision.

2. [Other Applications]: The same general considerations outlined above will control in respect of petitions for writs of certiorari to review judgments of the Court of Claims, of the Court of Customs and Patent Appeals, or of any other court whose determinations are by law reviewable on writ of certiorari.

B. CERTIORARI TO A COURT OF APPEALS BEFORE JUDGMENT: Rule 20.

A writ of certiorari to review a case pending in a court of appeals, before judgment is given in such court, will be granted only upon a showing that the case is of such imperative public importance as to justify the deviation from normal appellate processes and to require immediate settlement in this court.

C. REVIEW ON CERTIORARI—HOW SOUGHT—PARTIES: Rule 21.

1. A party intending to file a petition for certiorari may, prior to filing the case in this court or at any time thereafter prior to action by this court on the petition, request the clerk of the court possessed of the record to certify it, or any part of it, and to provide for its transmission to this court, but the filing of the record in this court is not a requisite for docketing the petition. If the petitioner has not done so, the respondent may request such clerk to certify and transmit the record or any part of it. Thereafter, the clerk of this court or any party to the case may request that additional parts of the record be certified and transmitted to this court. A copy of all requests for certification and transmission shall be sent to all parties to the proceeding.

2. When requested to certify and transmit the record, or any part of it, the clerk of the court possessed of the record shall number the documents to be certified and shall transmit with the record a numbered list of the documents, identifying each with reasonable definiteness. If the record has been printed for the use of the court below, such printed record plus the proceedings in the court below may be certified as the record unless one of the parties or the clerk of this court otherwise requests. The provisions of Rule 12(3) with respect to original papers shall apply to all cases sought to be reviewed on writ of certiorari.

3. Counsel for the petitioner shall file with the clerk of this court, with proof of service as provided by Rule 33, forty copies of a petition which shall comply in all respects with Rule 23, and shall enter his appearance and pay the docket fee. The case will then be placed on the docket. It shall be the duty of counsel for the petitioner to notify all respondents, on a form supplied by the clerk, of the date of filing and of the docket number of the case. Such notice shall be served as required by Rule 33.

4. All parties to the proceeding in the court whose judgment is sought to be reviewed shall be deemed parties in this court, unless the petitioner shall notify the clerk of this court in writing of his belief that one or more of the parties below have no interest in the outcome of the petition. A copy of such notice shall be served on all parties to the proceeding below and a party noted as no longer interested may remain a party here by notifying the clerk, with service on the other parties, that he has an interest in the petition. All parties other than the petitioner shall be respondents, but respondents who support the position of the petitioner shall meet the time schedule for filing papers which is provided for the petitioner, except that any response by such respondents to the petition shall be filed as promptly as possible after receipt of the petition.

D. REVIEW ON CERTIORARI—TIME FOR PETITIONING: Rule 22.

1. A petition for writ of certiorari to review the judgment of a state court of last resort in a criminal case shall be deemed in time when it is filed with the clerk within ninety days after the entry of such judgment. A justice of this court, for good cause shown, may extend the time for applying for a writ of certiorari in such cases for a period of not exceeding sixty days.

2. A petition for writ of certiorari to review the judgment of a court of appeals in a criminal case shall be deemed in time when it is filed with the clerk within thirty days after the entry of such judgment. A justice of this court, for good cause shown, may extend the time for applying for a writ of certiorari in such cases for a period not exceeding thirty days. If the original judgment in such a case was entered in a district court in Alaska, Guam, Hawaii, Puerto Rico, the Virgin Islands, or the Canal Zone, the petition shall be deemed filed in time if mailed by air-mail under a postmark dated within the thirty-day period or due extension thereof.

3. A petition for writ of certiorari in all other cases shall be deemed in time when it is filed with the clerk within the time prescribed by law.

4. An application for extension of time within which to file a petition for writ of certiorari must set out, as in a petition for certiorari [see Rule 23 (1), subparagraphs (b) and (f)], the grounds on which the jurisdiction of this court is invoked, must identify the judgment sought to be reviewed and have appended thereto a copy of the opinion, and must set forth with specificity the reasons why the granting of an extension of time is deemed justified. For the time and manner of presenting an application for extension of time within which to file a petition for writ of certiorari, see Rule 34, 35 (2), and 50. Such applications are not favored.

E. THE PETITION FOR CERTIORARI: Rule 23.

1. The petition for writ of certiorari shall contain in the order here indicated—

(a) A reference to the official and unofficial reports of the opinions delivered in the courts below, if any, and if reported. Any such opinions shall be appended as provided in subparagraph (i) hereof.

(b) A concise statement of the grounds on which the jurisdiction of this court is invoked, showing:

  (i) The date of the judgment or decree sought to be reviewed, and the time of its entry.

  (ii) The date of any order respecting a rehearing, and the date and terms of any order granting an extension of time within which to petition for certiorari; and

  (iii) The statutory provision believed to confer on this court jurisdiction to review the judgment or decree in question by writ of certiorari.

(c) The questions presented for review, expressed in the terms and circumstances of the case but without unnecessary detail. The statement of a question presented will be deemed to include every subsidiary question fairly comprised therein. Only the questions set forth in the petition or fairly comprised therein will be considered by the court.

(d) The constitutional provisions, treaties, statutes, ordinances, or regulations which the case involves, setting them out verbatim, and citing the volume and page where they may be found in the official edition. If the provisions involved are lengthy, their citation alone will suffice at this point, and their pertinent text shall be set forth in appendix.

(e) A concise statement of the case containing the facts material to the consideration of the questions presented.

(f) If review of the judgment of a state court is sought, the statement of the case shall also specify the state in the proceedings in the court of first instance and in the appellate court at which, and the manner in which, the federal questions sought to be reviewed were raised; the method of raising them (e.g., by a pleading, by request to charge and exceptions, by assignment of error); and the way in which they were passed upon by the court; such pertinent quotations of specific portions of the record, or summary thereof, with specific reference to the places in the record where the matter appears (e.g., ruling on exception, portion of the court's charge and exception thereto, assignment of errors) as will show that the federal question was timely and properly raised so as to give this court jurisdiction to review the judgment on writ of certiorari.

Where the portions of the record relied upon under this subparagraph are voluminous, then they shall be included in an appendix to the petition, which may, if more convenient, be separately presented.

(g) If review of the judgment of a federal court is sought, the statement of the case shall also show the basis for federal jurisdiction in the court of first instance.

(h) A direct and concise argument amplifying the reasons relied on for the allowance of the writ. See Rule 19.

(i) There shall be appended to the petition a copy of any opinion delivered upon the rendering of the judgment or decree sought to be reviewed, including all opinions of courts or administrative agencies in the case, and, if reference thereto is necessary to ascertain the grounds of the judgment or decree, opinions in companion cases. The opinions shall include the caption showing the name of the court or agency issuing the same and the title and numbers of the case and the date of their entry. If whatever is required by this paragraph to be appended to the petition is voluminous, it may, if more convenient, be separately presented.

(j) If review of the judgment or decree of a state court is sought, there shall also be appended to the petition a copy of the judgment or decree in question and any order on rehearing; and, if review of the judgment or decree of a federal court is sought, there shall similarly be appended a copy of such judgment or decree and any order on rehearing, which may, however, be limited to the portions thereof sought to be reviewed. The judgments, decrees, or orders on rehearing shall include the caption showing the name of the court issuing the same, the title and number of the case, and the date of entry of such judgment, decree and order.

2. The petition for writ of certiorari shall be printed in conformity with Rule 39.

3. All contentions in support of a petition for writ of certiorari shall be set forth in the body of the petition, as provided in subparagraph (h) of paragraph 1 of this rule. No separate brief in support of a petition for writ of certiorari will be received, and the clerk will refuse to file any petition for writ of certiorari to which is annexed or appended any supporting brief.

4. The failure of a petitioner to present with accuracy, brevity, and clearness whatever is essential to a ready and adequate understanding of the points requiring consideration will be a sufficient reason for denying his petition.

5. Where several cases are sought to be reviewed on certiorari to the same court that involve identical or closely related questions, it shall suffice to file a single petition for writ of certiorari covering all the cases.

F. BRIEF IN OPPOSITION—REPLY—SUPPLEMENTAL BRIEFS: Rule 24.

1. Counsel for the respondent shall have thirty days (unless enlarged by the court or a justice therof, or by the clerk under the provisions of paragraph 5 of Rule 34), after receipt of a petition, within which to file forty printed copies of an opposing brief disclosing any matter or ground why the cause should not be reviewed by this court. See Rule 19. Such brief in opposition shall comply with Rule 39 and with the requirements of Rule 40 governing a respondent's brief, and shall be served as prescribed by Rule 33. In cases where the United States or any agency, officer or employee thereof is the respondent, the respondent shall have an additional twenty days to file the said opposing brief.

2. No motion by a respondent to dismiss a petition for writ of certiorari will be received. Objections to the jurisdiction of the court to grant writs of certiorari may be included in briefs in opposition to petitions therefor.

3. Upon the expiration of the period for filing the respondent's brief, or upon an express waiver of the right to file, or upon the actual filing of such brief in a shorter time, the petition and brief, if any, shall be distributed by the clerk to the court for its consideration.

4. Reply briefs addressed to arguments first raised in the briefs in opposition may be filed, but distribution under paragraph 3 hereof will not be delayed pending the filing of such briefs.

5. Any party may file a supplemental brief at any time while a petition for a writ of certiorari is pending calling attention to new cases or legislation or other intervening matter not available at the time of his last filing.

G. ORDER GRANTING OR DENYING CERTIORARI: Rule 25.

1. Whenever a petition for writ of certiorari to review a decision of any court is granted, the clerk shall enter an order to that effect, and shall forthwith notify the court below and counsel of record of the granting of the petition. If the record has not previously been filed, the clerk of this court shall request the clerk of the court possessed of the record to certify it and transmit it to this court. A formal writ shall not issue unless specially directed.

2. Whenever application for a writ of certiorari to review a decision of any court is denied, the clerk shall enter an order to that effect, and shall forthwith notify the court below and counsel of record. The order of denial will not be suspended pending disposition of a petition for rehearing except by order of the court or of a justice thereof.

H. USE OF SINGLE APPENDIX: RULE 26.

After certiorari has been granted, any portion of the record to which the parties wish to direct the court's particular attention shall be printed in a single appendix prepared by the petitioner under the procedures provided in Rule 36, but the fact that any part of the record has not been printed shall not prevent the parties or the court from relying on it.

I. STAY PENDING REVIEW ON CERTIORARI: RULE 27.

Applications pursuant to 28 USC, §2101(f) to a justice of this court will normally not be entertained unless application for a stay has first been made to a judge of the court rendering the decision sought to be reviewed, or to such court, or unless the security offered below has been disapproved by such judge or court. All such applications are governed by Rules 50 and 51.

J. EXAMPLES OF RECENT CERTIORARI PROCEEDINGS BEFORE U.S. SUPREME COURT.

Cases have been reaching Supreme Court of the United States from wider scope of substantive law and of geographic areas than at any prior decade. The increasing volume, broader subject matter, and expanding concerns have triggered new emphasis toward use of certiorari as a vehicle of expediency in getting matters heard at the highest appellate level. Speed trends have focused attention on human hunger for "instant" justice along with instant basic necessities of food, shelter, and clothing. Impatient citizens clamor loud for bypass of every possible intermediate step toward final justice in lawsuits. A good hard look is therefore directed toward every avenue of approach.

Effort has been made throughout this handbook to answer the loud clear call from appellate advocates in cities and hinterlands of "show me." This has been done by the use of as many illustrations, examples, citations, and rule quotations as space could permit. We illustrate the broad scope of "What–Where" in applicable substance and source of origin by the following selection of certiorari matter appearing before the Supreme Court of the United States during one semester of mid-seventies:

1. Recent Proceeding from U.S. Circuit Court of Appeals from the District of Columbia, *Dave Pernell v. Southall Realty.* Decision below: 294 A. 2d 490 (1972), decided by the United States Supreme Court on writ of certiorari, Docket No. 72-6041, on April 14, 1974. This case originated in a summary eviction action brought in Superior Court of the District of Columbia by Southall Realty Company against Dave Pernell for non-

payment of rent. Pernell denied owing rent and requested a trial by jury. The Judge denied the request, tried the case himself and found for Southall Realty. On appeal the District Court affirmed. The Supreme Court granted certiorari, reversed and remanded for jury trial pursuant to the guarantee of the Constitution.

2. From the Second Circuit Court of Appeals, New York District: *Foley v. Blair & Co.* Decision below: 471 F. 2d 178 (1972), decided by the United States Supreme Court on writ of certiorari, Docket No. 72-1154, on December 5, 1973. This case raised the issue whether the appointment of a liquidator, under agreement between the New York Stock Exchange and the debtor, to liquidate the affairs of a financially troubled brokerage house, constituted an act of bankruptcy supporting adjudication of involuntary bankruptcy by the U.S. Referee in Bankruptcy. The District Court affirmed the arrangement with creditors. The Court of Appeals for the Second Circuit reversed, holding that the District Court had "erred in concluding that Blair had committed the fifth act of bankruptcy." It further held that "the liquidator did not meet what is usually regarded as essential to the status of a receiver, namely, appointed by the court."

The Supreme Court held that this question may become moot because the brokerage house subsequently made an "arrangement" with creditors under Chapter XI of the Bankruptcy Act. The case was thus remanded to determine whether the issues were moot in the light of the Chapter XI proceedings having been completed.

3. From the Fourth Circuit Court of Appeals (Virginia): *E. E. Falk v. Peter J. Brennan, Secretary of Labor.* On Writ of Certiorari to the Supreme Court of the United States. Docket No. 72-844. The Supreme Court reversed the Court of Appeals on December 5, 1973, and held in a 5-4 decision that the Fair Labor Standards Act does not apply to a managing real estate agent whose income from commissions is under the specified minimum of $500,000. The Court of Appeals had concluded that the proper measure of business activity was the total amount of rents collected by the managing agent, not the amount of his commissions. Hence, it was reversed in its holding that the employees in question were entitled to the benefits of the Fair Labor Standards Act.

4. From the Fifth Circuit Court of Appeals, Alabama District: *Cooper Stevedoring Co. v. Fritz Kopke, Inc.* Decision below: 479 F. 2d 1041 (1973), decided by United States Supreme Court on Writ of Certiorari, Docket No. 73-726, on May 28, 1974. This case in admiralty involved the right of a vessel to recover all or part of its loss from the stevedoring company, not the longshoreman's employer, which was jointly negligent in stowing cargo making the vessel liable for a longshoreman's injuries. Troy

Sessions, a longshoreman employed by Mid-Gulf Stevedores, Inc., in Houston, was injured on board a vessel when he stepped into a concealed gap between crates previously loaded by employee of Cooper Stevedoring Co. at Mobile, Alabama. The injured man brought an action against the owner of the vessel and the time charterer. The vessel brought a claim against the two stevedoring companies, seeking indemnity against them for any amount it was required to pay Sessions. The Supreme Court affirmed the decision of both lower courts and held that contribution was allowable, although the case did not involve collision.

5. From the Sixth Circuit Court of Appeals: *United States v. Calandra.* Decision below: 465 F. 2d 1218 (1972), decided by the United States Supreme Court on Writ of Certiorari, Docket No. 72-734 on January 8, 1974. This case was based on a grand jury witness refusing to answer questions on the ground that they were based on leads obtained from an unlawful search of respondent's place of business by federal agents who seized a card characterized as a "loan-sharking" record, as well as other books and records of the company. The District Court granted respondent's motion to suppress the illegally seized evidence and included a direction that he need not answer any questions based on suppressed evidence. The Court of Appeals affirmed. The Supreme Court granted certiorari and *reversed,* with three dissents.

6. From the Ninth Circuit Court of Appeals (Utah): *American Pipe and Construction Co., et al, Petitioners, v. State of Utah, et al, Respondents.* Decision below: 473 F. 2d 580 (1973) decided by United States Supreme Court, on Writ of Certiorari, Docket No. 72-1195, on January 16, 1974. This case involved the running of applicable statute of limitations in the question of timely filing of a class-suit. The certain exceptional circumstances under which the limitation period will be suspended or "tolled" is quite important to lawyers and their clients in a narrow category of cases factually similar to the *American Pipe Case.* The District Court allowed Utah to continue its suit on its own behalf but not on behalf of all other members of the proposed class. Over 60 Utah municipalities who would have been included in the class suit, then applied for leave to intervene in the Utah suit. The District Court determined statute of limitations had run, but the Court of Appeals reversed and held that the claims of the Utah municipalities were not barred by limitations. The Supreme Court affirmed the Judgment of Court of Appeals, holding that the commencement of the abortive class suit suspends the running of applicable statute of limitations as to all asserted members, who would have been members of the class had the requirement for class-suit statutes been fully satisfied.

K. SUMMARY.

Alarm is apparent from many authorities who are concerned about increased appellate court backlogs caused by escalated use of certiorari. We agree with the following which is quoted by published permission:[2]

> ... In current practice before the United States Supreme Court, a petition for a writ of certiorari is the most frequent means of requesting the Supreme Court to review a lower court's decision. The Court's practice is to grant a writ of certiorari if at least four justices vote in favor of its issuance. .... Substantive law reform has striven energetically of late to enlarge rights and to secure them more widely. That also has been the aim of much recent legislation. Thus, we have increased the occasions of justice, as has the sheer growth of the country itself. But the machinery of justice, if that is what it should be called, creaks. If we should let it reach the point of breakdown or, taking the term "machinery" seriously, let it transform itself into a high-speed, high-volume enterprise, we would mock the idea of justice and mock the substantive reforms of a generation.

---

[2] Alexander M. Brickel, *The Caseload of Supreme Court,* American Enterprises Institute for Public Policy Research, Domestic Affairs Study No. 21, Washington, D.C. 20004 (1973), p. 3; p. 37.

12

How to Prepare and Process the Record on Appeal

Time is of economic concern to the litigant, the advocate, and the court, in the big challenge of designation of record for appeal. Special attention can be given to avoid running an over-length on compilation of the record. Remind yourself that it is far better to follow the legal concepts and basic philosophy of the Honorable Roscoe Pound, than it is to try to impress today's court with a voluminous record transcribed from general designation to include "the whole thing" with hopes of gaining impression by paper weight pound.

A. STREAMLINED RECORD DEMANDED BY KEEN COMPETITION.

It is important that all extraneous matter and irrelevant details be eliminated. Appellate advocate can make careful review of the lower court record in order that designation may be made of those parts most vital to issues on appeal. Keeping the record to a minimum number of pages requires greater skill than a mere directive to transmit the entire record.

1. Appellate advocate competes with himself, his adversary, and his client in processing the record. Keen competition in all levels of complex society demands a more alert leadership to implement rules of the game for a higher quality of justice under law. The advocate anticipates stimulating competition with the adversary for proper record designation. Each hopes to tilt the scales of justice toward the heavier impact in favor of his client's cause. However, deletion should not be made of unfavorable factual portions

in client's trial court record, lest opponent make issue of the deletion regardless of irrelevance. It is better to remain on the open, frank, fair-minded approach in the hopes of deflecting any spotlight on ,the unfavorable portions.

If the cost estimate is expensive for record transcript, the appeal results very doubtful, and your client's finances depleted, the wiser course may be to dissuade appellant from perfecting the appeal. His unreasonable insistence might be indicative of nuisance or vengeance motives which must be discouraged.

2. The litigant's cause competes for scheduling with other cases in court dockets. One need only to look at various charts or tables of statistics to sense alarm in the escalating caseload and unavoidable delays for case dispositions at the appellate levels. Urgency of streamlining the record can be revealed by a study of the annual or semi-annual statistics in Tables released by the Aministrative Office of the United States Courts. This provides an insight by illustrious example from which each person can note his particular geographic litigation area for consideration. Questions can be weighed as to the advisability of processing the appeal, time potentialities, economic problems of the litigant, traumatic effect, possible impatience, loss of confidence on the part of the client, and many other elements. Your legal counsel and guidance at this point in his decision to proceed with the appeal are of great significance to him. He has a right to know the approximate cost and the escalated time elements which are beyond control of appellate advocate.

For best "show me" illustration of technical procedures in preparing the record on appeal, we direct reader's attention to the very concise new directives in Federal Rules of Appellate Procedure.

B. CHECK LIST OF INTERROGATIVES FOR ADVOCATE'S SELF-QUESTIONNAIRE ON RECORD "FRAP" TEST.

		Answer
QUESTION	1. What constitutes the record on appeal?	(10 a)
	2. What is time limit on ordering transcript?	(10 b)
	3. What circumstances determine designation of record?	(10 b)
	4. How does appellee supplement designation?	(10 b)
	5. What is procedure where no report was made?	(10 c, d)
	6. Can the record be corrected, if erroneous?	(10 e)
	7. When and by whom must record be transmitted?	(11 a, b)
	8. What is procedure for temporary retention of record?	(11 c, e, f, g)
	9. Who pays docket fee? When?	(12 a)

10. What does appellee do if appellant fails to cause timely
    transmittal or pay docket fee?   (12 c)
11. What "FRAP" Rules are applicable to Tax Court?   (13, 14)
12. Does Tax Court use same form for appeal notice as
    District Court?   (Form 2)

EXPLANATION:

Answers to our FRAP test questions as parenthetically referred, in above check list, may now be found on the following pages. Quotation is made of the exact rule as the most pragmatic means of presenting direct communication from the United States Circuit Courts of Appeal to the inquiring reader who seeks instant how-to-do-it guidance from top authority.

C. SOURCE BOOK ANSWERS TO SELF-STUDY QUESTIONNAIRE.

1. The Record on Appeal—Rule 10 (FRAP).

(a) *Composition of the Record on Appeal.* The original papers and exhibits filed in the district court, the transcript of proceedings, if any, and a certified copy of the docket entries prepared by the clerk of the district court shall constitute the record on appeal in all cases.

(b) *The Transcript of Proceedings.* Within 10 days after filing the notice of appeal the appellant shall order from the reporter a transcript of such parts of the proceedings not already on file as he deems necessary for inclusion in the record. If the appellant intends to urge, on appeal, that a finding or conclusion is unsupported by the evidence or is contrary to the evidence, he shall include in the record a transcript of all evidence relevant to such finding or conclusion. Unless the entire transcript is to be included, the appellant shall, within the time above provided, file and serve on the appellee a description of the parts of the transcript which he intends to include in the record and a statement of the issues he intends to present on the appeal. If the appellee deems a transcript of other parts of the proceedings to be necessary he shall, within 10 days after the service of the statement of the appellant, file and serve on the appellant a designation of additional parts to be included. If the appellant shall refuse to order such parts, the appellee shall either order the parts or apply to the district court for an order requiring the appellant to do so. At the time of ordering, a party must make satisfactory arrangements with the reporter for payment of the cost of the transcript.

(c) *Statements of the Evidence or Proceedings When No Report Was Made.* If no report of the evidence or proceedings at a hearing or trial was made, or if a transcript is unavailable, the appellant may prepare a statement of the evidence or proceedings from the best available means, including his recollection. The statement shall be served on the appellee who may serve objections or propose amendments thereto within 10 days after service. Thereupon the statement and any objections or proposed amendments shall be submitted to the district court for settlement and approval, and as settled and approved shall be included by the clerk of the district court in the record on appeal.

(d) *Agreed Statement as the Record on Appeal.* In lieu of the record on appeal as defined in subdivision (a) of this rule, the parties may prepare and sign a statement of the case showing how the issues presented by the appeal arose and were decided in the district court and setting forth only so many of the facts averred and proved or sought to be proved as are essential to a decision of the issues presented. If the statement conforms to the truth, it, together with such additions as the court may consider necessary fully to present the issues raised by the appeal, shall be approved by the district court and shall then be certified to the court of appeals as the record on appeal and transmitted thereto by the clerk of the district court within the time provided by Rule 11. Copies of the agreed statement may be filed as appendix required by Rule 30.

(e) *Correction or Modification of the Record.* If any difference arises as to whether the record truly discloses what occurred in the district court, the difference shall be submitted to and settled by that court and the record made to conform to the truth. If anything material to either party is omitted from the record by error or accident or is misstated therein, the parties by stipulation, or the district court, either before or after the record is transmitted to the court of appeals, or the court of appeals on proper suggestion or of its own initiative, may direct that the omission or misstatement be corrected, and if necessary that a supplemental record be certified and transmitted. All other questions as to the form and content of the record shall be presented to the court of appeals.

2. Transmission of the Record: Rule 11.

(a) *Time for Transmission.* The record on appeal, including the transcript and exhibits necessary for the determination of the appeal, shall be transmitted to the court of appeals within 40 days after the filing of the notice of appeal unless the time is shortened or extended by an order entered under subdivision (d) of this rule. After filing the notice of appeal the appellant shall comply with the provisions of Rule 10 (b) and shall take any other action necessary to enable the clerk to assemble and transmit the record. If more than one appeal is taken, each appellant shall comply with the provisions of Rule 10 (b) and this subdivision, and a single record shall be transmitted within 40 days after the filing of the final notice of appeal.

(b) *Duty of Clerk to Transmit the Record.* When the record is complete for purposes of appeal, the clerk of the district court shall transmit it to the clerk of the court of appeals. The clerk of the district court shall number the documents correspondingly numbered and identified with reasonable definiteness. Documents of unusual bulk or weight and physical exhibits other than documents shall not be transmitted by the clerk unless he is directed to do so by a party or by the clerk of the court of appeals. A party must make advance arrangements with the clerks for transportation and receipt of exhibits of unusual bulk or weight.

Transmission of the record is effected when the clerk of the district court mails or otherwise forwards the record to the clerk of the court of appeals. The clerk of the district court shall indicate, by endorsement on the face of the record or otherwise, the date upon which it is transmitted to the court of appeals.

(c) *Temporary Retention of Record in District Court.* Notwithstanding the provisions of subdivisions (a) and (b) of this rule, the parties may stipulate, or the district court on motion of any party may order, that the clerk of the district court shall temporarily retain the record for use by the parties in preparing appellate papers. In that event, the appellant shall nevertheless cause the appeal to be docketed and the record to be filed within the time fixed or allowed for transmission of the record by complying with the provisions of Rule 12 (a) and by presenting to the clerk of court of appeals a partial record in the form of a copy of the docket entries, accompanied by a certificate of counsel for appellant, or of the appellant if he is without counsel, reciting that the record, including the transcript or parts thereof designed for inclusion and all necessary exhibits, is complete for purposes of appeal. Upon receipt of the brief of the appellee, or at such earlier time as the parties may agree or the court may order, the appellant shall request clerk of district court to transmit the record.

(d) *Extension of Time for Transmission of the Record.* The district court for cause shown may extend the time for transmitting the record. A request for extension must be made within the time originally prescribed or within an extension previously granted, and the district court shall not extend the time to a day more than 90 days from the date of filing of the first notice of appeal. If the district court is without authority to grant the relief sought or has denied a request therefor, the court of appeals may on motion for cause shown extend the time for transmitting the record or may permit the record to be transmitted and filed after the expiration of time allowed or fixed. If a request for an extension of time for transmitting the record has been previously denied, the motion shall set forth the denial and shall state the reasons therefor, if any were given. The district court or the court of appeals may require the record to be transmitted and the appeal to be docketed at any time within the time otherwise fixed or allowed.

(e) *Retention of the Record in District Court by Order of Court.* The court of appeals may provide by rule or order that a certified copy of the docket entries shall be transmitted in lieu of the entire record, subject to the right of any party to request at any time during the pendency of appeal that designated parts of the record be transmitted.

If the record or any part thereof is required in the district court for use there pending appeal, the district court may make an order to that effect, and the clerk of district court shall retain the record or parts thereof subject to request of the court of appeals, and shall transmit a copy of the order and of docket entries together with such parts of the original record as district court shall allow and copies of such parts as the parties may designate.

(f) *Stipulation of Parties That Parts of Record Be Retained in District.* The parties may agree by written stipulation filed in the district court that designated parts of the record shall be retained in the district court unless thereafter court of appeals shall order or any party shall request their transmittal. The parts thus designated shall nevertheless be a part of the record on appeal for all purposes.

(g) *Record for Preliminary Hearing in Court of Appeals.* If prior to the time the record is transmitted a party desires to make in the court of appeals a motion for dismissal, for release, for a stay pending appeal, for additional security on the bond on appeal or on a supersedeas bond, or for any intermediate order, the clerk of the district court at the request of any party shall transmit to the court of appeals such parts of the original record as any party shall designate.

3. Docketing the Appeal; Filing of the Record—Rule 12.

(a) *Docketing the Appeal.* Within the time allowed or fixed for transmission of the record, the appellant shall pay to the clerk of the court of appeals the docket fee fixed by the Judicial Conference of the United States pursuant to 28 U.S.C. §1913, and the clerk shall thereupon enter the appeal without prepayment of fees; the clerk shall enter the appeal upon the docket at the request of the party or at the time of filing the record. The court of appeals may upon motion for cause shown enlarge the time for docketing the appeal or permit the appeal to be docketed out of time. An appeal shall be docketed under the title given to the action in the district court, with the appellant identified as such, but if such title does not contain the name of the appellant, his name, identified as appellant, shall be added to the title.

(b) *Filing of the Records.* Upon receipt of the record or of papers authorized to be filed in lieu of the record under the provisions of Rule 11(c) and (e) by the clerk of the court of appeals following timely transmittal, and after the appeal has been timely docketed, the clerk shall file the record. The clerk shall immediately give notice to all parties of the date on which the record was filed.

(c) *Dismissal for Failure of Appellant to Cause Timely Transmission or to Docket Appeal.* If the appellant shall fail to cause timely transmission of the record or to pay the docket fee if a docket fee is required, any appellee may file a motion in the court of appeals to dismiss the appeal. The motion shall be supported by a certificate of the clerk of the district court showing the date and substance of the judgment or order from which the appeal was taken, the date on which the notice of appeal was filed, the expiration date of any order extending the time for transmitting the record, and by proof of service. The appellant may respond within 14 days of such service. The clerk shall docket the appeal for the purpose of permitting the court to entertain the motion without requiring payment of docket fee, but appellant shall not be permitted to respond without payment of the fee unless he is otherwise exempt therefrom.

D. REVIEW OF DECISION OF THE TAX COURT: Rules 13, 14 (FRAP).

Rule 13(c) Content of Appeal Notice. . . prescribed in Rule 3. . . Form 2 as suggested is included herein on following page, for Notice of Appeal.

Rule 14. All provisions of [FRAP] rules are applicable to decision review on appeal except Rules 4-9, 15-20, and 22-23, which are not applicable.

FORM #16

[FRAP No. 2] NOTICE OF APPEAL TO COURT OF APPEALS FROM A DECISION OF THE TAX COURT

TAX COURT OF THE UNITED STATES WASHINGTON, D.C.

A.B., PETITIONER	)
	)
V.	) DOCKET NO._____
	)
COMMISSIONER OF INTERNAL REVENUE,	)
	)
RESPONDENT	)

NOTICE OF APPEAL

Notice is hereby given that A.B. hereby appeals to the United States Court of Appeals from the_____Circuit from [that part of___] the decision entered in the above captioned proceeding on the___day of _____ 19_ [relating to] _____

_____

_____

(s)_____

ADDRESS _____

COUNSEL FOR A.B.

FORM #17

[FRAP No. 3] : PETITION FOR REVIEW OF ORDER OF AN AGENCY, BOARD, COMMISSION OR OFFICER

UNITED STATES COURT OF APPEALS FOR THE_____CIRCUIT

A.B., PETITIONER	)	
	)	
V	)	*PETITION FOR REVIEW*
	)	
X. Y. Z, RESPONDENT	)	

A. B. hereby petitions the court for review of the Order of the X.Y.Z. BOARD (Describe the order.)

_____

_____

_____

_____

_____

entered on_____.

_____

ATTORNEY FOR PETITIONER

ADDRESS_____

FEDERAL RULES OF APPELLATE PROCEDURE, "Appendix of Forms," U.S. Government Printing Office #82-974-O-72-2, Washington, D.C. 20402

13

How to Prepare the Federal Court Briefs

Authorities on brief writing give extensive relevance for appellate success to the time and talent exhibited by the advocate in preparation of federal court briefs. It has been pointed out that the brief is generally the first exposure of the judge to the case and to the issues. However, time pressures and personal preference of the jurist may schedule your brief for attention after the presentation of oral argument. It must be considered as your vehicle of persuasion, first and last. Hopefully, the written brief will hold focal point of interest during the final stages of deliberations, decisions, and opinion writing. Appellate advocate will be gratified to see his words quoted and his conclusion highlighted in the judicial opinion.

Better briefs are being written because more concise rules are being constantly updated by circuit appellate courts and by the Supreme Court. These guidelines have been thoughtfully handed down by jurists for the benefit of appellate advocacy, and it is mandatory that they be followed.

There are numerous occasions when our reader's paperback FRAP book[1] may be unavailable, his small library may not contain USCA revisions, he may be writing his brief in transit, or at his home desk. In any of these instances, his need is supplied in our one volume wherein we take the advocate to self-enlightenment through a question-answer FRAP test as follows:

---

[1] *Federal Rules of Appellate Procedure,* printed for the use of The Committee on the Judiciary, House of Representatives, U.S. Government Printing Office #82-974 0 72-3, Washington, D.C. 20402 (October 1, 1972), pp. 18-23.

A. BRIEF WRITING CHECK LIST OF INTERROGATORIES FOR APPELLATE ADVOCATE'S FRAP TEST.

This questionnaire is to be self-administered, and the answerbook directives are to be accepted from Appellate Judges as the voices of authority in brief writing guidance on the following pages.

QUESTION	FRAP ANSWER
1. What are the 5 appropriate topics for appellant's outline of brief?	(28, a)
2. What are the 4 appropriate topics for appellee's outline of brief?	(28, b)
3. Under what circumstances are reply briefs filed by appellant and appellee?	(28, c)
4. What designation is preferred in parties?	(28, d)
5. How are references to part of the record indicated?	(30, a, c, f)
6. How are statutes, rules and regulations to be included in the brief?	(28, f)
7. What are maximum brief lengths?	(28, g)
8. Who has brief-writing responsibility for multiple appellants or appellees?	(28, i)
9. Who pays cost of producing appendix?	(30, b)
10. Who prepares appendix to briefs?	(30, a)
11. How many copies of Exhibits are filed?	(30, c)
12. Under what circumstances can appendix be dispensed with?	(30, f)
13. What is maximum time limit for filing brief after record is filed?	(31. a)
14. How many copies of briefs are to be filed and served?	(31, b)
15. Is it fatal to the cause if brief is not timely filed?	(31, c)
16. What are preferred formats as to size, duplicating, and color of brief covers?	(32)
17. List the items required on cover page.	(32)
18. Does one file the same number of brief copies in the Supreme Court of the United States as in Federal Appellate Circuit Courts? (Supreme Court Rule 41.)	
19. How many printed copies of appellant briefs on certiorari are to be filed in Supreme Court? Within what time limit?	*RULE 41:* (1)
20. How many printed copies of appellee briefs are to be filed, and within what time limit?	(2)
21. What is time limit on reply briefs?	(3)
22. What provisions are made for supplemental briefs on newly enacted legislation or other intervening matters?	(5)

1. Preparation of Briefs in U.S. Circuit Courts of Appeals: Rule 28.

(a) *Brief of the Appellant.* The brief of appellant shall contain under appropriate headings and in the order here indicated:

(1) A table of contents, with page references, and a table of cases (alphabetically arranged), statutes and other authorities cited, with references to the pages of the brief where they are cited.

(2) A statement of the issues presented for review.

(3) A statement of the case. The statement shall first indicate briefly the nature of the case, the course of proceedings, and its disposition in the court below. There shall follow a statement of the facts relevant to the issues presented for review, with appropriate references to the record [see subdivision (e)].

(4) An argument. The argument may be preceded by a summary. The argument shall contain the contentions of the appellant with respect to the issues presented, and the reasons therefor, with citations to the authorities, statutes and parts of the record relied on.

(5) A short conclusion stating the precise relief sought.

(b) *Brief of the Appellee.* The brief of the appellee shall conform to the requirements of subdivision (a) (1) through (4), except that a statement of the issues or of the case need not be made unless the appellee is dissatisfied with the statement of the appellant.

(c) *Reply Brief.* The appellant may file a brief in reply to the brief of appellee; and if the appellee has cross-appealed, the appellee may file a brief in reply to the response of the appellant to the issues presented by the cross appeal. No further briefs may be filed except by court leave.

(d) *References in Briefs to Parties.* Counsel will be expected in their briefs and oral arguments to keep to a minimum references to parties by such designations as "appellant" and "appellee." It promotes clarity to use same designations as lower court or agency proceedings, or actual names of parties, or descriptive terms such as "the employee," "the injured person," "the taxpayer," or "the stevedore."

(e) *References in Briefs to the Record.* References in the briefs to parts of the record reproduced in the appendix filed with the brief of the appellant [see Rule 30 (a)] shall be to pages of appendix at which those parts appear. If appendix is prepared after the briefs are filed, references in briefs to the record shall be made by one of the methods allowed by Rule 30(c). If record is reproduced in accordance with provisions of Rule 30(f), or if references are made in briefs to parts of the record not reproduced, the references shall be to pages of the parts of the record involved; e.g., Answer p. 7, Motion for Judgment, p. 2, Transcript p. 231. Intelligible abbreviations may be used. If reference is made to evidence the admissibility of which is in controversy, reference shall be made to the pages of the appendix or of the transcript at which the evidence was identified, offered, and received or rejected.

(f) *Reproductions of Statutes, Rules, or Regulations.* If determination of the issues presented requires the study of statutes, rules, regulations, or relevant parts thereof, they shall be reproduced in the brief or in an addendum at the end, or they may be supplied to the court in pamphlet form.

(g) *Length of Briefs.* Except by permission of the court, principal brief shall not exceed 50 pages of standard typographic printing or 70 pages of printing by any other process of duplicating or copying, exclusive of pages containing table of contents, tables of citations, and any addendum containing statutes, rules, or regulations. And except by permission of the court, reply briefs shall not exceed 25 pages of standard typographic printing or 35 pages of printing by any other process of duplicating or copying.

(h) *Briefs in Cases Involving Cross Appeals.* If a cross appeal is filed, the plaintiff in the court below shall be deemed the appellant for the purpose of this rule and Rules 30 and 31, unless the parties otherwise agree or the court otherwise orders. The brief of the appellee shall contain the issues and argument involved in his appeal as well as the answer to the brief of the appellant.

(i) *Briefs in Cases Involving Multiple Appellants or Appellees.* In cases involving more than one appellant or appellee, including cases consolidated for purposes of the appeal, any number of either may join in a single brief, and any appellant, or appellee may adopt by reference any part of the brief of another. Parties may join in reply briefs.

2. Preparation of Appendix to the Briefs: Rule 30 [FRAP].

(a) *Duty of Appellant to Prepare and File Appendix,* which shall contain:
    (1) the relevant docket entries in the proceeding below;
    (2) relevant portions of pleadings, charge, findings, or opinion;
    (3) the judgment, order or decision in question; and
    (4) other parts to which parties wish to direct particular attention.

The fact that parts of the record are not included in the appendix shall not prevent the parties or the court from relying on such parts.

Unless filing is to be deferred pursuant to the provisions of subdivision (c) of this rule, the appellant shall serve and file the appendix with his brief. Ten copies of the appendix shall be filed with the clerk, and one copy shall be served on counsel for each party separately represented, unless the court shall by rule or order direct the filing or service of a lesser number.

(b) *Determination of Contents of Appendix: Cost of Production.* The parties are encouraged to agree as to contents of the appendix. In the absence of agreement, appellant shall, not later than 10 days after date on which the record is filed, serve on appellee a designation of parts of the record which he intends to include in appendix, and a statement of issues which he intends to present for review. If appellee deems it necessary to direct particular attention of the court to parts of the record not designated by appellant, he shall, within 10 days after the receipt of the designation, serve upon the appellant a designation of those parts. The appellant shall include in appendix the parts thus designated. In designating parts for inclusion in appendix, the parties shall have regard for the fact that the entire record is always available to the court for reference and examination and shall not engage in unnecessary designation.

(c) Unless parties otherwise agree, the cost of producing appendix shall initially be paid by appellant, but if appellant considers that parts of the record designated by the appellee for inclusion are unnecessary for determination of issues presented, he may so advise appellee and appellee shall advance the cost of including such parts. The cost of producing the appendix shall be taxed as costs in the case, but if either party shall cause matters to be included in the appendix unnecessarily, the court may impose the cost on the party. . . .

(d) *Arrangement of the Appendix.* At the beginning of the appendix there shall be inserted a list of parts of record which it contains, in the order in which the parts are set out therein, with references to pages of the appendix at which each part begins. The relevant docket entries shall be set out following the list of contents. Thereafter, other parts of record shall be set out in chronological order. When matter contained in the reporter's transcript of proceedings is set out in the appendix, the page of transcript at which such matter may be found shall be indicated in brackets immediately before the matter which is set out. Omissions in the text of papers or of the transcript must be indicated by asterisks. Immaterial formal matters (captions, subscriptions, or acknowledgments) shall be omitted. A question and its answer may be contained in a single paragraph.

(e) *Reproduction of Exhibits.* Exhibits designated for inclusion in the appendix may be contained in separate volume suitably indexed. Four copies shall be filed with appendix and one copy served on counsel for each party separately represented. The transcript of proceeding before administrative agency, board, commission, or officer used in an action in district court shall be regarded as an exhibit for purpose of this rule.

(f) *Hearing of Appeals on Original Record Without Necessity of Appendix.* Court of Appeals . . . may dispense with requirement of appendix. . . .

3. How to File and Serve Briefs: Rule 31 [FRAP].

(a) *Time for Serving and Filing Briefs.* Appellant shall serve and file his brief within 40 days after date on which the record is filed. The appellee shall serve and file his brief within 30 days after service of the brief of appellant. Appellant may serve and file a reply brief within 14 days after service of brief of the appellee, but, except for good cause shown, a reply brief must be filed at least 3 days before argument. If a court of appeals is prepared to consider cases on merits promptly after briefs are filed, and its practice is to do so, it may shorten the period prescribed above for serving and filing briefs, either by rule for all cases or for classes of cases, or by order for specific case.

(b) *Number of Copies to Be Filed and Served.* Twenty-five copies of each brief shall be filed with the clerk, unless the court by order in a particular case shall direct a lesser number, and two copies shall be served on counsel for each party separately represented. If a party is allowed to file typewritten ribbon and carbon copies of the brief, the original and three legible copies shall be filed with the clerk, and one copy shall be served on counsel for each party separately represented.

(c) *Consequences of Failure to File Briefs.* If an appellant fails to file his brief within the time provided by this rule, or within the time extended, an appellee may move for dismissal of the appeal. If an appellee fails to file his brief, he will not be heard at oral argument except by permission of the court.

4. Form of Briefs, Appendix and Other Papers: Rule 32 [FRAP].

Briefs and appendices may be produced by standard typographic printing, or by any duplicating or copying process which produces a clear black image on white paper. Carbon copies of briefs and appendices may not be submitted without permission of the court, except in behalf of parties allowed to proceed *in forma pauperis.* All printed matter must appear in at least 11 point type on opaque, unglazed paper. Briefs and appendices produced by standard typographic process shall be bound in volumes having pages 6-1/8 by 9-1/4 inches and type matter 4-1/6 by 7-1/6 inches. Those produced by any other process shall be bound in volumes having pages not exceeding 8-1/2 by 11 inches and type matter not exceeding 6-1/2 by 9-1/2 inches, with double spacing between each line of text. In patent cases the pages of briefs and appendices may be of such size as is necessary to utilize copies of patent documents. Copies of the reporter's transcript and other papers reproduced in a manner authorized by this rule may be inserted in the appendix; such pages may be informally renumbered if necessary.

If briefs are produced by commercial printing or duplicating firms, or, if produced otherwise and the covers to be described are available, the cover of the brief of the appellant should be blue; that of appellee, red; that of an intervenor or amicus curiae, green; that of any reply brief, gray. The cover of the appendix, if separately printed, should be white. The front covers of the briefs and of appendices, if separately printed, shall contain:

(1) name of the court and the number of the case; (2) title of the case; (3) nature of the proceeding; (4) title of the document (e.g., Brief for Appellant, Appendix); and (5) names and addresses of counsel representing party on whose behalf the document is filed.

B. UNITED STATES SUPREME COURT: Rule 41 [2]

BRIEFS ON THE MERITS—TIME FOR FILING

1. Counsel for the appellant or petitioner shall file with the clerk forty copies of his printed brief on the merits, within forty-five days of the order noting or postponing probable jurisdiction or of the order granting the writ of certiorari.

2. Forty printed copies of the brief of the appellee or respondent shall be filed with the clerk within thirty days after the receipt by him of the brief filed by the appellant or petitioner.

3. Reply briefs will be received up to three days before the case is called for hearing; but only by leave of court thereafter, since later filing may delay consideration of the case.

4. Periods of time stated in paragraphs 1 and 2 of this rule may be enlarged as provided in Rule 34, upon motion duly made; or, if a case is advanced for hearing, the time for filing briefs may be abridged as circumstances shall require, pursuant to order of court. . . .

5. Whenever a party desires to present late authorities, newly enacted legislation, or other intervening matters that were not available in time to have been included in his brief in chief, he may file forty printed copies of a supplemental brief, restricted to such new matter and otherwise in conformity with these rules, up to the time the case is called for hearing, or by leave of court thereafter.

6. No brief will be received through the clerk or otherwise after a case has been argued or submitted, except upon special leave.

7. No brief will be received by clerk unless the same shall be accompanied by proof of service as required by Rule 33.

———————

[2]*Rules of the Supreme Court of United States,* including Revisions to December 1, 1971, Law Printing Co., 1117-1118 14th Street, N.W. Washington, D.C. 20005, p. 39.

14

How and When to Use Oral Arguments in U.S. Appellate Courts

Oral argument and final disposition of federal appellate decisions have come under close scrutiny in recent years because of increased demands. The unprecedented influx of appellate cases on issues of constitutionality now require more attention than in any other decade in our history. Statistical reports show that case backlogs in federal districts have grown from 69,000 in the mid-sixties to 127,000 in the mid-seventies.[1] This increase predicts potential appellate upswing on appeals by right. Responsibility for expeditious processing lies with the advocates, the courts, and the public.

The advocates are first in line as problem solvers. It is a great call to action for appellates at this point. The most helpful advice is to screen cases more carefully, and make oral arguments shorter. It is needless and unprofessional to clutter appellate levels with cases which do not belong there. "Practice may make perfect" but not at the expense of "creaking" the wheels of justice!

Appellate courts have adopted a variety of new procedures to speed disposition of those cases which have little hope of appellate reversal. Most circuits have adopted a screening process whereby a significant number of cases are relegated to "no argument" calendar. Other cases are being placed

---

[1] See: Mark W. Cannon, "Administrative Change and the Supreme Court," *Judicature,* The Journal of the American Judicature Society, Vol. 57, No. 8, 1155 E. 60th Street, Chicago, Illinois 60637 (March 1974), p.341.

on a summary calendar and only abbreviated arguments are permitted. These changing trends require greater skill of advocates facing challenges of time curtailment. A firm commitment will issue from all parties for strict compliance with up-dated rules. For ready reference of the reader, we quote the following as most pertinent:

A. ORAL ARGUMENT RULES AND REGULATIONS UNDER FRAP.

1. [How, When, Why, Who and What of Oral Argument] – Rule 34.

(a) *Notice of Argument; Postponement.* The clerk shall advise all parties of the time and place at which oral argument will be heard. A request for postponement of the argument must be made by motion filed reasonably in advance of the date fixed for hearing.

(b) *Time Allowed for Argument.* Unless otherwise provided by rule for all cases or for classes of cases, each side will be allowed 30 minutes for argument. If counsel is of opinion that additional time is necessary for the adequate presentation of his argument, he may request such additional time as he deems necessary. Requests may be made by letter addressed to the clerk reasonably in advance of date fixed for argument and shall be liberally granted if cause therefor is shown. A party is not obliged to use all of time allowed, and the court may terminate the argument whenever in its judgment further argument is unnecessary.

(c) *Order and Content of Argument.* The appellant is entitled to open and conclude the argument. The opening argument shall include a fair statement of the case. Counsel will not be permitted to read at length from briefs, records or authorities.

(d) *Cross and Separate Appeals.* A cross or separate appeal shall be argued with the initial appeal at a single argument, unless the court otherwise directs. If a case involves a cross-appeal, the plaintiff in the action below shall be deemed the appellant for the purpose of this rule unless the parties otherwise agree or the court otherwise directs. If separate appellants support the same argument, case shall be taken to avoid duplication of argument.

(e) *Nonappearance of Parties.* If the appellee fails to appear to present argument, the court will hear argument on behalf of appellant, if present. If the appellant fails to appear, the court may hear argument on behalf of appellee, if his counsel is present. If neither party appears, case will be decided on briefs unless court orders otherwise.

(f) *Submission on Briefs.* By agreement of the parties, a case may be submitted for decision on the briefs, but the court may direct that the case be argued.

(g) *Use of Physical Exhibits at Argument.* If physical exhibits other than documents are to be used at the argument, counsel shall arrange to have them placed in the courtroom before the court convenes on the date of argument. After the argument, counsel shall cause the exhibits to be removed from the courtroom unless the court otherwise directs. If exhibits are not reclaimed by counsel within a reasonable time after notice is given by the clerk, they shall be destroyed or otherwise disposed of as the clerk shall think best.

2. Examples of Local Rules Supplementing FRAP on Oral Argument.

(a) *First Circuit.* Local Rule 9 on "Calendaring"[2] provides that the clerk will contact counsel approximately three weeks prior to hearing, to advise calendar, amount of time for argument, and to ascertain the name of person who will present the oral argument. One week before the monthly sitting commences the Clerk will prepare and distribute an order assigning the cases for that session to a day certain for hearing. The court reserves the privilege of reducing the requested time for argument when the case is presented. Rule 10 provides that all motions will be decided without oral argument unless the court orders otherwise.

Rule 12 of First Circuit provides on "Summary Disposition" that at any time, on such notice as the court may order, on motion of appellee or *sua sponte,* the court may dismiss the appeal or other request for relief or affirm and enforce the judgment or order below if the court lacks jurisdiction, or if it shall clearly appear that no substantial question is presented. In case of obvious manifest error the court may, similarly, reverse. Motions for such relief should be promptly filed when the occasion appears, and must be accompanied by four copies of a memorandum brief. If the court concludes, after adequate opportunity for briefing, that even though there may be a substantial question, oral argument would not assist it, the Clerk will so advise counsel. *Rule 13* states that parties may expect the courts to have some familiarity with the briefs, prior to oral argument. In cases of no great complexity, the court may inform counsel at the call, or earlier, that not more than 15 minutes a side will be permitted for argument. Rebuttal is not encouraged, and must be limited to unexpected matters.

(b) *Second Circuit, Handbook on Appeals*[3] as prepared by the Committee on Federal Courts of the Association of the Bar of the City of New York (1972) encourages oral argument to be submitted with every case. It reports only 2% of cases in that circuit are submitted without oral argument, a smaller percentage than in any court except the U.S. Supreme Court.

---

[2] *Rules of the United States Court of Appeals for the First Circuit,* Blanchard Press, Inc., Boston, Massachusetts. (Revised November 6, 1973.)

[3] *Appeals to the Second Circuit,* Record Press, Inc., 95 Morton Street, New york, N.Y. 10014 (1971 Edition).

(c) *Third Circuit Local Rules,* with revisions effective January 1, 1974: Amended Rule 12(6) provides that oral argument[4] may be dispensed with or shortened, by unanimous order of panel to which the case has been assigned. The clerk notifies the parties or counsel of such action.

(d) *Fourth Circuit,* Local *Rule 7* provides for pre-argument review as a means of determining the advisability of allotting time for the oral argument. As revised, December 6, 1972, this rule states[5] that at any time before argument, the chief judge, in the interest of docket control and expediting the final disposition, may designate a panel to review any pending case for assignment or disposition under this rule. If all the judges of the panel to which pending appeal has been referred conclude that the appeal is wholly without merit, the appeal will be dismissed, or the judgment affirmed. If all the judges of the panel conclude that the judgment below was in error, they may reverse, or vacate the judgment, or grant any other appropriate relief; but if any judge of such panel is of the opinion that the issue is debatable and that full briefing and oral argument would be enlightening, or otherwise of assistance, the case shall be set for a regular hearing. A pending appeal may be dismissed, or the judgment appealed from affirmed, reversed, or vacated, or other appropriate relief granted before the filing of briefs or before oral argument.

(e) *Fifth Circuit,* local rules were amended on December 12, 1973.[6] Rule 11 provides that the court may on its own motion, or for good cause shown on motion of either party, advance any case for hearing and prescribe an abbreviated briefing schedule. It also provides that a party, or parties, may waive oral argument by communicating this fact to the clerk in writing in advance of date of hearing. Rule 18 provides a separate calendar for those cases to be considered without oral argument with notice to parties of this summary calendar placement.

(f) *Sixth Circuit* Practitioner's Handbook[7] sets forth a complete time schedule on civil cases from district court decision to the time for calendar on oral argument in Circuit Court of Appeals, as follows:

30 days — filing notice of appeal
40 days   transmittal of original record

---

[4] *Rules of the United States Court of Appeals for Third Circuit,* International Printing Co., Philadelphia, Pa. 19143. (Amendments to January 1, 1974.)

[5] *Local Rules of U.S. Court of Appeals for Fourth Circuit,* Lewis Printing Co., Richmond, Va. 23200. (Revised October 1973.)

[6] *Local Rules of U.S. Court of Appeals for Fifth Circuit,* published with compliments of West Publishing Co., St. Paul, Minnesota (1974 Pamphlet).

[7] *Practitioner's Handbook for Appeals to United States Court of Appeals for the Sixth Circuit,* Clerk's Office, U.S. Post Office, Cincinnati, Ohio.

40 days   filing of appellant's brief
30 days — filing of appellee's brief
14 days — filing of reply brief

Total 154 days. Extension of time is granted only in extreme situations, because of increasing pressure in coping with evergrowing dockets. Cases are screened in advance of oral argument by a panel of judges designated by Chief Judge under this Circuit Rule 3(e). Amount of time allowed for oral argument is determined by this panel, or by the panel which will hear the appeal.

(g) *Seventh Circuit* local rules[8] as amended to November 1, 1973; in Rule 11, only one counsel may argue on the same side unless notice has been given to the clerk 7 days before commencement of the argument. When permitted, the total time is apportioned. No request for additional time for oral argument will be entertained unless filed with the clerk within 10 days after filing of appellant's or petitioner's brief.

(h) *Eighth Circuit* local rules[9] have revisions to February 15, 1974. Rule 3 provides that no oral argument is allowed on motions unless requested by the court. Rule 9 on court motion provides for summary disposition with no oral argument and no notice except *in forma pauperis.*

(i) *Ninth Circuit Court of Appeals* made revisions of local rules[10] on January 22, 1974. Rule 13 provides that oral argument shall be waived whenever a party fails to file his opening or answering brief within time limits or extension thereof, and late filing is permitted. Waiver may be set aside, however, in the discretion of a judge of this court.

(j) *Tenth Circuit* local rules,[11] as amended through October 16, 1973, provide under Rule 8(2) that the court will receive a motion to affirm the judgment sought to be reviewed on the ground that it is manifest that the questions on which the decision of the cause depends, are so unsubstantial as not to need further argument. Rule 9(c) on calendar B for accelerated cases provides that each side will be allowed 15 minutes for oral argument. Calendar C assignments are made after briefs are filed, when a special panel of the court will screen Calendar B cases to determine if oral argument would not be of material assistance to the court in its ultimate determination

---

[8] *Practitioner's Handbook–Seventh Circuit,* Gunthrop-Warren Printing Co., Chicago, Ill. 60606. (As amended November 1, 1973.)

[9] *Rules of U.S. Court of Appeals for Eighth Circuit,* St. Louis Law Printing Co., St. Louis, Mo. 63101. (Revised by Court Order February 15, 1974.)

[10] *Rules of U.S. Court of Appeals for Ninth Circuit,* Clerk's Office, San Francisco, California. (Revised as of January 22, 1974.)

[11] *U.S. Court of Appeals, Tenth Circuit Rules,* Clerk's Office, U.S. Courthouse, Denver, Colorado 80202. (As amended October 16, 1973.)

of issues presented. Clerk then informs the parties of the reassignment to Calendar C to be submitted to the court for disposition on merits with oral argument.

B. UNITED STATES SUPREME COURT REGULATIONS ORAL ARGUMENT: Rule 44.

1. Oral argument should undertake to emphasize and clarify the written argument appearing in briefs theretofore filed. The court looks with disfavor on any oral argument that is read from a prepared text.

2. The appellant or petitioner shall be entitled to open and conclude the argument. But when there are cross-appeals or cross-writ of certiorari they shall be argued together as one case and in the time of one case, and the court will, by order seasonably made, advise the parties which one is to open and close.

3. Unless otherwise directed, one half hour on each side will be allowed for argument. Request for additional time shall be presented not later than fifteen days after service of petitioner's or appellant's brief on the merits, by letter addressed to the clerk (copy to be sent opposing counsel), and shall set forth with specificity and conciseness why the case cannot be presented within the half-hour limitation.

4. Unless additional time has been granted, one counsel only will be heard for each side, except by special permission when several parties are on the same side. Divided arguments are not favored by the court.

5. In any case, and regardless of the number of counsel participating, a fair opening of the case shall be made by the party having the opening and closing.

6. Oral argument will not be heard on behalf of any party for whom no brief has been filed.

7. Counsel for an *amicus curiae* whose brief has been duly filed pursuant to Rule 42 may, with the consent of a party, argue orally on the side of such party, provided that neither the time nor the number of counsel permitted for oral argument on behalf of that party under the preceding paragraph of this rule will thereby be exceeded. In the absence of such consent, argument by counsel for *amicus curiae* may be made only by special leave of court, on motion particularly setting forth why such argument is thought to provide assistance to the court not otherwise available. Such motions, unless made on behalf of the United States or of a State, Territory, Commonwealth, or possession, are not favored.

C. PRE-ARGUMENT PREPARATORY HINTS.

For advocate planning his oral argument, the following pre-argument activities are suggested:

1. Obtain typewritten transcripts of exemplary oral arguments delivered by predecessors, and read these for helpful hints to focus on your own case.
2. Obtain tapes of recordings which have been made of prior oral arguments in celebrated cases, and listen to these on your playback machine.
3. Take your own tape machine and record your voice as you practice your proposed argument. Listen to playback and pretend you are in the Judge's position.
4. In refreshing your memory on appellate court directives on oral argument, it may be helpful if you first interrogate yourself and record your answers on tape. The "tape and listen" self-appraisal will serve two purposes as you read into the tape from prior pages herein to obtain rule awareness and to plan voice thrust or modulation.
5. Follow your own case from trial court to final oral argument so that you will have mental mastery of all the facts, irrespective of which point is developed first, by opposing counsel.
6. Visit the court where your oral argument is to be scheduled, observe other appellate advocates, the procedure, and the judges.
7. More than one visit would be helpful if time permits. Listen as if you were a judge. Does the argument impress you?
8. Arrive early on the day you are to present your oral argument.
9. Be prepared! Planning, organizing, and selecting subject matter should begin as soon as you obtain copy of the record.

D. DO'S AND DONT'S IN ORAL ARGUMENT PRESENTATION.

1. Do adopt your own flexible system of oral argument, irrespective of opponent's point plan.
2. Do not repeat the written brief although the same points are projected in oral argument.
3. Emphasize a new approach to your points already on file in the written brief, and make different organization in order to stimulate and enliven the court's attention.
4. Do not read to the court, but use index topic cards to refresh memory.
5. Take your point rotation from on-the-spot developments, normally stressing your own strong points first.
6. Flank your argument with supporting secondary points to capitalize on court's attention at the proper moment.

7. If two or more lawyers have written the brief, try to avoid splitting oral argument time.

8. Observe the court closely as opponent's oral argument is presented, and pick your rotation of points in accordance with apparent interest trend of the judges.

9. Welcome any interruption by the court as your new opportunity of communicating in oral argument.

10. Do not delay an answer when a judge proposes a question; shift your card outline to his point of concern.

11. Do not hesitate to admit lack of information, if the court interrupts with a question for which you do not have the answer.

12. Do volunteer to research an unknown point, with the court's permission, and to submit written supplemental communication within____hours, should the court have desire thereof.

13. Do not belabor the point if the interruption is made with evident boredom. Switch immediately to other points in planned presentation.

14. Do not reflect any attitude of anger, despair, or frustration if one judge turns his attention elsewhere.

15. Do not appear annoyed if one judge leaves the bench; take courage in the thought that he may have a momentary health problem for which he is more embarrassed than you.

16. Do be courteous and proceed as expeditiously as possible to the close of your argument BEFORE your time elapses.

The basic thrust of this handbook is directed toward the population flow and the increased demands for service of appellate advocates in the outreach areas of the vast countryside of the United States. Thousands of American people are moving annually away from metropolitan areas of North and East, and into the smaller communities of South and West. Statistical surveys of the early seventies reveal that people with college education are moving more frequently now than the low income labor force. Some of these will be lawyers establishing new residences. Some are potential clients in new communities. They will need lawyers in all levels, particularly the appellate practice where former "country lawyers" had only an occasional appeal. The United States Survey reveals that 4.68 million Americans moved out of metropolitan areas while only 3.73 million Americans moved in, during 1970-73. The more sophisticated client is coming into the outreach areas. The better-prepared advocate will accept the challenge of more legal services in the Federal appellate courts and more opportunities for developing new talents of persuasion by effective oral arguments.

Index

A

B